Small Business Server 2008 Installation, Migration, and Configuration

Set up and run your small business server making it deliver big business impact

David Overton

BIRMINGHAM - MUMBAI

Small Business Server 2008
Installation, Migration, and Configuration

Copyright © 2009 Packt Publishing

First published: April 2009

Production Reference: 1150409

Published by Packt Publishing Ltd.
32 Lincoln Road
Olton
Birmingham, B27 6PA, UK.

ISBN 978-1-847196-30-9

www.packtpub.com

Cover Image by Vinayak Chittar (vinayak.chittar@gmail.com)

Credits

Author
David Overton

Reviewers
Alex Stanier

Ian Watkins

Leslie Cupitt

Dr. Simon J Orebi Gann

Steve Davis

Vijay Singh Riyait

Acquisition Editor
Douglas Paterson

Development Editor
Dilip Venkatesh

Technical Editor
Ajay Shanker

Editorial Team Leader
Abhijeet Deobhakta

Project Team Leader
Lata Basantani

Indexer
Rekha Nair

Project Coordinator
Rajashree Hamine

Proofreader
Chris Smith

Production Coordinators
Aparna Bhagat

Dolly Dasilva

Cover Work
Aparna Bhagat

About the Author

David Overton has been in the IT industry for over 20 years and has worked at Microsoft in the UK for more than nine years. David fell in love with Small Business Server in 2003 when he was given the responsibility of engaging with journalists at the time of the launch of SBS in the UK. For the next four years, David was responsible for improving SBS deliveries by Microsoft partners. David has since has moved on to other roles inside Microsoft, but still continues to be part of the SBS community, helping users answer and resolve questions.

As well as his day job, David is also a writer: he has written for consumer publications *Windows XP* and *Windows Vista* magazines, and he blogs at `http://davidoverton.com`, where he helps readers find solutions to questions and problems.

When not working or writing, David likes to spend time with his family and also tries to fit in sailing any time of the year in any weather.

This book would not have been possible without the interaction of customers, the UK SBS group leads, SBSC partners who work together to improve IT for small businesses, and finally, my colleagues at Microsoft.

I could not have started this project without the support of all three members of my family who agreed to lose me for even more days each month. Once I started the book, I relied on seven people to give their guidance to ensure the content was the most useful possible.

Simon was my ultimate customer guide helping me keep an eye on the owner manager's perspective. Kate Bevan, a journalist, helped improve my writing style and reminded me to keep it simple. The people who are in business supplying and maintaining SBS for their customers every day were Leslie Cupitt of Business Solutions IT, Vijay Riyat of iQuebed, Ian Watkins of Oxbridge Technology Ltd, Alex Stanier of IT 4 Business, and Steve Davis of Sytec.

I need to thank Nick King at Microsoft for answering the questions I could not, and the staff at Packt Publishing Ltd, including Douglas, for the encouragement and guidance that finally led to this book being published.

About the Reviewers

Alex Stanier has worked in the IT industry for twenty years. He started with Ford Motor company on mainframes and minis, and on artificial intelligence solutions before discovering PCs and networks. He spent ten years in the BBC, running an outsourced IT support contract before starting a new company to service the SME market. For the past five years, he has been providing consultancy to a variety of smaller and larger clients. He plays an active and vocal part in the SBSC community.

Ian Watkins started working with computers in 1983 when he worked for Thomas Cook as an Analyst/Programmer writing in COBOL and CICs. Since then, he has moved to working on the Microsoft Platform for many small businesses and charitable organizations helping them to derive real value from the money they spend on IT. He is passionate about seeing IT used effectively in small organizations and helping them solve their real-world problems to drive their organizations forward.

Leslie Cupitt is a veteran of IT, earning his living from IT since 1981. He is a graduate in Management & Economics from the University of Bath. After various marketing roles in large companies, he moved into the marketing of IT, first at the UK's National Computing Centre, then with a large distributor, and then with a large IT retailer.

He has run Business Solutions Ltd. since its formation in 1988. Business Solutions Ltd. is a Microsoft Small Business Specialist. The focus is on supporting small businesses and building the return from their IT investment.

Leslie is an active member of the North West Small Business Community.

Dr. Simon J Orebi Gann is a Non-Executive Director and Senior Executive with a background of extensive commercial and IT experience in BP, Marks and Spencer, and the London International Financial Future Exchange (LIFFE). He has Board experience, which includes US public and UK private company non-executive roles, as well as line roles on company operating boards. With a doctorate in high energy physics, which gave him his first experience of the power of computing, he always seeks opportunities to use new technology early, aiming to gain the longest economic life and maximize return from investment. He ensures that he remains up-to-date with technological developments to identify and assess new commercial opportunities.

With a background of successful delivery of many major IT programs in the Retail, Finance, and Energy industries, Simon assists businesses that are considering or engaged in technology-enabled change to ensure that their strategy is appropriate, goals set are both challenging and achievable, and that the approach and governance will deliver. As well as working at a major international scale, he also undertakes small business projects and often pioneers key technology in his own business. He is an active advisor to venture capital firms on potential investments and on exit strategies.

Steve Davis is a passionate believer in business computing and a member of the British Computer Society. He is also a close colleague of David Overton and the pair often collaborate on Small Business Server issues. Steve has the advantage of working in the "wilds" of IT, with responsibilities towards a wide variety of customers including many business critical applications.

Vijay Singh Riyait is a Chartered Engineer and a Member of the Institution of Engineering & Technology (IET), which is the largest professional Engineering institution in the UK. He is the Technical Director of Ardent iSys, which is a Microsoft Small Business Specialist. He has over 15 years experience as a software developer. He graduated from the University of Wales, Bangor where he studied Electronic Engineering, having won a sponsorship from Marconi Radar Systems Ltd.

He spent five years as a Research Associate at the University of Newcastle upon Tyne, where he was researching signal processing techniques for underwater sonar systems. He is the author of a number of academic papers and first author of a paper published by the IEEE Transactions on Image Processing. Vijay has also worked for GPT, Ericsson, Concept Design (a Nottingham-based software consultancy specializing in GSM/3G telecoms), and ID Data on Smartcard Technologies.

Vijay is currently a Microsoft SBSC PAL (Partner Area Lead) for the UK, which is a recognition by Microsoft of his commitment to promoting engagement between Microsoft Small Business Partners and Microsoft.

Vijay is a Microsoft Certified Professional (MCP) and a Microsoft Certified Technology Specialist (MCTS) on Windows SharePoint Services 3.0 and Microsoft Office SharePoint Server 2007.

Table of Contents

Preface

SBS 2008 has the potential to deliver real business value to a business, but to enable this, you need to implement it correctly while ensuring it is delivered in a secure manner. While SBS 2008 is designed for small businesses, understanding how to make it fit your business is still vital. This means you need to correctly install SBS 2008 or migrate from SBS 2003 and then configure it to meet your needs.

This book will walk you through your journey ensuring you complete all the necessary actions to successfully complete this task.

What this book covers

Chapter 1 sets out to ensure that you are prepared for your journey into SBS 2008, and then plot the route you will be taking and explain why.

Chapter 2 is a brief chapter covering the basics of SBS 2008. You will understand the technologies that you will be interacting with while installing and configuring SBS 2008, and have all the technology that you need to complete the task at hand.

Chapter 3 will cover the preparation required to migrate from SBS 2003 to SBS 2008. This will consist of the following steps: checking if your SBS 2003 server is healthy, backing up the server, installing the required software, changing SBS 2003 to prepare it for migration, and completing the migration tools. We will also see the answer to some questions that enable you to decide when and how to perform a migration. At the end of this chapter, we'll see the two areas that I will not be covering in the migration steps, namely ISA and the variety of anti-malware that may be installed.

Chapter 4 covers the installation of SBS 2008 on a new system, either as a first server in an organization or as a new server into an organization with SBS 2003. We will cover: installing the operating system, installing the SBS components, migrating network settings, getting updates, confirming company information, creating an administration account, naming servers, installing anti-malware tools, and resolving installation issues. The steps involved will get you to the point where you are connected to the Internet.

Chapter 5 covers the migration of the configuration settings from the SBS 2003 system to SBS 2008. This will require activity on both servers. We will cover the following areas in this chapter: starting the Migration Wizard, initially configuring the SBS 2008 network, configuring Internet Access, migrating the SBS 2003 network settings across, and cleaning up the group policy settings.

Chapter 6 covers the migration of email in Exchange 2003 on the SBS 2003 server to Exchange 2007 on SBS 2008.

Chapter 7 covers the migration of data in the CompanyWeb — `http://CompanyWeb`, a Windows SharePoint Site, from SBS 2003 to a site called OldCompanyWeb on SBS 2008.

Chapter 8 covers the finalizing of the migration tasks with the migration of the users and the remaining data from the SBS 2003 system to SBS 2008. We will cover the following tasks in this chapter: migrating file shares, migrating the fax data, migrating users and groups, migrating LOB applications, and finishing the migration.

Chapter 9 covers the process of finalizing the network setup — moving all the network services to be served from the SBS 2008 server. In this chapter, we will carry out the following tasks, some of which are optional: accepting the customer feedback option, configuring your Internet domain name for remote access and email, checking your Internet network settings, enabling email routing via your ISP (smart hosts) if required, installing a paid-for SSL certificate (optional), configuring Office Live for Small Business for SBS 2008 (optional), and configuring a VPN (also known as RAS) for external access (optional).

Chapter 10 covers the process of finishing the network protection and routing setup and configuring the protection of the data on the server. We will cover: configuring the firewall ports, configuring and testing backups, and configuring anti-malware.

Chapter 11 covers the tasks required to add and manage users as well as the tasks to add and manage their desktop and notebook computers.

Chapter 12 covers the following areas: email, calendar, and contacts, file management, and remote access to the server, network, and services.

Chapter 13 covers: daily maintenance checks via the built-in reports, maintenance areas, and troubleshooting common problems.

What you need for this book

This book is designed as a hands-on manual when implementing SBS 2008; so you will need an SBS 2008 server and access to the Internet.

Who this book is for

This book is designed for anyone who needs to install and configure SBS 2008. You don't need to be a technical consultant who wants to tweak every setting to become an SBS success. This book will help those with a basic understanding of technology and a desire to install and use SBS 2008 quickly and continue with their business.

Conventions

In this book, you will find a number of styles of text that distinguish between different kinds of information. Here are some examples of these styles, and an explanation of their meaning.

New terms and **important words** are shown in bold. Words that you see on the screen, in menus or dialog boxes for example, appear in our text like this: "clicking the **Next** button moves you to the next screen".

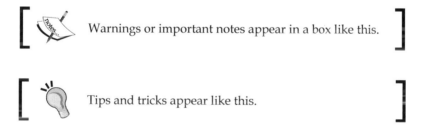

Warnings or important notes appear in a box like this.

Tips and tricks appear like this.

Reader feedback

Feedback from our readers is always welcome. Let us know what you think about this book—what you liked or may have disliked. Reader feedback is important for us to develop titles that you really get the most out of.

To send us general feedback, simply drop an email to feedback@packtpub.com, and mention the book title in the subject of your message.

If there is a book that you need and would like to see us publish, please send us a note via the **SUGGEST A TITLE** form on www.packtpub.com, or send an email to suggest@packtpub.com.

If there is a topic that you have expertise in and you are interested in either writing or contributing to a book on, see our author guide on www.packtpub.com/authors.

Customer support

Now that you are the proud owner of a Packt book, we have a number of things to help you to get the most from your purchase.

Errata

Although we have taken every care to ensure the accuracy of our contents, mistakes do happen. If you find a mistake in one of our books—maybe a mistake in text or code—we would be grateful if you would report this to us. By doing so, you can save other readers from frustration, and help us to improve subsequent versions of this book. If you find any errata, please report them by visiting http://www.packtpub.com/support, selecting your book, clicking on the **let us know** link, and entering the details of your errata. Once your errata are verified, your submission will be accepted and the errata added to any list of existing errata. Any existing errata can be viewed by selecting your title from http://www.packtpub.com/support.

Piracy

Piracy of copyright material on the Internet is an ongoing problem across all media. At Packt, we take the protection of our copyright and licenses very seriously. If you come across any illegal copies of our works in any form on the Internet, please provide us with the location address or website name immediately, so that we can pursue a remedy.

Please contact us at copyright@packtpub.com with a link to the suspected pirated material.

We appreciate your help in protecting our authors, and our ability to bring you valuable content.

Questions

You can contact us at questions@packtpub.com if you are having a problem with any aspect of this book, and we will do our best to address it.

1
Introduction

I've always had a passion for computers and solving the problems that they present and create when put into a workplace. I started working with Microsoft's Small Business Products in 2003, leading the technical presentation to journalists of the, then new, Small Business Server (SBS) 2003 product. Since then, I have worked with small business customers and Microsoft partners to ensure high quality Small Business Server implementations.

When SBS 2008 was launched in November 2008 with updated technologies, I had already been working for two years with the SBS 2008 team inside Microsoft and a select group of Microsoft partners to ensure that the quality of delivery for small businesses would continue.

I've installed Microsoft products many, many times, and I've seen many people deploy SBS. Through my own installations and other people's, I've learned some simple guidelines that should lead you to a successful completion of your project to deploy SBS 2008 today.

Today, I still work for Microsoft, although I've moved on since I was the Head of Technology for Small Business. However, small business still has a large place in my heart, so I visit SBS groups around the country, where I listen and offer my experience of seeing people deploy SBS—both 2003 and now 2008.

This book is the culmination of the useful and valuable experience that I've gained, delivered in the easiest way to consume that I could devise without actually being there.

This chapter sets out to ensure you are prepared for your journey into SBS 2008, and then plot the route you will be taking and why.

Who should read this book...and do the work?

This book is for those people who are about to install and use SBS 2008—either migrating from a SBS 2003 server or installing their first SBS 2008 server—and want to know how to set up an SBS 2008 system that works.

If you have no IT experience, I warn you, it will be a tough journey, although not an unachievable one if you are determined. However, a word of advice: if you are the small business owner or an employee and you're concerned about your skills, go and find someone with the "SBSC" blue badge below and get them to explain why they should do some, if not most or all, of the work for you and then you will more confident of success.

1

SBS 2008 server should be the IT foundation on which your business can survive and thrive. Like all foundations, it needs to be reliable. It should also be serviceable and expandable in the future. You may be able to save money doing all the work and management yourself, but this will, at the least, cost time and in the worst case, wasted money or lost customers. Time is often more precious in a small business than money, which is often pretty tight too, so spending a little bit more at the beginning may well save you a whole lot in the near future if you get it wrong.

Finally, you might think in some parts of this book that I'm teaching my grandmother to suck eggs. Experience has taught me that people sometimes gloss over details and then can't find their mistakes. If you stick with me and use those more familiar sections as revision for what needs doing, you should end up with a problem-free installation.

Why are you installing a server?

To avoid a server installation being a technical decision, it is important to identify your business reasons and then ensure you understand how SBS 2008 will fit in. This might sound obvious, but it's a step people, especially technical people, often miss out.

There are two things that drive the deployment of new IT: first is a wish to do something differently, where SBS 2008 can assist; second is a need to replace old kit that is either not living up to its promises or is getting old and failing.

If your reason is "I want IT to make things better", then you need to work out more precisely what you want to do with your server—otherwise, you're setting yourself up for failure. I will go into what SBS 2008 can deliver for a business in Chapter 2.

How to get the return on your server investment

It's about the money, or, to use the business jargon, the return on investment (ROI). If you invest £5,000 on your IT project, how long will it be before your business sees the incremental benefit of at least £5,000 in return? If you can't answer that question, how will you know that SBS 2008 is giving a benefit to your business? Remember that the return could be as simple as "more sales", or it could be as complex as reducing staff churn and, therefore, the cost of training new team members. It can also be against "the cost of losing business" if the need for IT is critical to continuing and competing in today's more competitive markets.

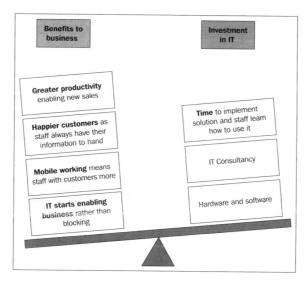

To help drive out this process, keep asking yourself or your IT consultant *why you are doing this*. What are the changes and what will be the benefits of those changes? Then, sit down and put a value on each change—and the cost of not making the change. Normally, you'll find that the financial benefits make themselves plain pretty quickly.

The list of *whys* can also help you to prioritize the order you make changes in. It will also help with your bank manager if you're after a loan to roll out the new technology: bank managers love to know what financial benefits the new technology will be delivering.

Book goals

In writing this book, I wanted you to be able to achieve a simple set of goals:

- Install or migrate to SBS 2008 without any emergencies
- Understand the decisions behind your actions
- Enable your users to interact and gain benefit from SBS 2008
- Enable SBS 2008 to be supported and reliable after the installation

In the installation and configuration sections, I endeavor to explain why we need to carry out a task and how you will carry it out. Where possible, I also explain what the options are, what might go astray, and in such situations, how you would understand or recover.

This should lead to a system that not only works today, but with good ongoing tender loving care remain reliable through its lifetime.

Because I do believe that every SBS 2008 system should have a business ROI plan behind it, enabling users to make the most of the system is also vital and has a whole chapter devoted purely to it.

Navigation route through book

The book is split into sections that roughly cover the following topics:

- Installation and migration
- Configuration of SBS 2008
- User enablement
- Ongoing server management

While you can dip in and out of the various chapters, if you are performing a clean install then you can skip the migration chapters as shown.

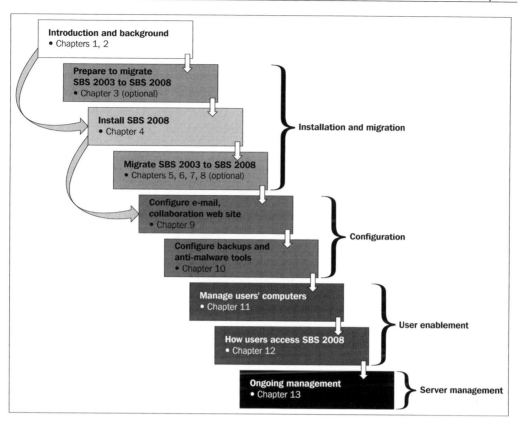

The migration and installation chapters follow the prescribed migration methodology from Microsoft; however, I offer alternative processes to achieve some of the tasks to reduce the manual work and the possibility for mistakes, through the use of scripting.

The configuration chapters will ensure that your SBS 2008 server is functional in the services it can offer and that the security settings and software are correctly installed and configured. Security includes both the blocking of malware and the ability to recover from data loss through the use of backup software.

The user enablement chapters will cover both the management of users and their computers, and the tasks that a user can carry out that will utilize the services of SBS 2008. The user and computer management is something that you will need to implement when you first install SBS 2008, and then again every time you add a new computer or user to your network. This chapter will enable you to do so quickly and securely with minimum of trouble using the wizards and tools provided by SBS 2008. On the other hand, the information in Chapter 12 will need to be imparted to staff to ensure they get the most from the SBS 2008 server.

Finally, but by no means the least, you will need to continue to maintain your server to keep it in perfect running order. There will be tasks that require a daily check and some checks that need to be carried out on a less regular basis. Chapter 13 will give you a reasonable idea of the tasks and more important, what to do as errors arise.

How to ask more questions

I write a blog, which can be found at `http://davidoverton.com` where I write about all things that interest me in technology and there is also a special forum to ask questions relating to this book at `http://davidoverton.com/book`. I may not be able to talk to every owner of a small business or installer of SBS 2008 personally, but I'm very happy for you to contact me via the blog, whether it's about SBS 2008 or another Microsoft product. I can't promise that I'll be able to answer your question, but I'll try.

Summary

So, we've reached the end of this chapter. Before turning to the next one, let's go over the three things you need to have got your head around:

- You now understand how you want to change your business and you understand how SBS 2008 will help you achieve those changes.
- You have planned the investment you need to make and where the money is going to come from.
- You should understand which sections of the book you are going to work through.

The first two aren't really within the scope of this book—your business is up to you, but the rest of the book should help you achieve your business goals using SBS 2008.

2

Introduction to SBS 2008

SBS 2008 is a collection of standard Microsoft technologies designed to deliver benefits that larger businesses enjoy at a price point that is desirable for small businesses. There is nothing new in the concept, but the magic in SBS 2008 is that these enterprise technologies have been carefully orchestrated so as to make them manageable by a small business owner or partner through automatic configuration and a set of interfaces that manage the enterprise complexity for you.

SBS 2008

You are able to look to SBS 2008 to deliver the following:

- Provision of a robust email system to a small (up to 50) group of users
- Support for easy collaboration between those users: email, shared calendars, document repository, and Internet access to all facilities
- A single source of common data across the customers and suppliers of a business, with easy tools to manage that data in one place
- Provision of a web site for customers, suppliers, and staff
- Management of the company's PCs for security, efficiency, and backup
- Enabling staff to be productive while working away from the office

To explain a bit more about how this is done, I will briefly describe the role each component technology has to play in the overall solution.

Each technology provides much more than the short description below.

Windows Server 2008

Windows Server provides much of the infrastructure that is used by SBS 2008. All the networking components that enable PCs to find each other, the server, and the Internet are managed by Windows Server.

All the user information is stored in the Active Directory on Server 2008. This includes their usernames, email details, and security access. Active Directory has the potential to be an extremely complicated tool to manage, but SBS 2008 pre-configures almost all of the settings to ensure the solution matches the business needs. By using Active Directory, you ensure the security of data as access is controlled by a centrally managed user list.

Windows Server 2008 provides the platform for the other technologies mentioned below, so without it, you could not run Exchange 2007 or Windows SharePoint Services. Those core platform technologies also include file and printer management to enable the base level of collaboration and sharing.

Exchange Server 2007

Exchange Server 2007 is the primary information sharing platform, providing email, calendar, and contact functionality across the business. This enables both individual and shared accounts, and securely managed access to each other's calendars and contacts when desired.

This is then presented via Microsoft Outlook as part of Office, via the web interface known as Outlook Web Access or to mobile phones that support the ActiveSync protocol.

Windows SharePoint Services

Windows SharePoint Services provide the information collaboration services outside of email, calendars, and contacts. These are delivered through a web-based portal that can be accessed both internally and externally via the Internet. This portal is secure and searchable, so once a file is shared on the site, provided you have the permission, you can quickly find it.

SharePoint is also a platform for applications and more ISVs are delivering their software to run on top of SharePoint.

A pre-built portal is provided in SBS 2008 called CompanyWeb.

Windows Software Update Services

SBS 2008 centrally manages the update process for all the computers in the business, ensuring that they are updated in a timely fashion and only when approved by the administrator.

This is delivered using the Windows Software Update Service, which evaluates the updates that should be delivered to machines on the network, downloads them to SBS 2008, and then deploys them to the right machines on the network. The success or failure of the update is monitored and reported back to you.

Windows SBS Console

The Windows SBS Console is the one-stop shop to manage all of the technologies mentioned above. It covers 90%+ of the configuration and management that you will need to do on SBS 2008 as will be seen in the later chapters of this book.

One of the key strengths of the console with its wizard-based approach to configuration is that it can coordinate several facets of the embedded technologies to make what would be a complex configuration on Windows Server 2008 into a simple check box or two on SBS 2008.

Premium Server technologies

The final piece of the puzzle is the Premium technologies, which consists of a second Windows Server and SQL Server. This server is designed to run applications in the SBS network. Since some applications will not run on the latest versions of Windows Server or SQL Server, you get the disks for Windows Server 2003 and 2008, and SQL 2005 and 2008; however, you can only install one version of Windows and SQL onto the server.

Solution Checklist

While every installation of SBS 2008 will have its own unique facets, you will find a similar set of technologies in the business for it to exist.

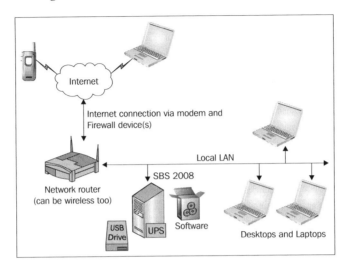

In terms of a typical solution, you will need:

- SBS Server
    - X64 hardware with >4 GB RAM

- Backup
- USB Backup device
    - Optional Uninterruptable Power Supply (UPS) to manage power outages and spikes

- Network
- Internet connectivity
- Firewall (can be embedded in an Internet connectivity device)
- Routers
    - Optional wireless routers

- Internet
- Domain name
- Name server for DNS management
- Remote devices
- Mobile phones with ActiveSync

- Laptops and home computers
- Software
- Anti-virus software and subscription
- SBS 2008 server and CALs

I'm hoping that your solution has all of these; if not, then double-check that you do not need them and then continue through the book.

Support

I've mentioned this before, but I will mention it again, if you are not a Microsoft partner, then you must know where you will go for quality support. I would always recommend a Microsoft Partner with the SBSC blue badge as mentioned in Chapter 1 as they have taken exams and provided case studies to gain the SBSC status. While no certification can guarantee the competency of a partner, it does at least show that the partner has invested time and money in becoming reasonably expert.

It is also often worth understanding what your support contract with the partner covers—that is, what is included in your monthly or annual fees and what will cost you extra. Make sure you're clear on this and how additional fees are calculated: if you have a user who constantly rings for help on something small, be aware that he or she could be quite expensive in terms of your extra support bill. You might need to find a support package that includes a certain number of that kind of phone calls.

Summary

Once again a brief chapter, covering the basics of SBS 2008. You should now understand the technologies that you will be interacting with while installing and configuring SBS 2008, and should have all the technology that you need to complete the task at hand.

3

Preparing to Migrate from SBS 2003

There are two ways to install SBS 2008, one is into a "green field site" where no server exists and the other is to migrate an existing Windows Server or Small Business Server 2003 to Small Business Server 2008. This chapter will cover the preparation required to migrate from SBS 2003 to SBS 2008. This will consist of the following steps:

- Checking if your SBS 2003 server is healthy
- Backing up the server
- Installing the required software
- Changing SBS 2003 to prepare it for migration
- Completing the migration tools

We will also see the answer to some questions that enable you to decide when and how to perform a migration. At the end of this chapter, we'll see the two areas that I will not be covering in the migration steps, namely ISA and the variety of anti-malware that may be installed.

When to migrate and when to perform a clean installation

This is an often asked question. If you have an existing server, but consider the setup to be messed up, then starting again can be an option. However, if you chose to start again, you will need to perform the following tasks on every machine in your network:

- Back up the machine (just in case you need to restart the process)
- Back up all useful data and settings

- Remove the machine from the SBS 2003 domain
- Join the machine to the SBS 2008 domain
- Restore the data and settings

For files and data stored on the servers, you will need to modify all security settings as these will be set for the old users and not the new users on the SBS 2008 system. This is a very lengthy and manual process, and one that often leads to data or settings being lost if careful planning is not carried out first.

Only migrating a part of a system

The migration process is one that happens at many levels, with stages that can be skipped if you wish to clean up a system. You can avoid much of the clean installation pain by selecting what you migrate.

If you migrate only the Active Directory components, you will avoid the lengthy process described. You can still clean up all other aspects of a system as if it were a clean installation. For this reason, I will almost always recommend a migration for even a handful of users.

Why do you have to migrate to SBS 2008?

SBS 2008 is a 64-bit operating system that requires 64-bit hardware and plenty of memory. SBS 2003 is a 32-bit operating system and there is no supported mechanism to perform an in-place upgrade from a 32-bit Windows Server to a 64-Bit Windows Server. Instead, a migration from one server to another must occur.

While this can be performed in such a way that the existing server becomes the SBS 2008 server, this adds a great deal of complexity to the migration process. The steps to achieve migration of SBS 2003 to SBS 2008 in this complex scenario are still almost the same. So, these chapters will help should you choose to re-use the SBS 2003 server as your SBS 2008 server.

Once the migration process is finished, you will have to turn off the SBS 2003 server as SBS 2003 and SBS 2008 cannot both exist on the network for more than 21 days without the occurrence of significant errors.

You can add other Windows Servers onto the network, which includes converting the old SBS 2003 server into an ordinary Windows Server and continuing to use it. SBS 2008 Premium edition includes the ability to install Windows Server 2003 or 2008 onto another system, which could be your old server system. Just remember that you may have limited life out of the old server.

Impact on users

I would recommend doing this work when you don't expect the server to be heavily loaded as some items, such as the network reconfiguration, can stop people from being able to connect to the server for a short while. Outside of the updates and networking steps, the server will be fully functional during this process.

Fourteen steps of migration

There is an excellent migration guide from Microsoft and a help file in SBS 2008, which formed a part of the basis for the migration steps in this book. While they provide a good start, I found several items that need additional explanation, alternative solutions, or more information to complete them successfully. That is one of the purposes of these chapters.

The Microsoft Migration whitepaper can be found at
`http://davidoverton.com/r.ashx?X.`

There are fourteen steps that you need to complete to prepare your server for migration and these are as follows:

1. Plan the migration process including how you will move third-party applications.
2. Communicate plan and impact to users and get an agreement on impact
3. Check the health of SBS 2003 Active Directory.
4. Back up the existing server.
5. Change network configuration to match SBS 2008 design requirements.
6. Update software on SBS 2003.
7. Change Active Directory functionality level.
8. Confirm SBS 2003 is currently configured at best-practice levels.
9. Remove unnecessary email from Exchange.
10. Check permissions are set to allow a migration.
11. Prepare SBS 2003 Time Synchronisation.
12. Run the migration tool on SBS 2003.
13. Prepare migration of line-of-business applications.
14. Complete the answer file for SBS 2008 migration.

Many of the steps are quick and simple, while others require a real attention to detail and an understanding of the issues in hand. I will walk you through them however, there is potential for your SBS 2003 system to be configured in a way that things will appear slightly differently. Your creativity may be required to get to the right end point.

All the listed tasks need to be carried out as a system administrator, which is normally the Administrator login.

Practise makes perfect

If you have a number of customer systems to migrate, then I would recommend working on a test system before you finally start on a customer system. The first time you will find yourself taking longer than you might have thought. You will discover some corners of SBS 2003 that you did not know about, and learn the new console and tools in SBS 2008. By working on a trial system, any mistakes and time overruns do not impact real system users.

Doing two things at once

Many of the steps in this process take some time to run through. You can choose to do things in a very singular linear way or you may choose to use the time while downloads are installing and the machine is reconfiguring to either start the installation of the new SBS 2008 server or read more background information on the Microsoft web site at http://www.microsoft.com/sbs/en/us/default.aspx.

If you wish to install the SBS 2008 server, you must jump to the end of this chapter and create the migration answer file before you start installing the SBS 2008 server. Since SBS 2008 will take at least 30 minutes to install and as much as 2 hours for the entire process, it is a potential good use of time only provided you are confident with the process.

Migrating from SBS 2003 to SBS 2008 on the same server

Before I delve into the detail of the migration, I wanted to cover the subject of a single box upgrade in slightly more detail, where you load SBS 2008 onto the SBS 2003 hardware. Provided the existing hardware is up to scratch, this is possible.

You have two choices here. One is to use Hyper-V to create two virtual machines on the same system, one for SBS 2003 and the other for SBS 2008. The other is to move the SBS 2003 system to a virtual machine, temporarily, during the course of the migration.

Both of these solutions require a very good understanding of virtualisation technology, but I will describe the processes briefly for each scenario.

Migration with Hyper-V running SBS 2003 and SBS 2008 on the same system

Your system will need to conform to the minimum requirements of Hyper-V and have at least 6 GB of memory in the system as well as two additional disks. You need to feel confident that the server is capable of running for the next two years, at a minimum, to make it worthwhile. The minimum requirements of Hyper-V can be found on the Microsoft web site at `http://www.microsoft.com/servers/hyper-v-server/system-requirements.msp`.

 This process is not supported by Microsoft, but the server produced at the end will be.

Process to migrate on one system

1. Take a full system backup before starting.

2. Take existing system and add RAM and two disks.

3. Install Hyper-V Server onto one disk.

4. Install Hyper-V manager onto a client PC.

5. Configure the network so that both systems can connect to a real physical network that has your Internet router and firewall on it as well as each other.

6. Configure a virtual machine with pass-through disks that point to each of your SBS 2003 disks. You will only need to configure 1 GB of memory as you only need enough to perform a migration.

7. Start and boot the SBS 2003 virtual machine.

8. Check that all services start (or can be started if there is a timing issue) and that all data is available.

9. Install the Integration Services Setup disk, run the setup, and reboot when asked.

10. Create another virtual machine with 4 GB of RAM that points to the other new disk, again as a pass-through volume. This will be the SBS 2008 boot disk and can be booted with or without Hyper-V later.

11. Perform the migration as per the chapters of this book.

12. Finish the migration to the point where the SBS 2003 box is turned off.

13. Turn off the SBS 2003 virtual machine and store, recycle, or dispose of the disks.

 More information on this process along with links to further information can be found on my web site at `http://davidoverton.com/r.ashx?U.`

Migration by moving SBS 2003 to a temporary virtual environment

You will need virtualisation software, such as Microsoft Virtual PC and you will need to ensure that your license for SBS 2003 enables you to run it on another machine, the virtual machine, such as with Software Assurance.

 This process is not supported by Microsoft, but the SBS 2008 server produced will be as will the migration process itself. I have used this process many times myself.

Once again, I will not cover all the details and you will need some third-party tools to complete the process.

The SBS 2003 system will not be available to users during this process.

Process for installing SBS 2008 on the same box as 2003

1. Back up the SBS 2003 server.

2. Ensure you have a temporary machine (such as a laptop) with enough storage to have all the SBS files from your SBS 2003 system and at least 2 GB of memory.

3. Run a third-party P2V (Physical to Virtual) tool to copy your SBS 2003 disks into Virtual Hard Disks (VHDs).

4. Download, install, and run Microsoft Virtual Server and start the SBS 2003 system using the VHDs created above.

5. Install new disks on the old system.

6. Carry out the migration tasks as documented in this chapter.

7. Turn off the SBS 2003 virtual machine.

Planning the migration and communicating the plan

It is always a much better experience for everyone if the migration is understood on paper before the actual event takes place. To this end, I would recommend reading through the migration steps in these chapters and then going back to the beginning of these steps to further evaluate the impact upon the users.

There will be moments of down time as the server is rebooting and the network is reconfiguring, and while files, data, users, and settings are moved between systems. It is not possible for me to put an actual time on this as it all depends on how much data there is to move. My first migration took me 5 days, spread over two weekends, while my second migration took a little over a day.

If you have a vanilla SBS 2003 system then all stages will be very simple, but if you have a number of line-of-business applications then you will also need to plan on how to move these.

I can't provide guidance on these applications, but they normally consist of one or more of the following items and will need steps to migrate them that are provided by the suppliers:

- **Program files** that will need to be re-installed on SBS 2008. Ensure these are compatible with a 64-bit Windows Server 2008.

- **Web files**. These may need to be copied from the location on SBS 2003 to a similar location in SBS 2008 and then have the web site properties migrated.

- **Database files**. These are normally very simple to stop, move the files and restart after SQL has been reloaded on SSB 2008.

- **Windows SharePoint Services** can be migrated using the information for CompanyWeb as a template.

Informing the users

Once you have understood the steps for your particular migration, you will need to inform the users when their system will not be available and what will be changing. Most changes will not require user intervention as you can make the SBS 2008 server appear to have the same name as the SBS 2003 server from the point of view of network shares and web sites, but printers and new policies may require some education.

If the system is going to be unavailable to users, you will probably be limited to working in the evening and at weekends to reduce the impact on users.

Checking the health of the SBS 2003

You cannot migrate from an unhealthy SBS 2003, so it is vital you check the health of your SBS 2003 system. There is currently no documented method to carry this out, but I recommend the following steps:

1. Run the SBS 2003 Best Practise Analyser and resolve any issues identified.
2. Run a full virus scan of the system.
3. Check that the Active Directory is functioning correctly.

The Best Practices Analyzer can be found at
`http://davidoverton.com/r.ashx?V`.

If you have previously installed Exchange 2007 onto the SBS 2003 network, you need to ensure it is completely removed. You can follow instructions at `http://davidoverton.com/r.ashx?Y` to do this.

Checking Active Directory

There are many steps to checking out Active Directory, but the following should get you started. You will need to install the support tools from the SBS first CD to complete the tests. Start by opening up a **Command Prompt** from the **Start** menu:

1. Run the **NSLookup** command and check that it returns the correct IP address when you type in your server name. Then type **Exit**.

2. Run **DCDIAG /v/c** and carefully check through the results for issues. You should also run **DCDIAG /test:DNS /DNSALL /e /v, DCDIAG /test: DcPromo /e /v, DCDIAG /test:RegisterInDNS.** Some errors may be fixed by running **DCDIAG /fix**.

3. Run **NETDIAG /v** and carefully check through the results for issues. Some issues may be fixed by running **NETDIAG /fix**.

[There are more tests and some discussion on my web site at
http://davidoverton.com/r.ashx?W.]

Backing up the existing server

While it is very unlikely that there will be a need to recover using this backup, not having it in place is very foolish. Should the migration fail or deliver undesirable results in any way, the ability to go back to a known good state is vital. There is nothing worse than discovering months after the installation of the new server that you have lost something and have no way to recover it. This way, you know you have a good copy you can go back too to either reset the clock or recover lost data.

Doing the backup

You can either perform a normal backup using the SBS 2003 backup tools or you can manually produce a backup with the NTBackup software provided on SBS 2003 to ensure that you have captured all files. To start **NT Backup**, go to the **All Programs** menu on the **Start** menu, select **Accessories**, **System Tools**, and then **Backup**.

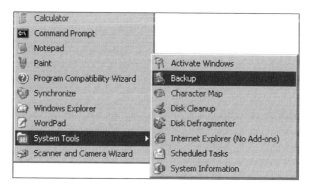

In the backup tool, select all the drives that have data on them, as well as the system state and the **Microsoft Information Store for Exchange**. Click on the **Browse** button next to the **Backup media or filename** text box and choose external USB disks or other backup devices. Now, go to the **Options** item on the **Tools** menu and ensure that the **Verify data after the backup completes** option is selected. If you do not verify a backup, you might find that it is corrupt just when you need it.

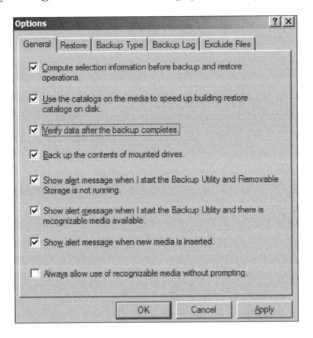

Click on **Start backup** to start the process. After about a minute, the tool should give you a reasonable indication as to how much time you will be waiting for the backup to finish. Depending on the amount of data, the backup can take between 10 minutes and 3 hours.

 Ensure that you have enough space on your backup media for the backup otherwise you will have to start again. You could purchase a new removable USB drive specifically for the purpose of this backup—to provide a long term backup and ensure you have enough space.

 You should perform a quick test restore of some of the files to ensure the backup really does work. Better to spend a few minutes now rather than regretting it later.

Changing network configuration to match SBS 2008 design requirements

There are two simple ways in which the connection between SBS 2003 and the client PCs can be configured to connect to the Internet. One has two network cables connecting to the back of the SBS 2003 and is called a twin NIC (Network Interface Card) or duel homed solution. This has the SBS 2003 system as the controlling gateway and firewall to the Internet.

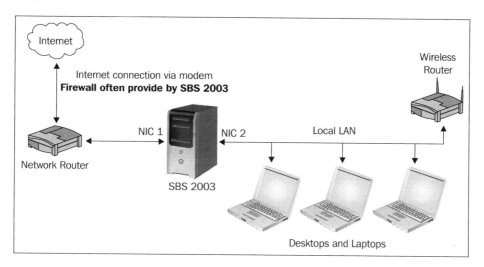

SBS 2008 only supports a configuration using a single NIC in the SBS 2003 and SBS 2008, and the firewall and router must be one or more external devices.

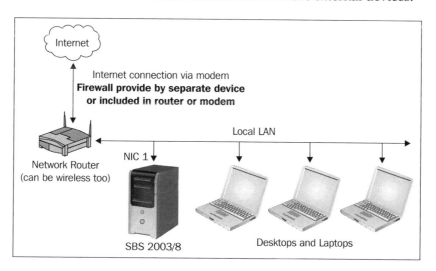

If you have a single NIC solution, you don't need to carry out the work of this section; however, if you do have two NICs that are in use, then you need to follow this process to change to a single NIC solution.

1. Install your firewall and router and ensure DHCP is turned off on these devices. You will need to refer to the device-specific manual to disable DHCP as it is normally on by default.
2. Physically re-configure SBS 2003 to use a single NIC.
3. Re-configure SBS 2003 network settings.
4. Check that the router has the correct firewall settings.
5. Check that the DHCP settings are correct.

It is vital that you install and configure the firewall before making any other changes otherwise you will expose your systems to malware. Any amount of time connected to the Internet without this protection is likely to lead to problems.

Installing your firewall and router and ensuring DHCP is turned off on these devices

Ensure that you have the new firewall and (or) router in place. Now, remove the cable that connects your SBS 2003 server to the Internet. This should leave just one network cable between the SBS 2003 server and your network.

Follow the instructions in your router and firewall manual(s) to configure the IP address of the router. I would recommend 192.168.x.1 as the router IP address where x matches your existing network connection settings.

You will often connect to the configuration settings for these devices via a web page. It may be easier to initially connect the device to a PC, make the changes, and then plug it into the SBS 2003 Server.

Now, disable DHCP on the router and check to ensure that SBS 2003's DHCP service is still running. SBS 2003 will stop the DHCP server if it becomes aware of the router DHCP service. If you are unsure, run the command **NET START DHCPSERVER** and it will be started if necessary.

It is important that the router's gateway to the Internet is presented as an address of 192.168.x.1 or 192.168.x.254 as SBS 2008 expects one of these addresses to be the Internet router connection.

Your networking infrastructure should now be set up as per one of the options below.

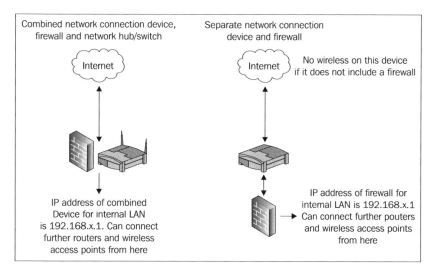

Physically re-configuring SBS 2003 to use a single NIC

The next step is to disable one of the network adapters in SBS 2003. Go to **Control Panel**, right-click on **Network Connections** and select **open**. You will see that you have two network adapters. One will still be connected to the network and one will have a red cross to show that the cable is removed. This was the port that was connected to the Internet and now has the cable removed from it. Select this network device, right-click on it, and select **Disable**.

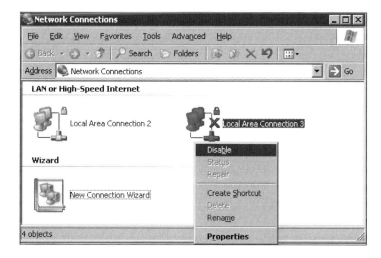

Your SBS 2003 system will now not be routing to the Internet correctly and Internet connections will not resume until you reconfigure the settings.

If you wish, you can later remove this network card from the SBS 2003 server; however, for now it is perfectly safe to simply disable it, especially since the server will be turned off at the end of the migration. The IP address of the server is recommended as **192.168.x.2**. This can be confirmed by right-clicking on the network connection to your LAN and selecting **Properties**.

Re-configuring SBS 2003 network settings

We now need to re-configure SBS 2003. Assuming the IP address of the server has not changed, this is simply a case of re-running the **Configure E-mail and Internet Connection** wizard.

Start the **Server Management** tool and click **Connect to the Internet** in the **To-Do list**.

When the wizard starts, it might inform you that you have a UPnP router and offer to configure this for you. I prefer to be in control, so I always select **No**; however, if you are comfortable with SBS 2003 configuring this for you, you can select **Yes**.

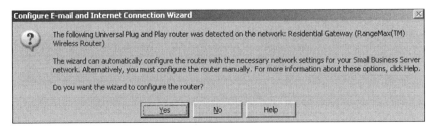

Select **Broadband** as the **Connection Type** and then click on **Next**. Then, change the **My server uses** option to **A local Router with an IP Address** and click on **Next** to continue.

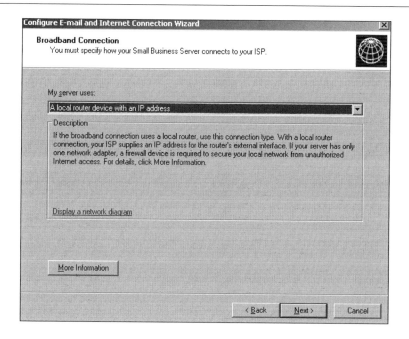

You should be able to leave the DNS settings the same on the **Router Connection** page; however, you will need to change the **Local IP address of router**. For my network, this was **192.168.0.1**.

Ensure that the **My server uses a single network connection for both Internet access and the local network** box has a check mark in it and then click on **Next**.

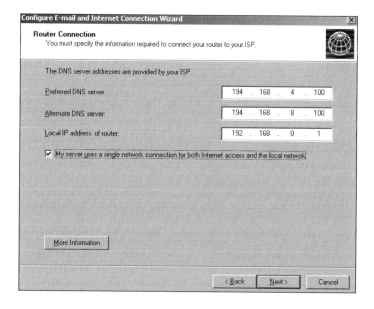

Double-check which services you wish to expose through your firewall.
These should be the same ones as were previously selected, but it is always
worth double-checking and then clicking **Next** when you are happy.

 If the wizard had detected a UPnP router, then this will configure
the router with the settings here, potentially changing your carefully
hand-crafted setting.

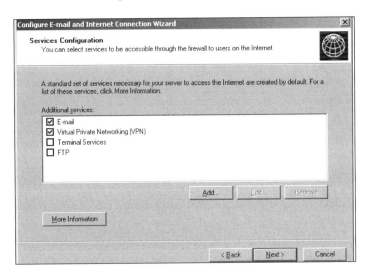

For the **Certificates** and **Internet E-mail** screens, you can simply select the **Do not
change** option and click on **Next**.

Finally, you will see a summary screen where you need to check that the right
options are selected and then click on the **Finish** button.

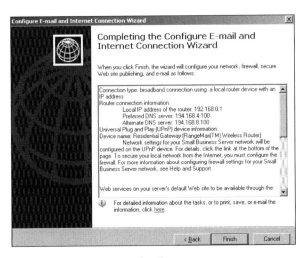

Changing VPN Server

If you had previously enabled VPN, you will also need to disable this via the **Configure Remote Access** option in the **Internet an E-mail** section of the **Server Management** tool as this will now be managed by the SBS 2008 server.

Checking that the router has the correct firewall settings

If you do not have a UPnP router or if your UPnP routers are not quite up to spec., you will need to verify and change the firewall settings. Your router will only need the ports opening that match the services you selected.

Port	Usage
25	Email coming into the server
80	Web traffic that is NOT secure
443	Secure web traffic, such as Remote Web Workplace and mobile services for phones
444 (optional)	Secure access to the CompanyWeb SharePoint site
1723 (optional)	VPN Access
4125 (optional)	Remote Access to computers inside the network, provided as a feature of Remote Web Workplace

Each of the above ports, if used by you, will need to be set to point to the IP address of your server, which is normally 192.168.x.2.

If you have statically assigned router or IP address information on workstations or printers, these should be checked to ensure they are still correct.

Checking if network settings are correct

If this has all been correctly configured, then you should be able to perform the following tests on a PC in the office. To do this, we will:

1. Check if PCs can connect to the server
2. Check that the right IP Address information is sent to each PC
3. Check local and Internet web browsing
4. Check email settings.

The first step is to reboot a PC and check how long it takes to log in. If the DHCP information is correct, it will log in quickly. If it does not, then this suggests that the DNS addresses are not pointing to the SBS Server or that DNS is not running on the SBS server.

The next step is to manually check the DNS addresses. You can see the IP Address information on the PC by using the IPConfig command. To run this command, you can simply run **cmd.exe** on Windows XP or if you are running Windows Vista, you will need to find **Command Prompt**, right-click on it, and select **Run as Administrator**. Then, type **IPCONFIG /ALL**. The following screenshot shows the key items where the server has an IP address of **192.168.0.2** and the router was configured as **192.168.0.1**.

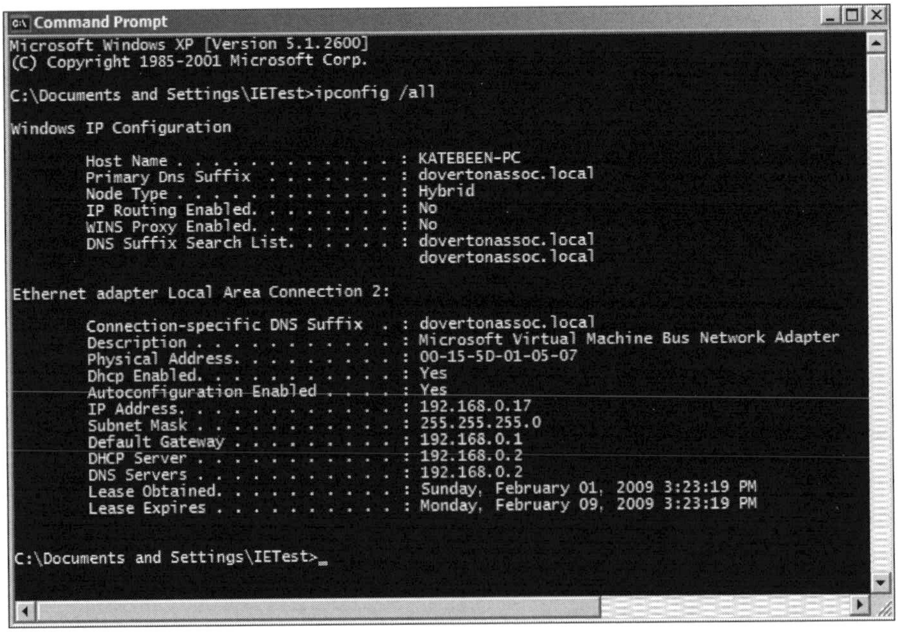

```
Command Prompt                                                      _ □ X
Microsoft Windows XP [Version 5.1.2600]
(C) Copyright 1985-2001 Microsoft Corp.

C:\Documents and Settings\IETest>ipconfig /all

Windows IP Configuration

        Host Name . . . . . . . . . . . . : KATEBEEN-PC
        Primary Dns Suffix  . . . . . . . : dovertonassoc.local
        Node Type . . . . . . . . . . . . : Hybrid
        IP Routing Enabled. . . . . . . . : No
        WINS Proxy Enabled. . . . . . . . : No
        DNS Suffix Search List. . . . . . : dovertonassoc.local
                                            dovertonassoc.local

Ethernet adapter Local Area Connection 2:

        Connection-specific DNS Suffix  . : dovertonassoc.local
        Description . . . . . . . . . . . : Microsoft Virtual Machine Bus Network Adapter
        Physical Address. . . . . . . . . : 00-15-5D-01-05-07
        Dhcp Enabled. . . . . . . . . . . : Yes
        Autoconfiguration Enabled . . . . : Yes
        IP Address. . . . . . . . . . . . : 192.168.0.17
        Subnet Mask . . . . . . . . . . . : 255.255.255.0
        Default Gateway . . . . . . . . . : 192.168.0.1
        DHCP Server . . . . . . . . . . . : 192.168.0.2
        DNS Servers . . . . . . . . . . . : 192.168.0.2
        Lease Obtained. . . . . . . . . . : Sunday, February 01, 2009 3:23:19 PM
        Lease Expires . . . . . . . . . . : Monday, February 09, 2009 3:23:19 PM

C:\Documents and Settings\IETest>_
```

Now, check that you can connect to the internal web site http://companyweb and confirm that the internal Windows SharePoint Services site appears as expected and that you can navigate around it. If you cannot browse the internal web sites, check that the **IISAdmin** service is running on SBS 2003 by running **Services.msc**. If it is running, check that the web site has started within the **Internet Information Services** tool from the **Administration Tools** menu on the **Start** menu.

To confirm that the connection to the Internet is working, try browsing an Internet web site, such as http://davidoverton.com and ensure your access.

Finally, open Outlook and send and receive email. If you have an account outside of the SBS 2003 environment, such as an MSN account, send a test email using that account to your SBS 2003 email account.

Assuming that all the tests work, your network is now configured so that it can be migrated to SBS 2008.

Updating software on SBS 2003

The migration process requires the latest software updates on SBS 2003. Although updating and patching a system just prior to turning it off might seem a little unusual, it is required as the migration tools rely on the latest updates.

We need to install all the updates we know about and then double-check the system afterwards.

Installing Updates

The easiest way to do this is to go to Microsoft Update and select **Custom**.

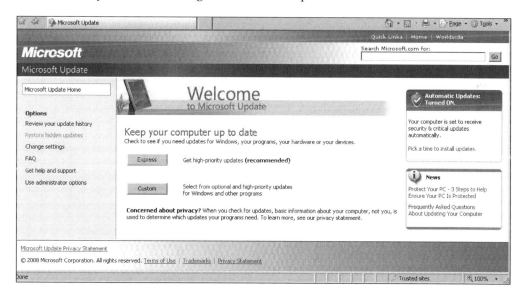

If you have **Windows Update** on your system in the **Start** menu, it will only check the core Windows files and not those of Exchange and SQL. To change this, click **Change Settings** and scroll down to choose updates for **All Microsoft products**, which will result in Microsoft Update being provided as an icon in your **Start** menu instead of **Windows Update**.

Once the custom list is built, install all security and recommended updates except those for hardware items such as graphic cards and sound systems. If your network card is showing, you should consider doing updates for this too.

This will do 90% of the work for you, but it will not do everything. You will still need to download the following:

- Exchange 2003 Service Pack 2—http://davidoverton.com/r.ashx?Z
- SQL Server Management Studio Express Service Pack 2—http://davidoverton.com/r.ashx?10

You will need to install each of the tools above. For the Exchange update, you should simply be able to click **Next** to get it to update Exchange.

 Note that while this is working, Exchange will be unable to receive email.

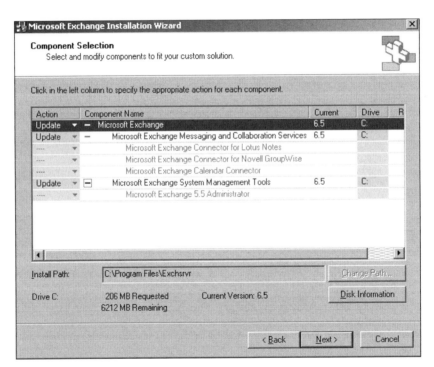

Once it has started, you will see the following screen until it is complete.

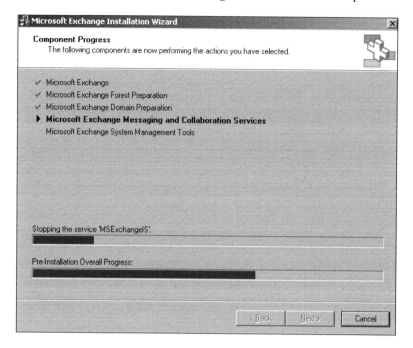

The SQL Server update comes in two flavors; ensure you download the 32-bit version.

Again, clicking **Next** will continue the update. You may have to reboot once these updates have been loaded.

Keep Updating

Once you have loaded this software onto your server, go back to Windows Updates to check if there are more that need to be updated as a result. Keep doing this until Windows Updates believes there is nothing more to update. Because the system will be restarting, this process should only be performed when users are not using the system.

Checking Versions

To some extent, you should find that all items in this section are at the required versions and therefore, there will be no action required. However, I prefer safe to sorry and to avoid errors later on, so here are the checks we need to make to ensure that the migration tools work successfully. The checks we will perform are:

- Check SBS 2003 is at Service Pack 1 or greater.
- Check Windows Server is at Service Pack 2 or greater.
- Check Exchange 2003 Service Pack 2 is installed.
- Check that .NET Framework 2.0 is installed.
- Check the version for Microsoft Core XML Services.
- Check Windows SharePoint Services 2.0 Service Pack 3 is installed and used.

Checking SBS 2003 is at Service Pack 1 or greater

There are various ways to do this, but if you execute this command, it will tell you the answer:

```
reg query HKLM\SOFTWARE\Microsoft\SmallBusinessServer /v
ServicePackNumber
```

if all is well, then you should see the response:

```
HKEY_LOCAL_MACHINE\SOFTWARE\Microsoft\SmallBusinessServer
Service PackNumber    REG_DWORD    0x1
```

The highlighted line above is the key where the number of 0x1 (or greater in the future) is what we are looking for.

Checking Windows Server is at Service Pack 2 or greater

SBS is build on top of Window Server and we also need to confirm that Windows Server has the correct service pack installed. Run the command **WINVER** and you should see the results as shown in the following screenshot. The item to note is that the version has the text **Service Pack 2** in it.

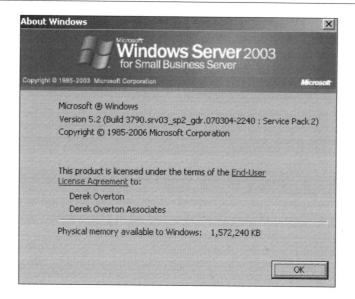

Checking Exchange 2003 Service Pack 2 is installed

We installed the service pack above so this should not be an issue. If the service pack has failed to install, the version will show as service pack one. To check the settings, follow these steps:

1. Go to the **Start** menu and run the **Server Management** tool.
2. Close the **Standard Management** list by clicking on the **+/-** box.
3. Expand the **Advanced Management** section.
4. Navigate down the levels by clicking on the name of your **Exchange Server administration group** (below Computer Management).
5. Expand **Administration Groups, first administrative group, Servers** and finally, your SBS 2003 system.
6. Right-click on your server and select **Properties** from the menu.
7. Select the **General** tab and check that it states **Service Pack 2.**

The following screenshot shows the navigation tree expanded with the **Properties** window open and the **General** tab showing **Service Pack 1**. If this is the case, then you need to either reboot, or load the service pack as described above.

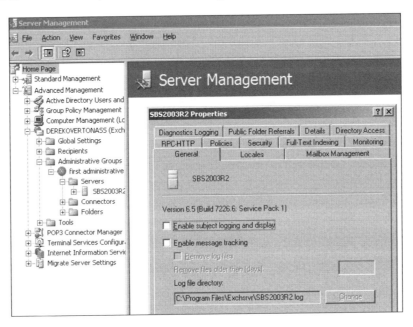

Checking that .NET Framework 2.0 is installed

The next few checks all start in **Add or Remove Programs** in the Control panel. Open this up and then go searching for **Microsoft .NET Framework 2.0 Service Pack 1**.

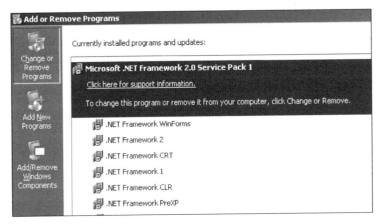

Checking the version for Microsoft Core XML Services

Next, scroll down in the Add/Remove program screen to find the **MSXML 6.0 Parser (KB9337579)**. The KB Article number may well be different, but you need to click on this and then click on **Click here for support information**. A little yellow box appears and one item is the version number. This needs to be greater than "6.10.1129.0", so in the following screenshot **6.10.1200.0** is ok. If it is not, check your updates as the updates for this are provided via Microsoft Update.

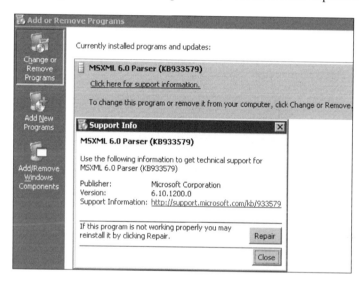

Checking Windows SharePoint Services 2.0 Service Pack 3 is installed and used

Finally, in Add/Remove programs, we need to check on Windows SharePoint Services 2.0. It should be just above the MSXML entry. If it states Windows SharePoint Services 2.0, and then in the detail, when you click onto it, Service Pack 3 or higher then this is at the level needed.

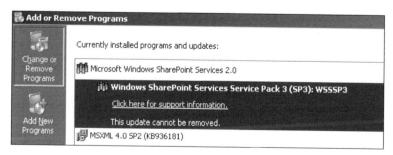

There is one more to check to perform with SharePoint Services and that is to ensure that CompanyWeb is running at the right version too. To do so, click the **Start** menu and find the **SharePoint Central** menu item on the **Administrative tools** menu to open the **Windows SharePoint Services Administration** page. Click **Configure virtual server settings** and double-check that the version number next to **CompanyWeb** is at least **6.0.2.8165**.

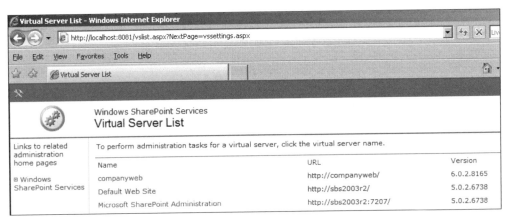

If it is not at the correct level then open a command prompt and enter the following commands:

```
cd /d "C:\Program Files\Common Files\Microsoft Shared\Web Server
Extensions\60\Bin"
stsadm -o upgrade -forceupgrade -url http://companyweb
exit
```

Changing Active Directory functionality level

Active Directory is a very powerful and complex tool for large organizations. SBS 2003 protects the user from needing to be knowledgeable in configuring Active Directory and takes care of this for the user. However, this complex nature means that for the upgrade we need to adjust some of the configuration settings relating to the versions of Windows Server on the network. If you are not familiar with Active Directory, then I would simply follow the instructions.

If you have a Windows Server 2000 system on the network as a domain controller, you will need to demote it using **DCPROMO** before you can continue here. Running **DCPROMO** will offer to demote the server it is run on for you.

As a little bit of background, Active Directory is built with the intention that it will increase in functionality and scope as newer versions of Windows Server are released. For SBS 2008 to function correctly, it requires that level to be at least that of Windows Server 2003, while SBS 2003 is configured to a level suitable for Windows Server 2000. SBS 2003 is designed out the box to work with Windows Server 2000 Domain Controllers without having to tweak these settings. SBS 2008 is designed to work with Windows Server 2003 Domain controllers without issues.

You then need to raise the "functional level" of the domain and the forest. This basically means that Active Directory supports newer functionality by removing support for Domain controllers before Windows Server 2003. Since SBS 2008 will be in control, you do not need to do anything for this functionality to be used.

Raising the functional level for the domain and Forest

Open the **Active Directory Domain and Trusts** tool from the **Administrative Tools** on the **Start** menu. You should see your domain listed under the first heading of **Active Directory Domain and Trusts**. Right-click the domain and select **Raise Domain Functional Level**.

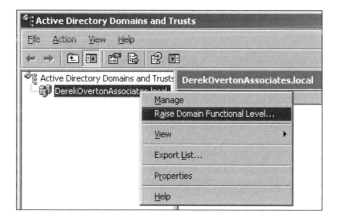

The functional level will be shown as Windows 2000 native. In the drop-down box, change this to Windows Server 2003 and click **Raise**.

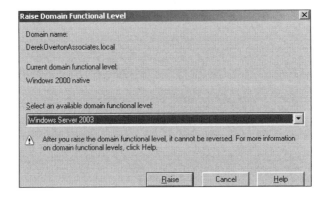

This should take a few seconds to complete. Then, right-click on **Active Directory Domain Trusts** and select **Raise Forest Functional Level**.

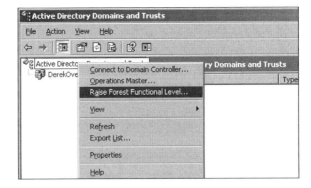

The functional level will again be shown as Windows 2000 native. In the drop-down box, change this to **Windows Server 2003** and click **Raise**.

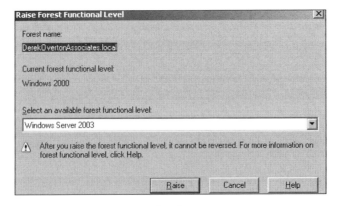

Confirming SBS 2003 is currently configured at best practice levels

I've tried to cover most of the default settings that need to be examined, but there are still further checks that can be carried out via the Best Practise Analyser tool to ensure a smooth migration.

To help maintain a well-run SBS 2003 system, Microsoft produced the "Best Practices Analyzer", which will do a more thorough investigation into your system. This tool can be downloaded from `http://davidoverton.com/r.ashx?11` and should be installed and run.

Select **Start Scan** to kick things off and wait while it investigates your settings. This will take a few minutes to complete.

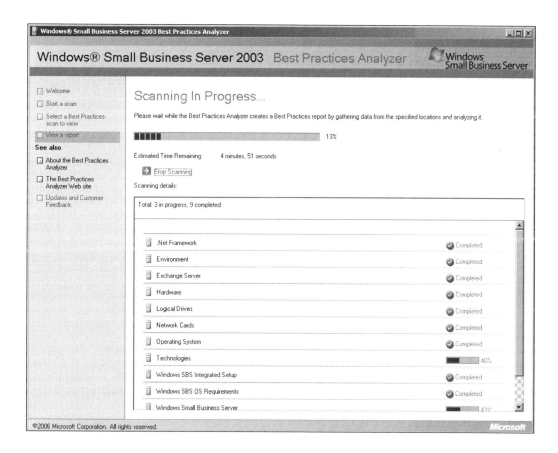

Once the analyzer has run, you can judge if any of the issues warrant further action. In the following example, I was not concerned about the number of network cards, DNS comments, or Task Offloading. I had more than 2 network cards in the system because this was a test machine and the DNS entries are due to me previously hosting my own DNS domains. The Task Offloading has been known to provide issues, but not on my network cards, so no further action there. However, I did update Outlook Web Access as all security updates should be performed in my opinion and while I had not run the SBS 2003 backup tool, I had taken a manual backup.

You also need to use your judgement to decide what actions, if any, you take from this report, but always action product updates to keep your system secure and stable.

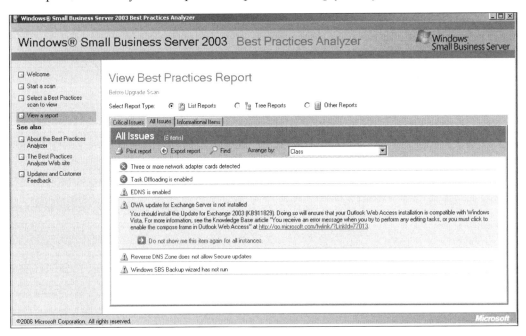

Removing unnecessary email from Exchange

Migrating all the email mailboxes will take time so removing unnecessary email is vital. Ask all the users to archive older emails and empty their deleted items folder to shorten the migration task. Each user will need to do this on his/her own, from Outlook, although you may have to assist in the process. While it is not vital to carry out this task, if they do not, then expect significantly longer email database checks and actual migration times later in the process.

The process for each user is very simple assuming they are using Outlook as their email program.

- Empty the deleted items by clicking the **Tools** menu and selecting **Empty "Deleted Items" Folder**.

- Archive emails to a PST file by selecting the **File** menu and clicking **Archive**.

  - Select **Archive this folder and all subfolders** and select the top item (normally, something like Mailbox—David Overton).

  - Set a date, such as **1st January 2008**, that all items older than will be stored in the archive file.

  - Ensure the box with **Include items with "Do not AutoArchive" checked** has a check mark in it.

  - Check or change the **archive file** location to somewhere the user can find the later.

  - Click on **OK**.

 Once the email has been archived, the PST file created can be accessed by the user. You may also wish to create a new PST file for the user and drag-and-drop mail. Note that while the archive is running, a user may continue to use Outlook, but when dragging and dropping, you have to wait for each move to finish.

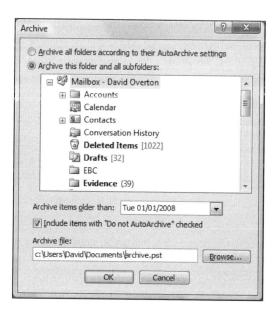

Checking that the permissions are set to allow a migration

The migration process will only run a number of tools with the logged in user being an administrator and sometimes not all the right permissions are in place for this user. To check the permissions, open **Server Management** and click **Users** in the left-hand pane.

Right-click on the **Administrator account** (or the account you use to administer SBS 2003) and select **Properties**. Now, switch to the **Member Of** tab and verify that **Enterprise Admins**, **Schema Admins**, and **Domain Admins** at the minimum are in the tab. If one is missing, click the **Add** button and add it, otherwise you can simply click **Cancel**.

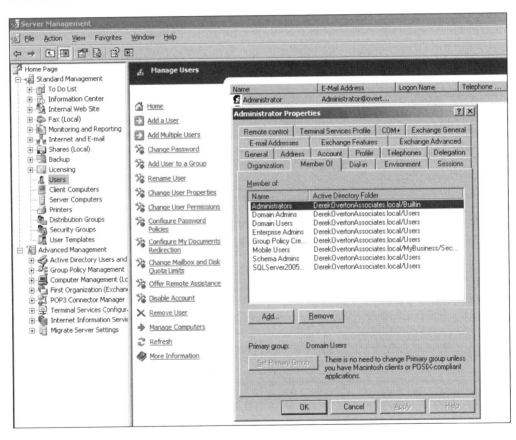

Preparing SBS 2003 Time Synchronisation

Good timekeeping might seem like a *nice* feature, but with computer security, it is a must. Both servers must keep themselves within 5 minutes of each other on their clocks otherwise the security communications will fail. To achieve this, we will synchronize the SBS 2003 system to the SBS 2008 system. While the SBS 2008 system is not yet present, this command is needed before the two systems start communicating, which will happen during installation of SBS 2008. To prepare for this, you will need to enter the following commands into a **Command Prompt** by running **cmd.exe**. The **w32tm** command re-configures the time synchronization service and tells it to synchronise to the Active Directory domain. Starting and stopping the **w32time** service will re-synchronize the time to the new settings.

```
w32tm /config /syncfromflags:domhier /reliable:no /update
net stop w32time
net start w32time
```

You should see the output like this:

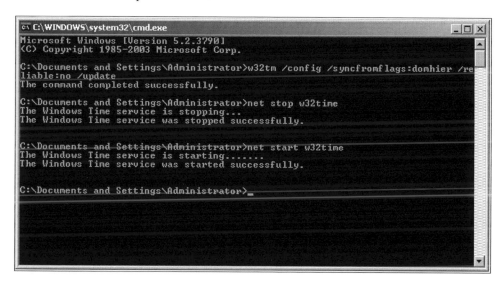

Running the migration tool on SBS 2003

We are now on the final stage of the migration preparation on the SBS 2003 server. Depending on how much work was required, it may have taken some time to get to here. This last step will further update Active Directory and Exchange 2003 as well as install an update to the server enabling SBS 2003 and SBS 2008 to co-exist for 21 days.

To run the tool, insert the SBS 2008 DVD and navigate to the **Tools** folder. Here, you will find the file **SourceTool.exe** that you need to run.

 The SBS 2008 DVD may not work on your SBS 2003 server if it only has a CD-ROM drive. If this is the case, put the DVD into a PC with a DVD drive and copy the **Tools** folder across the network onto the SBS 2003 server. Now, you will be able to run from the hard disk.

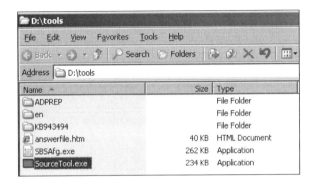

The tool starts off by re-emphasizing the importance of a backup. Assuming you have made a reliable backup, check the box and click on **Next**.

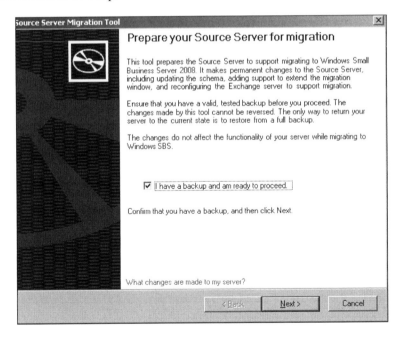

Once the tool has finished, it will confirm completion.

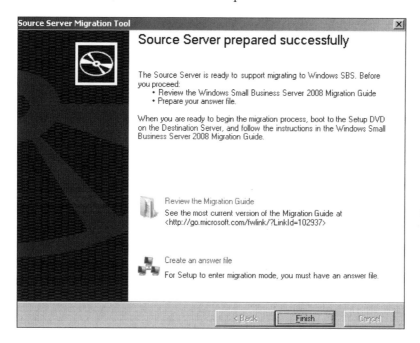

You will now need to restart the server before you start the actual migration process. You can still create the answer file described overleaf before rebooting.

Preparing to migrate line-of-business applications

We have now gone through all the steps required to prepare the Microsoft applications and settings that would normally be installed on a SBS 2003 system; however, if you have installed SQL Server 2000 or SQL Server 2005 or any other applications, you need to consult with the vendors for those applications on how to move them to a new system.

At this point, you may decide to install these applications onto a second system as part of SBS 2008 Premium edition or again onto the first server of SBS 2008. If you are planning to do the latter, bear in mind that you are moving from SBS 2003 to SBS 2008, which means from Windows Server 2003 32-bit to Windows 2008 64-bit and that the impact of the applications on the first server could be high. If you wish to use only one physical system, then you can consider loading the Premium server inside a virtual machine so it can be managed and easily transferred at a future date.

Each application will require its own unique preparation before it is migrated. Without the vendor's support, you will find this task very difficult. Having discussed with the vendor the recommended process, if there are required tasks to prepare for the migration, now is the time to execute those tasks.

Completing the answer file for SBS 2008 setup

 If you are completing a migration, you **must** create an answer file, which makes this a mandatory step.

When SBS 2008 is installing, it looks for the answer file on all drives, including every USB stick or floppy drive in the system. It provides the information required for the SBS 2008 setup program to perform a migration rather than a clean installation. There is no way to perform a migration without using the file produced by the answer file tool.

Navigate back to the **Tools** folder on the DVD and run the SBSAfg.exe program to create the answer file.

 You will require either a floppy disk, USB drive, or the ability to create your own SBS 2008 DVD with the answer file embedded on it.

There are three important sections in the answer file, namely the first and last two sections, but the others enable you to enter information once now so that you don't have to enter it again.

Once the tool is started, ensure that the type is set to **Migration from Existing Server** in the **Installation Type** section.

```
Installation type
 ○  New installation
 ⦿  Migration from existing server (Join existing domain)
```

In the **Installation Settings** section, I would normally check both boxes to enable the installation to automatically get updates and avoid being asked answers to the questions I am completing in this tool. If you would rather check each step of the installation process then do not put a check mark in the **Run unattended** box.

For the clock settings, I would set the time zone automatically. During the migration, you get a chance to confirm that the clock is correctly set.

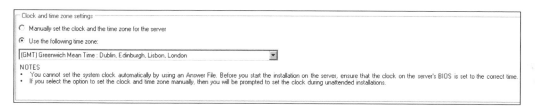

Unless you have some specific security software already in place, check to use both the trial services. They can be removed later if desired, but it gives you immediate security out of the box after installation

 While you can install OneCare, Microsoft has announced that new licenses for OneCare will not be provided after the middle of 2009 and a replacement product for SBS 2008 has not been communicated. If you intend installing alternative anti-malware software on your SBS 2008 server, do not check the OneCare box

While you can choose how much or little you enter into the **Company Information**, entering the information now will save you having to update several places later in the installation process. This information is used to populate the fax services and the internal and external web site information.

Due to a bug in the handling of the process to create certificates and digitally sign the SSL certificates, I would advise that you to not put anything in the **Certificate Authority Name** section. This is the name that is used to describe which authority will guarantee the security of your certificates. If you were to enter your domain name or the name of your server for remote access, you will block yourself from using these names later on, yet they would be the default names used.

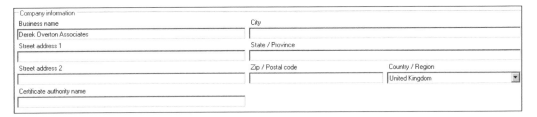

The **Source Server** section is one of the most vital sections. You must complete this section correctly with the username and password that you have been using, the name of your SBS 2003 server, and the domain name. Note that the username and password will become the recovery password should you have to boot the server in **Directory Services Restore Mode**, that is, without Active Directory loaded.

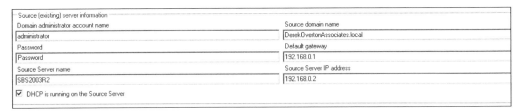

If you are not sure of the server name and domain name, then right-click on **My Computer** and select **Properties**. The **System Properties** window will appear that has the computer name in the **Full computer name** before the first full stop and then, the **Domain** listed as follows.

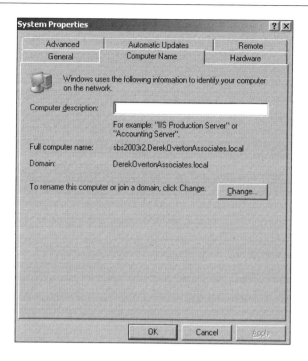

Finally, you have to insert some information about the new server you will be creating, such as the name you plan for it and the IP address it will use.

 The IP Address of the SBS 2008 server cannot be the same as the IP address for the SBS 2003 server. For me, this meant that SBS 2003 was 192,168.0.2 and SBS 2008 was 192.168.0.3. If desired, you can change the IP address once the migration is fully completed.

Once all these sections are completed, save the file as sbsanswerfile.xml to a USB stick or a floppy disk and everything is finally prepared for the migration to a new server.

Obviously, the answer file has some very sensitive information about the security to your system and should not be left around or loaded on media that people can browse at later. Consider deleting the answer file once you have successfully migrated the system.

What is not covered

There are two areas that I will not be discussing in the migration steps as they either impact only a few users or are too broad to cover in detail.

ISA configuration

ISA Server is an optional component of SBS 2003 Premium Edition that provides an intelligent firewall to the system. ISA Server 2004 is found only on a small proportion of SBS 2003 systems. As the network will need a firewall that is not installed on the server, the simplest solution is to remove ISA Server 2004 from SBS 2003 before migration.

Other Security & Firewall software

Network security and firewall settings can cause problems during migration especially if they are not configured to the standard SBS 2003 settings. For example, when writing the chapters on migration, the system I was working with had Symantec security software on that continually blocked network communications. In the end, I disabled the network security to enable the migration to continue once I was sure the existing network was secured and after a full anti-virus scan was complete. I was only confident to do this as the new server had security software installed and a firewall was in place to protect the network from external malware.

Just to be clear, ensure your network is secure before you disable this protection. With SBS 2008, you will need a separate firewall before you install SBS 2008 and this needs to be in place and configured before you start. Without doing this, your new server will be compromised within minutes.

Summary

Finally, the server is ready for the next stage of the migration, which is to install SBS 2008 on the new server using the answer file.

By running through this migration preparation process, you should have a well-running SBS 2003 system that is secure and functional for all your users, but also ready for the migration. Many of the steps are best practice for keeping a server up to date, so hopefully, it was not too long a process.

The items such as checking Active Directory and running the Best Practices Analyzer should significantly reduce the likelihood of problems when migrating across.

The next stage is to start the installation of SBS 2008 with the answer file.

4

Installing SBS 2008 and Connecting to the Internet

This chapter covers the installation of SBS 2008 on a new system, either as a first server in an organization or as a new server into an organization with SBS 2003. We will cover:

- Installing the operating system
- Installing the SBS components
- Migrating network settings
- Getting updates
- Confirming company information
- Creating an administration account
- Naming servers
- Installing anti-malware tools
- Resolving installation issues

The steps involved will get you to the point where you are connected to the Internet. There are some steps that are different, depending on whether this is a new installation or a migration.

SBS 2008 installation

The installation process is split into two sections:

- Installation of the operating system and other files to the disk
- Installation of everything that makes it SBS 2008

You cannot separate the two or stop the second half from happening; although, you will be required to provide input to the server at each stage.

Operating system installation

If you are performing a migration from SBS 2003 to SBS 2008, you must have your USB memory stick with the SBSAnswerFile.xml file loaded onto the root directory. The process to create this is covered in the previous chapter.

You must also have a network cable plugged into the SBS server, connected to a hub or switch, for the installation to succeed.

Migrating to SBS 2008 in a virtual environment

If you are installing SBS 2008 into a virtual machine, such as under Hyper-V from Microsoft then you cannot simply plug in a USB memory stick as USB ports are not available within the virtual machine. For the install process to read it, either you must add it as a pass-through hard disk or you can create a Virtual Floppy Disk with the file on it. To add the USB Disk as a hard disk in Hyper-V, mark it as offline in the **DISKPART** tool and then add it as a drive before starting the virtual machine. For detailed instructions, take a look at http://davidoverton.com/r.ashx?12.

If you have a DVD for the system, insert the DVD and boot the system and follow the instructions to boot from a DVD for your system. You will normally have to press a key to start the process. You will see the grey bar progressing across the screen as the DVD is read. If you have a system from a hardware manufacturer then the operating system may already be installed on the hard disk. If this is the case, simply turn on the machine.

If your machine will not boot from the DVD and you have a DVD drive on the system, then check the BIOS settings to ensure that the DVD is the first boot drive.

You will then be asked to set the **Language to install**, **Time and currency format**, and **Keyboard or input method** to match your needs.

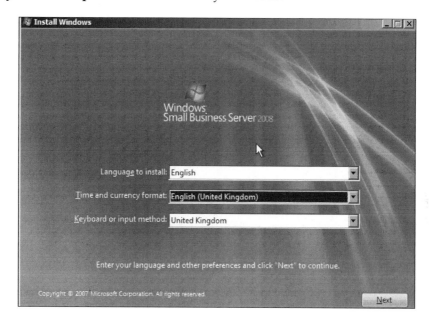

If you are migrating, you must ensure that you have installed the USB memory stick before you click on the **Install Now** button. However, if you are performing a clean installation, then simply press the button.

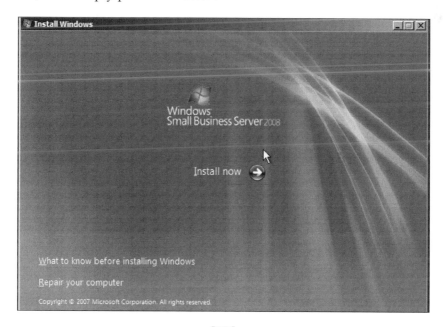

If you wish to carry out a trial installation that gives you 30 days without activating your installation and fixing your hardware to your product key, do not enter a product key into the **Product key** box. If you are performing your final installation, then enter the key from the SBS 2008 package or the **Certificate of Authenticity** on the system case if SBS was pre-installed on the server.

 If you do not enter a product key, you will be prompted to enter the key within 30 days. You can extend the time without a key, but ultimately, you will need to activate SBS 2008 to continue using it.

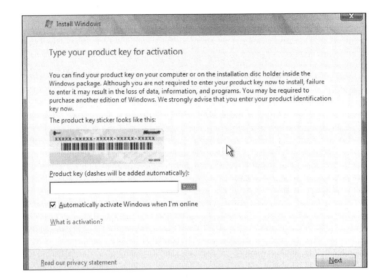

Next, accept the license and click on **Next**.

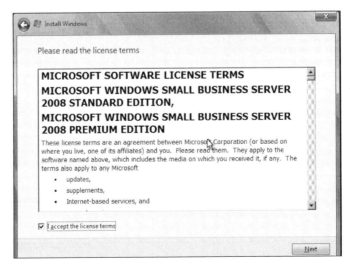

Select the **Custom (advanced)** installation option.

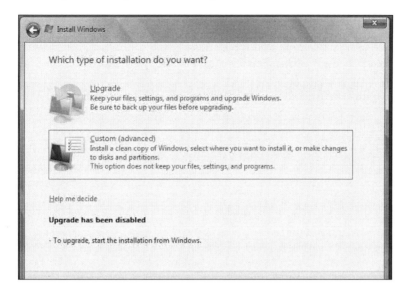

You should see one or more disks presented to you in a list. There are two schools of thought here on how to configure the first disk. One school has all the data on the first (or primary) partition and the other creates two partitions and splits the data and the operating system. The idea here is that the system partition can be correctly sized and backed up with a different strategy to the data partition. You can also easily move the second partition onto larger disks should there be a need to in the future.

There are merits to both arguments, but if you only have a single disk, I would simply select this and install SBS 2008 to this disk without partitioning first. For SBS 2008, this should be absolutely fine as your data needs are not going to grow too rapidly. If you do have significant data requirements with multiple disks, then having the data and system separate does make sense.

No hard disks showing

If you do not see a hard disk shown in the screen, maybe because you need to load RAID disk drivers, click on the **Load Driver** button and insert the CD or floppy disk that came with your computer or motherboard. Provided your system supports Windows 2008, this will resolve this problem.

Let's have a look at the following screenshot:

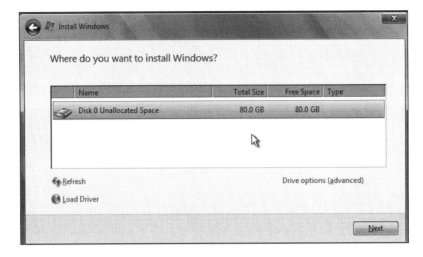

Click on **Next** and the actual installation will finally start and take over an hour to complete. You will find yourself watching the progress on a screen similar to the one shown in the following screenshot. There is no interaction to this process, which means it can just be left on its own; however, it is best to check in ever so often to ensure that an error message has not interrupted the installation. The only error I've seen was when there was a read error from my DVD (I had scratched it!). I cleaned the disk and re-started the install again without any issue.

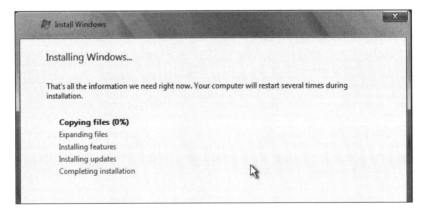

SBS 2008 installation continued

Once the system has rebooted, you will see a screen informing you that the installation was successful and that it is now time to continue. Some of the screens shown only relate to a system that is part of a migration, while others only relate to a clean installation. If this is a clean installation and not a migration, then you simply need to click on **Next**.

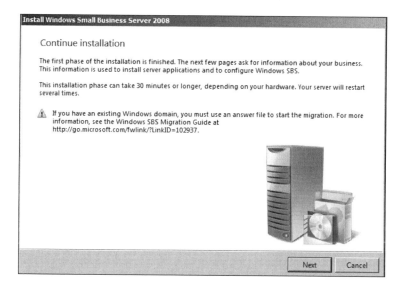

If you are performing a migration, you will see the **Start the Migration Guide** screen that re-affirms the importance of a backup. I'm assuming you do have a backup.

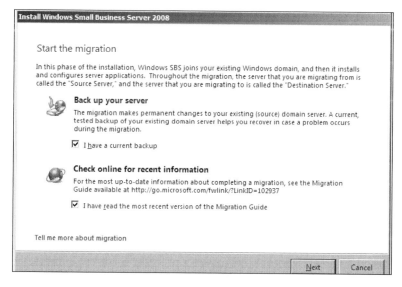

Check the two boxes regarding a backup and the migration guide, and click on **Next**.

The Microsoft migration guide can be downloaded from `http://davidoverton.com/r.ashx?X`. This was used in putting together the information for this book. If you are keen to explore more details around the installation process, then this guide is a valuable source of information. I also have a forum on my web site at `http://davidoverton.com/r.ashx?13`.

If you have selected to run unattended in the answer file settings, then you will not see many of the following settings screens. If you did not ask for an unattended install, then all the answers you have entered will still be used, but you will be asked to verify the details. The next sections cover off those sections you will need to complete.

Time Verification

Even if you selected an unattended install, you could have still set for the time to be manually confirmed. As with the SBS 2003 system you are migrating from, you are next asked to verify the time for the migration to work. Correct time is an essential part of the security settings.

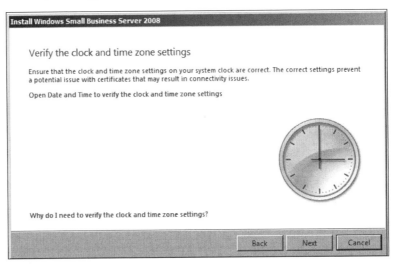

The small clock picture does not show the time, so the only way to verify the date and time is to click on the **Open Date and Time** link. This brings up the normal date and time dialog box scene as shown in the following screenshot. As this is a new system, it is quite probable that the date and/or the time will be wrong or the time zone will not be correct, so verify all the items.

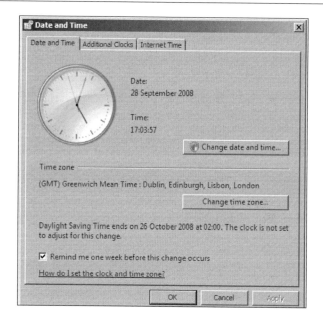

Network settings for migrating systems

For the migration to work, the source (SBS 2003) and destination (SBS 2008) servers need to have their IP or network addresses confirmed. Since this information was in the Answer File, it should simply be a case of confirming it if the unattended installation is not selected. Normally, the IP addresses should both be of the form of 192.168.x.y where x is the same for both addresses and y is different.

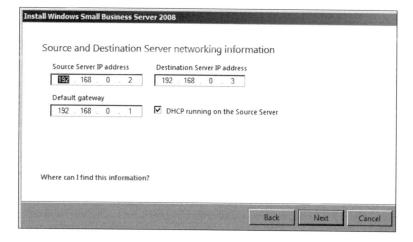

The next items that may need confirmation are the settings for the domain. Do not add certificate information as it can cause issues; leave this setting blank. Again, this should simply be a case of clicking on **Next** to confirm the settings from the Answer File.

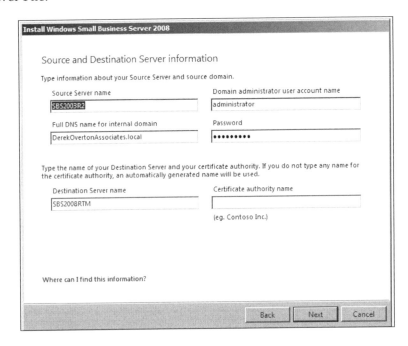

Getting installation updates

You are now presented with an opportunity to download updates for your server. These updates can cover both the process of the installation and the security of the server. Since it can take only minutes for a machine connected to the Internet to be compromised, I strongly suggest that you get the installation updates. Select **Go online and get the most recent installation updates** to get updates.

 You will need a working Internet connection to be able to get updates.

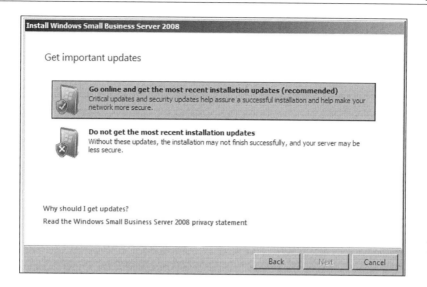

Confirming Company information

The Company information is used to populate information in the Fax settings, the intranet site, and Exchange 2007. Even if you are using an Answer File, you may be prompted to re-confirm these settings. Fill in the details and click on **Next**.

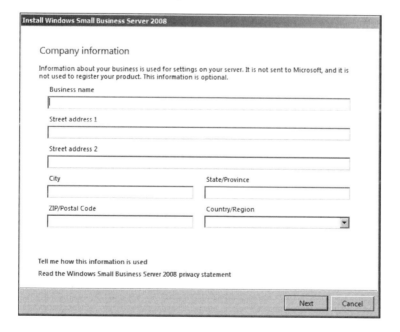

Creating an administrator account for new installations

If you're performing a clean installation, you need to create the administrator account. To do this, fill in the **First name** and **Last name** fields with the name of the administrator of the system. The **Administrator user name** should be related to the administration of the system, but should not be *Administrator* as this is a security risk.

Think carefully about the name of the administrator as this will be the name used to manage the system. It should not be *administrator*, and it should not be a regular user's account either. It may be that someone is both a user and administrator of the system, which should mean that two accounts are created.

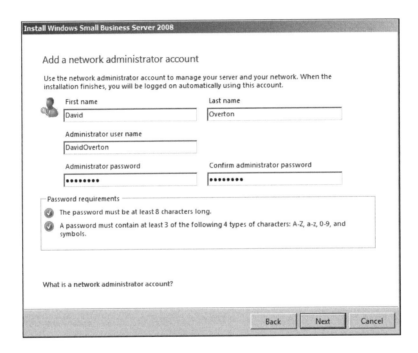

Naming your server and domain for new installations

If this is a new installation, you will need to name your server in the **Server name** box and enter an **internal domain name**, which should not be confused with the Internet domain name. If your Internet domain name was mycompany.com then your internal domain name might be **mycompany**. Enter this and then click on **Next**.

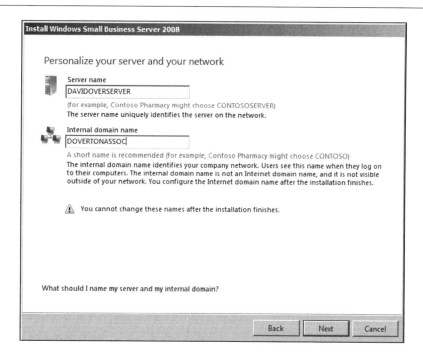

Installing OneCare and Forefront Trials

You always have the option as to whether to use the Microsoft security products or those provided by a third party. If you intend to use third-party products that are suitable for SBS 2008, do not check these boxes, but ensure you install those products and sign up to the subscription as soon as possible. The Microsoft products are trial products, which means you can use them to secure your machine for 3+ months without paying any additional money; however, after that time you will need to purchase the subscription licenses. You can de-install the Microsoft products to replace them at any time.

 Microsoft has announced the end of OneCare, but you can still use it to give three months free anti-malware support. You will need to purchase anti-malware software for your SBS 2008 system eventually.

Paying for security products on an ongoing basis

Whether it is Microsoft or other third-party products you use for security, they will need constant updates to deal with the ever changing threat to your server and network. For this reason, you should purchase a subscription with monthly or annual payments no matter who the provider is.

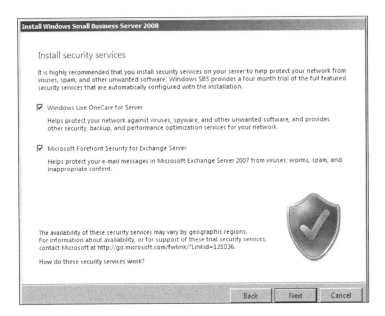

You may see a summary screen confirming the settings. Click **Next** on this screen and once this has finished expanding and installing, click on the **Finish** button.

Installation finished, possibly with errors

Now, you have finally finished the last part of the installation before you actually migrate data and settings across. It might have all gone smoothly or some errors may have been reported as **installation issues**. If the installation process goes severely off the rails then SBS 2008 will stop the installation; however, there are some errors or issues that are acceptable during the installation process. A log of these errors will be made and you will be told about them on the final screen as shown in the following screenshot. To view the errors, click on the **View installation issues** text.

You can read the installation issues at any time from the SBS 2008 console, so you do not need to note all the detail, at this stage of the process, if you decide to resolve some of them later.

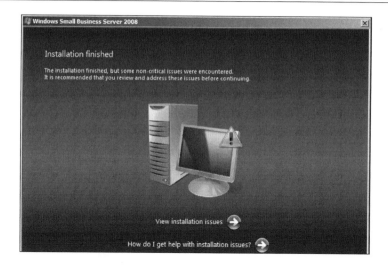

Resolving errors and installing SBS 2008 updates

Having finished the installation, you can check the issues in the **Windows SBS Console** by clicking on **View installation issues**. Most of the installations I have carried out have shown at least one issue, ranging from network errors to update failures.

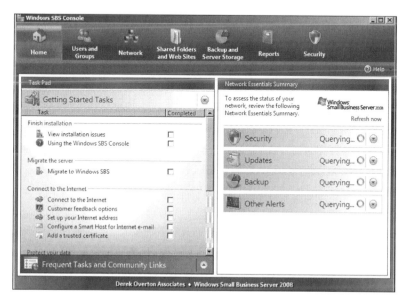

Click on the link **View installation issues** to see any issues.

You need to take the action recommended or other appropriate action. Click on **How do I fix this issue** to get advice on the specific issue and how to fix it. Given that errors are unexpected, I can't script all the answers here; however, there is one I have frequently seen, about updates that did not run.

If the issue, as shown in the following screenshot, is **One or more updates cannot be installed** then the best option is to run **Windows Update**. You can find this by typing **Windows Update** into the **Start menu**.

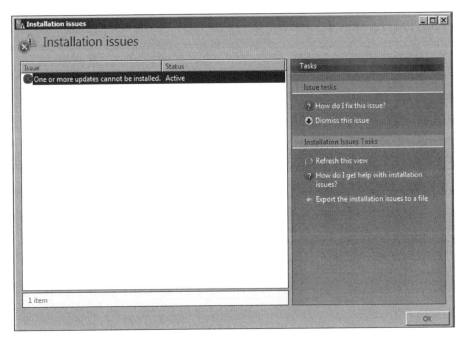

You should see that your system is waiting to install updates as shown in the following screenshot and then, you simply need to click on the **Install Updates** button. If there are no updates listed, click on the **Check for Updates** button. If this fails to connect to find updates, then you need to check your network cables and network settings.

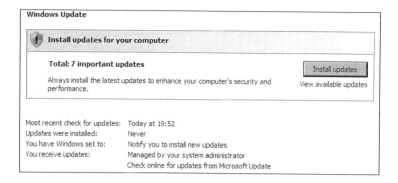

Once the updates are installed, you will probably be prompted to reboot the system, which you should do so by clicking on the **Restart Now** button.

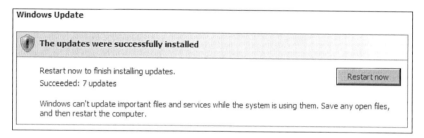

Setting up IP addresses for clean installations

If you are running a new installation, you will need to configure your Internet settings to continue with the setup. For migrations, this will have already been done automatically, so this step can be skipped. To complete this step, your SBS 2008 system must be wired into your network.

DHCP Settings

SBS 2008 should be configured as the only DHCP server on your network. It is possible that your router, wireless hub, telephone system, or other network component will be fulfilling this role at the moment. You will need to disable this for SBS 2008 to be correctly configured.

If you have restarted the system, log back in and open the **Windows SBS Console** from the **Start** menu. In the **Task Pad** on the **Home** screen, click on the task **Connect to the Internet**.

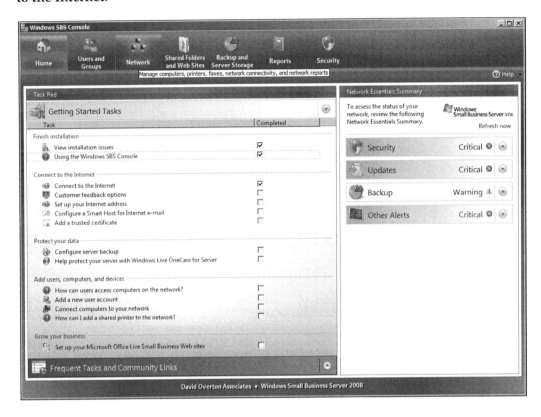

The initial screen requires you to confirm that you have the **IP address of the internal interface on your router**. This is also known as the router gateway address. This is used to configure the access to the Internet for the server, and if you have a UPnP router to also configure various settings on it.

 If you configure a router with UPnP, you might remove any customizations you have made to it. It might be easier to configure the network by hand.

Once you have confirmed you have this information, click on **Next**.

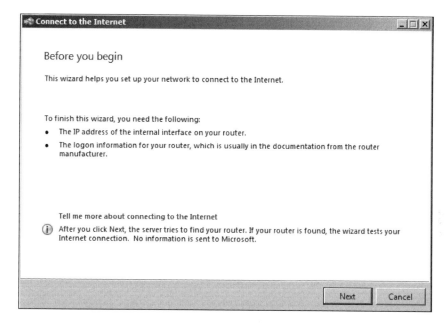

SBS 2008 will try to detect your existing network settings. It should take no more than 30 seconds to do so.

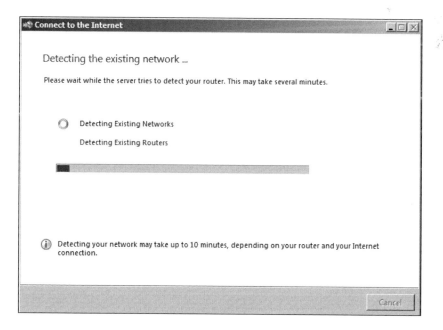

If it cannot find your settings, it will offer some default settings that you can accept or change. Once you have what you believe are the correct settings, click on **Next.**

 SBS 2008 checks for routers on 192.168.x.1 and 192.168.x.254 only, so I advice using one of those. You should also plan the IP addresses of fixed devices on your network, such as printers.

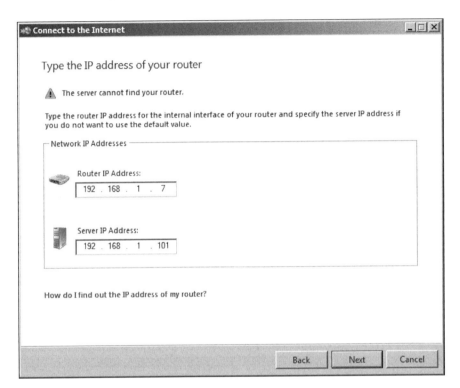

SBS 2008 will try to verify the router gateway address and use the IP address that you suggested. If it is still not able to detect these settings, you will be told that **a router was not found on your local network**. If you have not yet set up your Internet connection, then click on the **Yes** button. If you have configured your router, then click on **No** and check your settings.

 If you have problems here, then you can check settings by using **Ping** or **Tracert** to check the network's ability to carry messages and then **Nslookup** to check DNS settings.

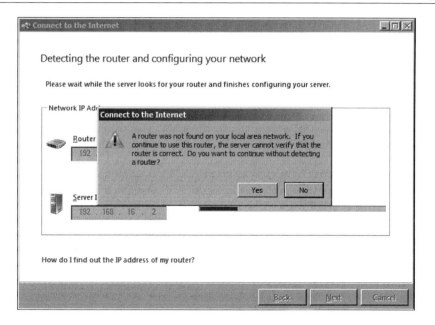

If the settings are correct, SBS 2008 will show the settings and confirm that the router was found with a large green check mark at the top of the **Connect to the Internet** wizard. Click on **Next** to start the configuration process.

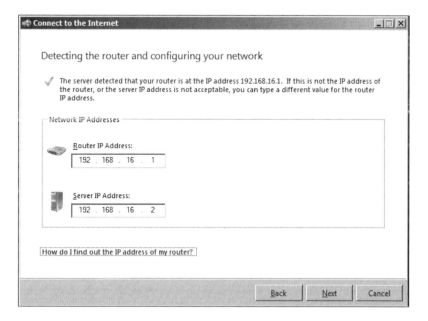

Once the configuration is complete, you will see a green check mark and be able to click on the **Finish** button.

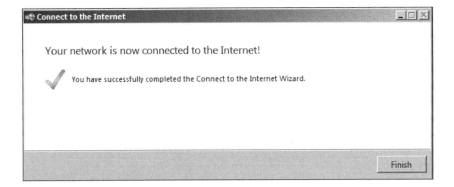

Summary

You now have a system that is part of a network domain, either an existing domain if you're running a migration or a new domain, your first, if this is a clean install.

The server should be able to send and receive information with the Internet, but is not yet configured to take advantage of the many abilities that SBS 2008 offers a small business. If you are running a migration, you will need to run through the migration wizard over the next four chapters to migrate all the settings and data.

If this is a clean installation, you will need to continue with the configuration by following the **Windows SBS Console** check list, and then migrate each business PC's data into the SBS domain. To follow the checklist, go to Chapter 7 to configure the server and secure it.

5

Migrating Systems and Settings from SBS 2003

This chapter covers the migration of the configuration settings from the SBS 2003 system to SBS 2008. This will require activity on both servers.

We will cover the following areas in this chapter:

- Starting the Migration Wizard
- Initially configuring the SBS 2008 network
- Configuring Internet Access
- Migrating the SBS 2003 network settings across
- Cleaning up the group policy settings

Impact on users

This part of the migration will see users being impacted from the perspective of incoming email and network routing. I would strongly advise that users were not trying to use the system while this was performed. If all goes well, it should not take more than an hour to complete.

Assumptions

The assumption here is that the preparations for migration went smoothly or all issues that were raised have been fully resolved. Since the migration process builds on previous steps, if something has failed it needs to be resolved otherwise later steps will fail too. It is also vital that your server is fully patched as per the Windows Update and the Best Practices Analyzer tool and that all the pre-requisites as described in Chapter 3 have been met.

I'm also assuming that the installation, other than needing updates, went smoothly as described in Chapter 4. If not, you should re-run the installation rather than trying to continue when the foundations are flawed.

There are a number of checks in the migration process, for which if they throw up an error the recommendation is to stop and fix the problem. If the problem is particularly severe or points to a flaw in the original SBS 2003 system, then the most likely way to avoid further issues in the migration would be to follow this process:

- Back up any changed data on either server, such as file shares, email, or data in the CompanyWeb SharePoint site.

- Restore the original server to its original state from the backup taken prior to starting the migration.

- Rectify the situation on the original SBS 2003 server.

- Apply all the preparation steps.

- Restore the updated data from the SBS 2003 and SBS 2008 servers.

- Take another backup of the SBS 2003 server, but don't destroy the earlier one you took.

- Start the SBS 2008 installation and re-start the migration.

This might sound very severe, but I've seen some people end up with an unusable server by plowing on through error after error when fixing an original small problem and re-starting the whole process would have saved time and frustration. Having said that, very few errors require such extreme action. Most issues can be fixed and the failed migration step can be re-started.

 Microsoft provides information on common error messages, with some resolution tips at http://davidoverton.com/r.ashx?18. Additional troubleshooting tools and the repair guide can be found at http://davidoverton.com/r.ashx?17.

21-day time limit

It is important that the migration process is completed in less than 21 days. You should be able to complete the whole migration process in a concerted effort of between one and three days depending on the amount of data that needs moving. There is often no reason why you can't leave the process and come back to it later providing users can access their data, email, and web sites when you stop. If the process is not finished within in 21 days, you will see the following error message and your SBS 2003 system will start rebooting every 60-90 minutes. While you can be productive between the reboots, this should be a completely avoidable situation. If errors have stopped the successful migration, the recovery process opposite should be used, which would reset the timers as well as give you a platform to repair and restart from.

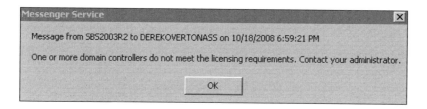

User Access Control

User Access Control (or UAC as it is often called) is a security feature of Windows
Server 2008 and Windows Vista. The prompts that are displayed are color coded to
highlight the level of risk associated with accepting or continuing the process. While
we are performing the many administration tasks for the migration, you will see
a number of these prompts. Once the configuration is completed, you should then
see very few; however, when you do, you should carefully consider if you intended
on something changing the core system settings. If you are not sure, always stop or
block the action.

During the migration, should you see a blue prompt similar to the one shown in the
following screenshot as you start a new task from the menu or click a menu item
with the shield on it, you should be safe to continue. If you see any orange or red
prompts, this seems suspicious to me and is something to question.

I do not highlight when you will see UAC prompts during the migration, which is
why I am covering them in detail here. While you can turn off UAC prompts, you
do not get to see if a UAC prompt was blue or orange if you do so, which is a vital
security benefit, so I strongly recommend leaving UAC enabled and clicking on
Continue as appropriate.

Following is an example of a blue colored UAC prompt, which is common for
applications and tools signed by third parties as well as the Microsoft tools.

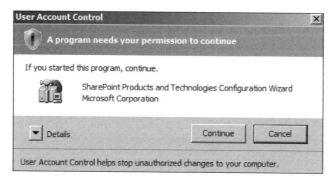

Below is an example of an orange colored UAC prompt, which tells you that the application is not signed or "trusted". Any application that gives a prompt like this should be carefully considered, although this prompt does not mean the application is bad.

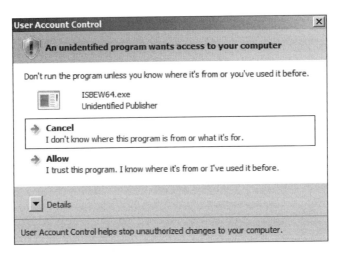

Preparing to run the Migration Wizard

There are still two more tasks that you might have to finish off before you can run the Migration Wizard without issue. The first is to change the folder redirection group policy and the second is to create a new user with administrator ability.

Changing folder redirection

If you have folder redirection enabled, it means that all your documents are stored on the server as well as the user's PC. This needs to be pointed to the new server before the migration is started by checking and changing group policy in your domain. If you are not sure if it is enabled, simply follow this process and if the policy does not exist, then you are fine.

Having logged on the SBS 2008 system, find the folder **Administrative Tools** on the **Start** menu and then click **Group Policy Management** from the menu.

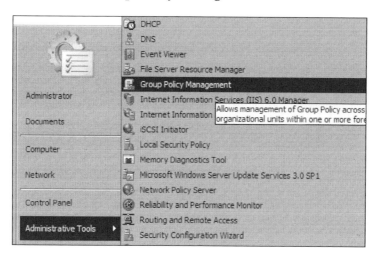

This will open up the GPO (Group Policy Object) Management tool. Here, you will see a combination of all the policies that were defined on the SBS 2003 server, including folder redirection and firewall settings as well as and the new policies loaded by SBS 2008. While we will remove the policies that conflict later in the book, right now, we just need to change the folder redirection policy.

 Changing the Group Policy Objects can cause your system or users' abilities to change. You should only make changes that you are confident are required, such as the one described here.

Navigate to the **Group Policy Objects** in the lefthand navigation pane and find the **Small Business Server Folder Redirection** item and click on it.

If it is not present, then you do not need to continue the process of changing folder redirection and can skip forward to creating a new administrator account.

If you do not have this feature enabled, but having read about it in Chapter 2 would like to do so, this will be covered in Chapter 11.

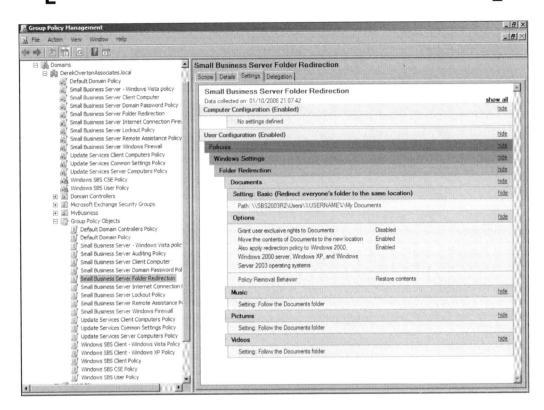

Right-click on the **Small Business Server Folder Redirection** GPO and select **Edit**.

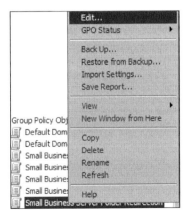

This will load the Group Policy Management Editor. Navigate to **User Configuration**, **Windows Settings**, **Folder Redirection**, and finally, **Documents**. Right-click **Documents** and select **Properties**.

Set the **Setting** dropdown to **Basic – Redirect everyone's folder to the same location** and change the **Root Path** to **\\<Destination ServerName>\RedirectedFolders** where you put in the name of your new server for **<Destination ServerName>**.

 Until you migrate the files, which is described in Chapter 8, users can load and save files, but their existing files will not be stored on the new server.

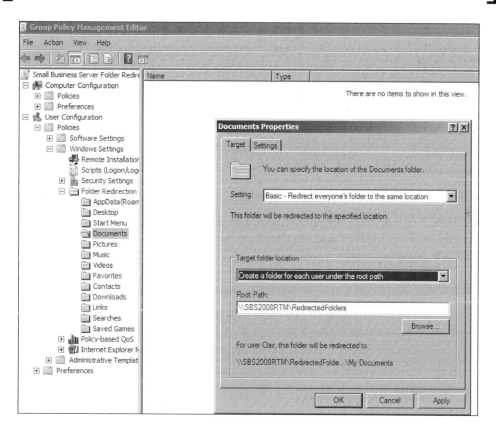

When you click on **OK**, you will receive a warning, which you can simply accept.

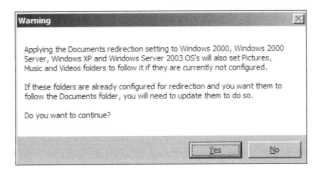

Creating a new administrator account

If you try to run the migration wizard when you are logged into the SBS 2008 system with the default SBS 2003 system administrator user of **Administrator**, the tool will display this error message:

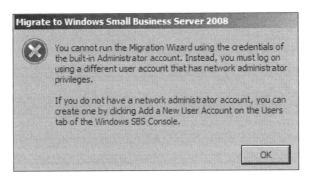

 SBS 2008 attempts to avoid simple security errors by enabling restrictive policies to enforce good practice. One of those items is that the system administrator user is not called administrator. This means a would-be hacker has to know what the administrator username is rather than simply knowing what it would be.

Go to the **Users and Groups** tab in the **Windows SBS Console** and add a new user who will be an administrator. Since we have not yet migrated across any of the existing SBS 2003 users, we can simply make one of them an administrator; however, that would not be a recommended solution, so we need to add a new user for the administrator.

Click on the **Add a new user account** link to start the process.

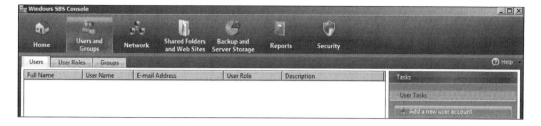

Fill in the details on the screen, which should be self explanatory.

Ideally, the administrator user should not simply be a normal user's name as you do not want someone logged in as the domain administrator when working. While the user can still include a person's name, it should clearly identify itself as an administrator rather than a normal user. In the following example, I used **David Overton Admin** as the name and user so they are not confused with David Overton the user.

The SBS 2008 wizard suggests a potential **user name**; however, you can freely type into this box to change it should you desire. You also need to ensure that the **User Role** is set to **Network Administrator** before clicking on **Next**.

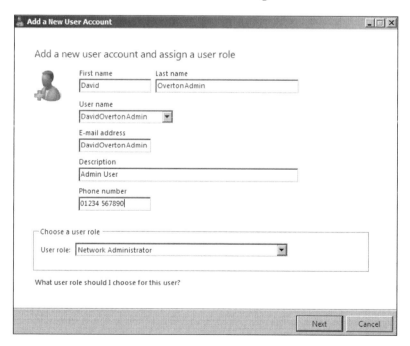

The wizard will execute a number of steps to create the user, including creating shared folders and configuring email.

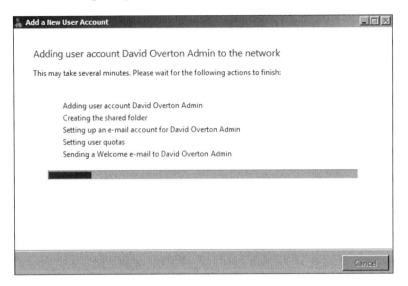

The user will be created, but once again there may be a warning associated with the user and the current early state of migration.

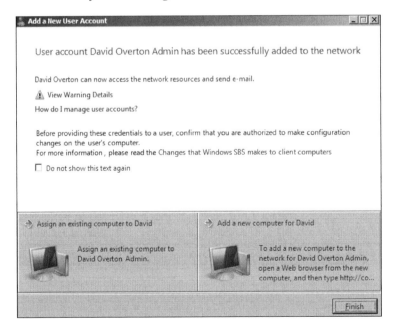

If you click on the **View Warning Details** link, you will see the errors (if any). If the error relates to the inability to send a welcome email, this is an expected error and can be ignored as this will be rectified later through the migration process. Other errors will require further investigation.

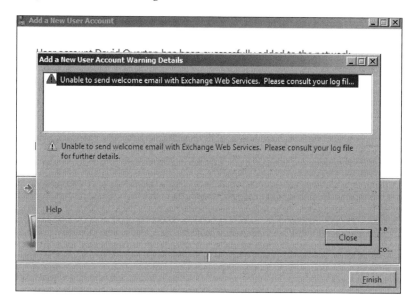

We're now ready and able to start the Migration Wizard!

Working through the Migration Wizard

You do not have to use the Migration Wizard to perform the migration; however, the wizard guides you through a reliable and supported process that ensures that all the standard settings and content from SBS 2003 are migrated. I would never attempt a migration without going through this process.

Start back on the **Home** tab in the **Windows SBS Console** and you will see that the third option is the **Migrate to Windows SBS 2008** link. Click on this to start the wizard.

If you do not see the Migrate task on the list, then SBS 2008 was not installed in a migration configuration. You will need to restart the process ensuring the answer file is prepared and available to the server during installation as required.

The Migration Wizard

You should now see a screen similar to the one shown below:

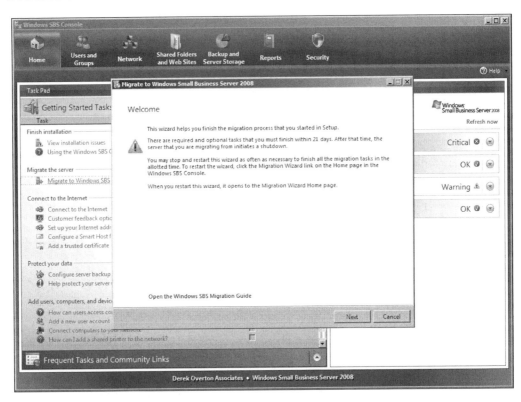

This presents you with a number of tasks that should be completed to reliably migrate the data and settings from SBS 2003 to SBS 2008 and enable the SBS 2003 server to be decommissioned. Some steps are mandatory and others optional, but all should be considered before ignoring. You should only ignore a step if you believe there is no impact or because you are concerned about the quality of the data that you would be migrating across.

To help understand what must be done, even if you have concerns about the integrity of the source server, look at the following table. I would strongly recommend all items that I have marked as mandatory even if you have some concerns about the SBS 2003 server settings. You might choose to perform the migration in a non-standard way for the mandatory tasks, but they should still be performed. An example for this might be the Exchange mailboxes migration. You might not use Exchange to perform the migration if you considered this as a suspect and might export all the mail into PST files, but you will still need to ensure that the user's mail is migrated.

Migration Task	Mandatory or optional task	Manually or automatic process
Change where to store data on the Destination Server	Optional	Automatic
Configure the network	Mandatory	Manual
Configure the Internet address	Mandatory	Manual
Migrate network settings	Optional	Automatic
Migrate Exchange mailboxes and settings	Mandatory	Both
Remove legacy group policies and logon settings	Mandatory	Manual
Migrate Users' shared data	Mandatory	Manual
Migrate SharePoint Web site	Optional	Manual
Migrate Fax data	Optional	Manual
Migrate Users and Groups	Mandatory	Both

Changing where to store data on the SBS 2008 server

While it is possible to manage the data storage locations, I normally do this once I have completed the migration tasks. The movement of all data except Exchange is governed by commands you type in, so these steps do not govern where the data is migrated to. I will cover in more detail how to move data locations in Chapter 13.

To start the migration, highlight the first task on the list and then click on the **Next** button.

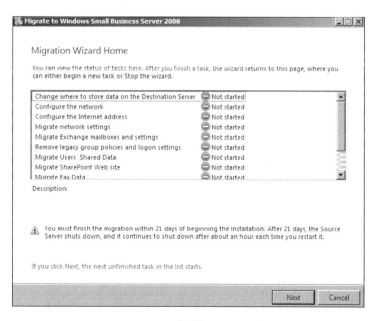

If you do want to change data locations before you have started the migration, click the links on the screen. If you wish to skip this task, click on the **Skip task** radio button at the bottom of the screen, followed by **Next**.

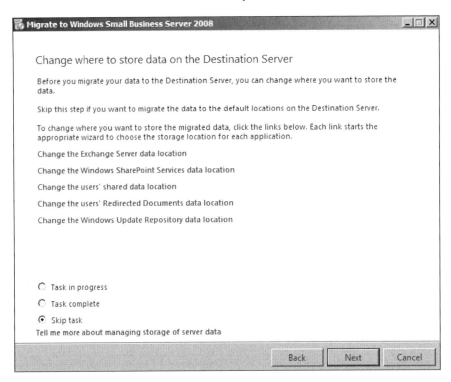

If you move data, you will need to ensure you have at least two disks that are formatted with NTFS before you start the process. Click on **Next** on the getting started page to continue.

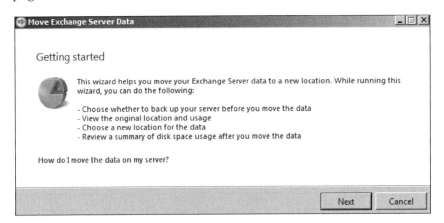

SBS 2008 will search for disks that could have the data moved to them and then present these in a list for you to choose from. Choose a disk from the **New location** selection and click **Move**.

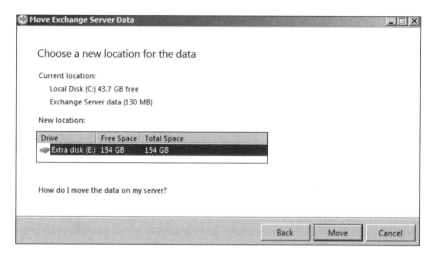

Once the data movement is complete, you will see a summary of the movement carried out.

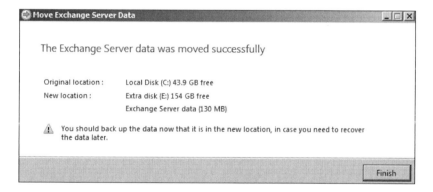

Finally, click on **Finish** to get back to the task options. Select other locations that you might want to move and when you have completed all you desire, click **Task completed** and then click on **Next** to get back to the migration task list.

Initially configuring the SBS 2008 network

Now, we need to confirm and configure the network settings. On the Migration Wizard, select the second option of **Configure the network** and then select **Next**.

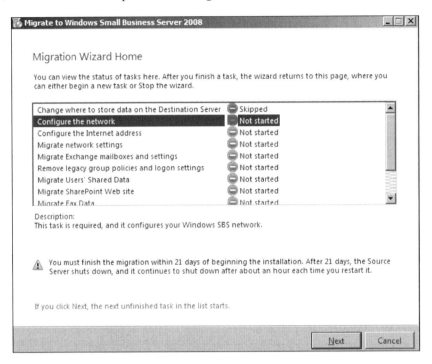

This step simply gives you a link to the standard SBS 2008 *Connect to the Internet Wizard*. In this section, we will walk through the steps as if you have a UPnP network router (one that can be configured by SBS automatically). If you want to see how to configure the network without a UPnP router, take a look at Chapter 4 for the section on *Setting up IP Addresses for clean installations*. Click the **Start the Connect to Internet Wizard** link to start the task.

 UPnP routers can be reconfigured by any system on the network at any time. This presents a management and security issue. Even if your router supports UPnP, you can choose to manually configure it.

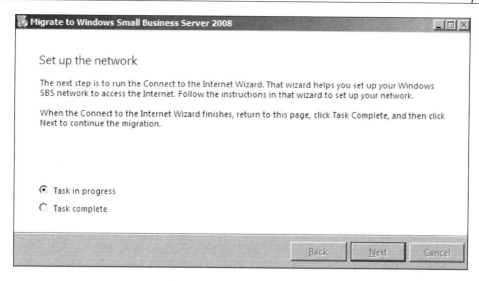

Just in case you've forgotten it since you ran the tool to create the answer file, you will need to know the IP address of your server and your Internet router. Click on the **Next** button to start SBS 2008's detection routine.

 The term router and gateway are interchangeable in meaning for small business networks. What is important is the IP address of the hardware that connects your internal network to the Internet.

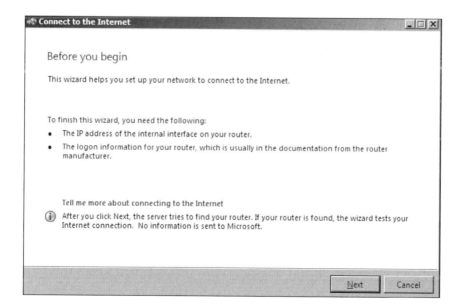

Assuming the wizard finds a router, it will ask you to confirm the two IP addresses. Simply click on **Next** to continue. If no router is found, check your cables and ensure that your router is plugged in. SBS 2008 attempts to find the router with the following process. You might consider changing your router IP address to enable it to be found by the tools.

- It sends an ICMP Router Discovery Message on multicast address 224.0.0.2 and waits for a Router Advertisement if the protocol is supported.

- It sends the Simple Service Discovery Protocol Discovery Service (SSDP) to find routers that do not support RFC 1256.

- It sends ARP requests to 192.168.*.1 and 192.168.*.254, looking for routers with those IP addresses.

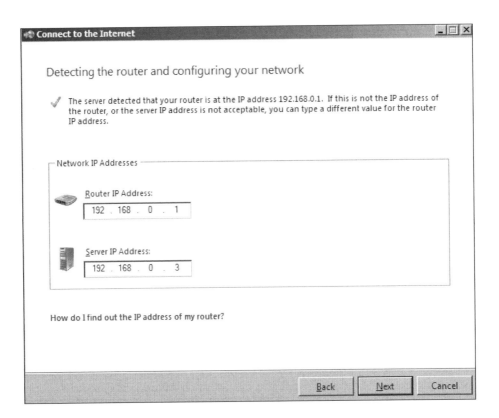

The configuration will be checked while the following screen appears:

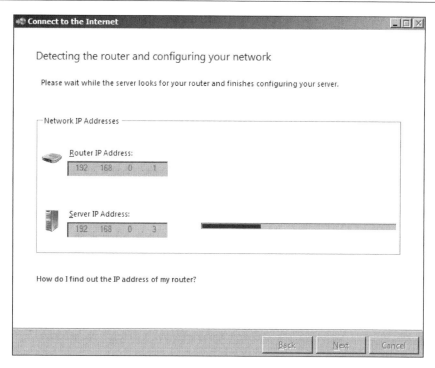

Once the process is complete, you will see a screen with a large green check mark:

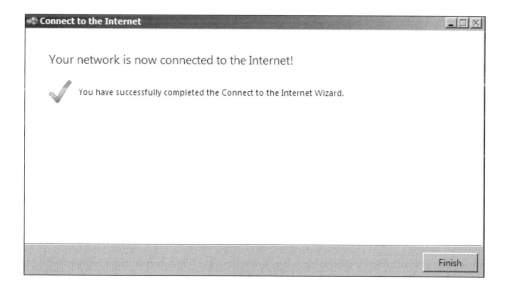

If requested to do so, select **Task Completed** on the screen and click on **Next**.

Configuring Internet Access

The Configure Internet Access wizard configures the following items:

- Internet Domain Name
- DNS management for Domain Name
- Firewall ports
- Email addresses

I am assuming that you already have a domain name as you would have used it with SBS 2003 and it will continue to be used once you have migrated to SBS 2008. If you don't, then you can again follow the information in Chapter 9 in the section on *Configuring your Internet domain name for remote access and email*. Select **Configure Internet Access** and then click on the **Next** button.

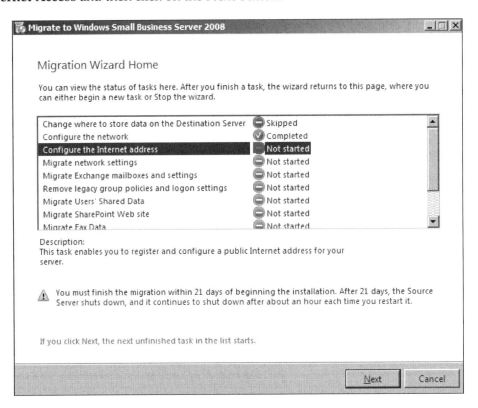

Since we have not imported an SSL certificate, the configuration steps will enable the creation of an SSL certificate that is signed by SBS 2008. This certificate will automatically be distributed to all machines as they log onto the network to enable correct installation of the certificate into their trusted root list.

Anyone using secured network services, such as VPNs, accessing the Remote Web Workplace, or connecting to email without having their PC logged onto the physical network in the office with the SBS 2008 system, will see security errors as their machines will not yet trust the certificate. Since this will also impact Outlook collecting email, the certificate cannot simply be sent to users. It will need to be copied to physical media, such as a CD and mailed to people so they can continue working securely. To learn more about this, click on **How do I distribute certificates to remote users?** from the first screen in the task.

Once you have read this, or if you do not need to, click the **Start the Internet Address Management Wizard** link to start the wizard.

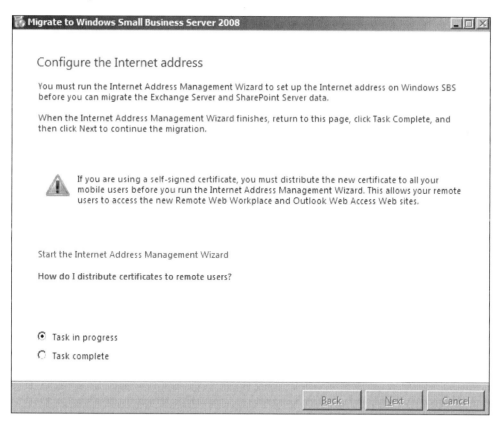

Since you have a domain name that you wish to use, select the **I already have a domain name I want to use** radio button and click on **Next**.

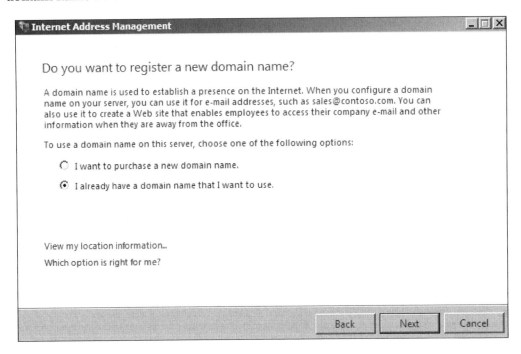

SBS 2008 works equally well with static or dynamic IP addresses and provides tools for managing the Internet domain DNS entries that SBS uses. If you have a dynamic IP address and the IP address changes, then SBS 2008 has the ability to update the DNS servers with the new IP address so that people can continue to find the server. It also fully understands the desire to have a domain where the public web site is hosted elsewhere, potentially by Office Live, and the SBS is found at a sub-domain of the main domain name. To provide all these features, your DNS must be managed by one of the supported partners for SBS 2008.

If your DNS address is not going to be managed by one of the partners, then you can continue to manage your DNS settings in the same way as you did with SBS 2003, using either your ISP or a domain registrar to provide this service. You may have a dynamic IP address and use a tool to update your DNS settings. You can continue to use these tools with SBS 2008 without any changes to your service.

You can also transfer your domain to one of the registrars supported by SBS 2008. If you do perform a transfer, later in the process select the domain registrar provider of your choice and when you **Visit Web Site**, you can transfer your domain.

Domain Registrar Transfers: time and risks

Some domain to domain transfers can be immediate, but they can also take more than 5 days. During this time, your domain might be left in limbo. Talk to the current owner of your domain registration to see if they can make the transfer quicker if desired.

It is also worth understanding that you may have many settings or sub-domains that may require transferring to and you must ensure that your new provider will be able to fulfil your requirements, otherwise, you will experience issues when other services try to connect to certain Internet services.

Choosing SBS 2008 to manage your DNS

Select the option of **I want the server to manage the domain name for me** and click on **Next**. If you want to manage it yourself, skip to the next section.

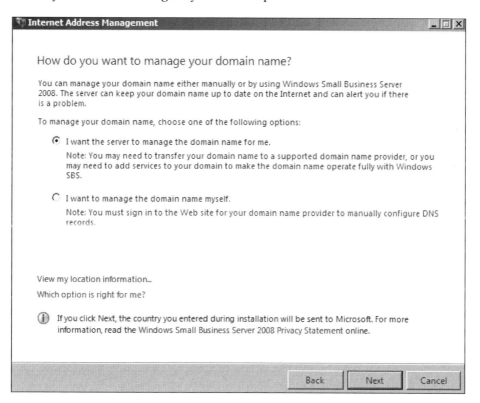

You now have to confirm your external domain name. Note that remote access to your site will be `https://remote.`**Domain Name**`.com`, while if you configure Office Live, it will be `http://www.`**Domain Name**`.com` and your email addresses will all be `<username>@`**Domain Name**`.com`. Type in your domain name without the extension, then select the extension from the list and click on **Next**.

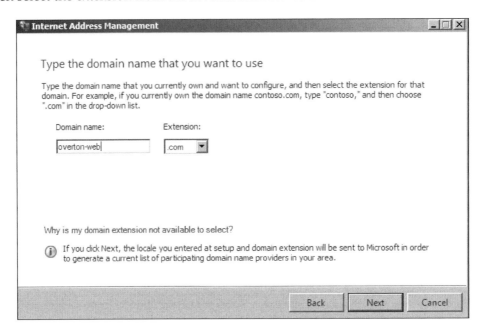

Pick your domain name provider from the list. If you have transferred it, you can still use the settings, it will just take some time to finalize. If you are unsure which provider to choose, click on the links to learn more about each provider. Once you have the right provider, click on **Next**.

 The providers in the screenshot will change over time as more providers are signed up to the service.

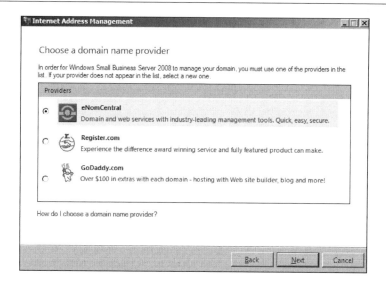

If you need to carry out further configuring of your domain name at your chosen provider, click on **Visit Web Site**, otherwise simply click **Next**. If you do need to complete some configuration, a web page will open for you to make the changes. Close the web page and then click on **Next** when complete.

 If you are performing a transfer, then you can create an account, perform the transfer, and gather your username and password when you visit the provider's web site.

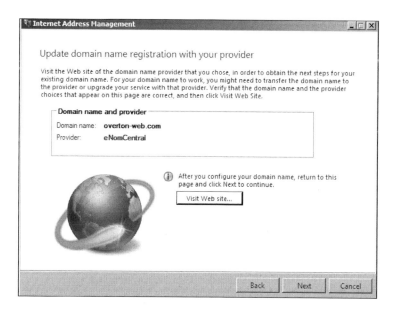

Having visited the web site, you will have either created a new account and have been provided with a user name and password or you will have used one that you already had for that provider. Now, type in your username and password for that provider and click on the **Configure** button.

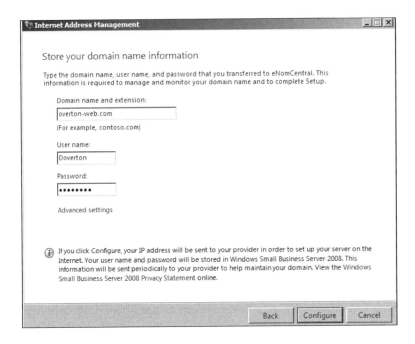

The configuration may take several minutes as the following screen completes for each option.

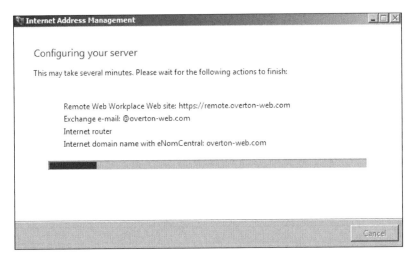

Once the configuration is completed, you may have to deal with a few issues. In the following example, there are issues with the Internet Router and Domain Name management.

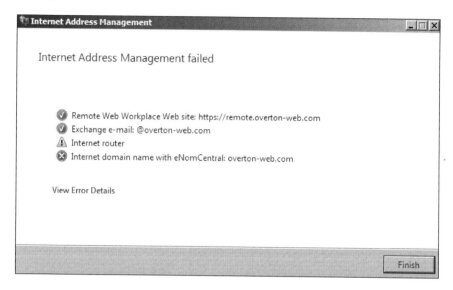

Clicking on **View Error Details** shows the errors incurred by the wizard task. SBS 2008 offers a very sophisticated diagnosis system for any error that might be experienced by a wizard. This example highlights two common errors you will see.

The first error message stating that **Windows Small Business Server 2008 cannot open ports 25, 80, 443 and 987 to the IP ad...** is caused by the inability to program the firewall as it is not yet fully configured and is not a UPnP firewall.

The second error message stating that the **DNS configuration is not yet complete** is common if you have just created your account with the domain provider or have just moved a domain for management by the provider.

If you are experiencing either of these errors in the same situations, then you can simply click **Close**. If there are other errors or the situation is different, then click on **Help** to learn about further diagnosing of the errors and the potential solution.

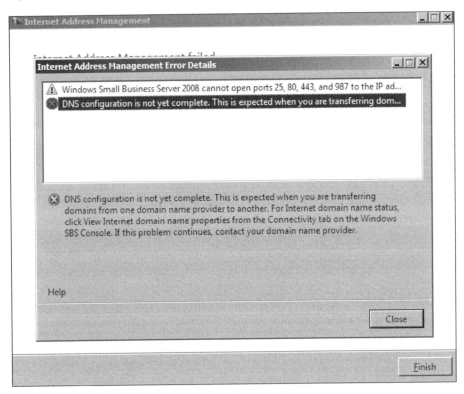

Choosing to manage your DNS settings yourself

If you choose *not* to let SBS 2008 manage your DNS settings, then you will need to select **I want to manage the domain name myself** from the list and then click on **Next** to move to the next screen.

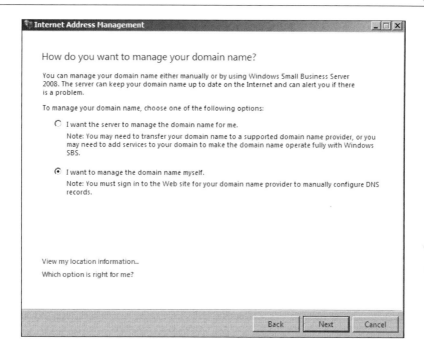

Type in your domain name, including the extension, and then click **Next** to start the configuration of Internet settings for SBS 2008. Once again the process will complete and may show some warnings as per the following example.

Clicking on **View Warning Details** shows the errors incurred by the wizard task. SBS 2008 offers a very sophisticated diagnosis system for any error that might be experienced by a wizard. This example highlights a common error stating that **Windows Small Business Server 2008 cannot open ports 25, 80, 443 and 987 to the IP ad...**It is caused by the inability to program the firewall as it is not yet fully configured and is not a UPnP firewall.

If you are experiencing these errors in the same situation, then you can simple click on **Close**. If there are other errors or you think the reason might be different, then click **Help** to learn about further diagnosing of the errors and the potential solution.

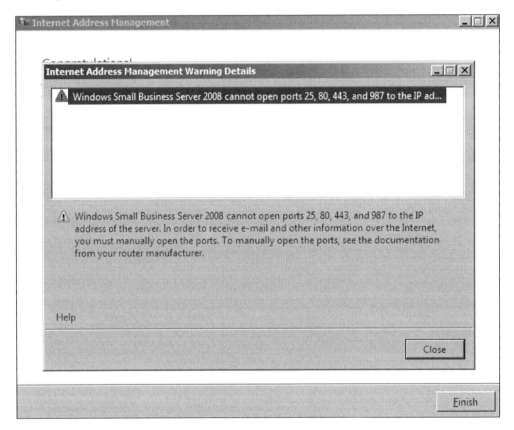

Finishing the Configure the Internet section

Select **Task Completed** on the screen and click **Next** to take you back to the list of tasks remaining.

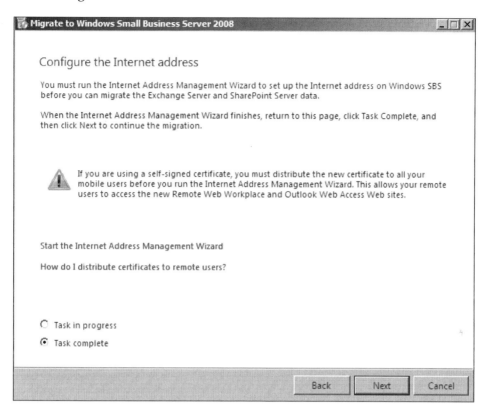

Migrating the SBS 2003 network settings across

In this section, I'm keeping it simple by continuing to use the self-generated certificate. If you have or want a certificate that is trusted outside your SBS network, then look at Chapter 10 *Securing the server*.

To get through this section, select **Migrate Network Settings** and then click on **Next**.

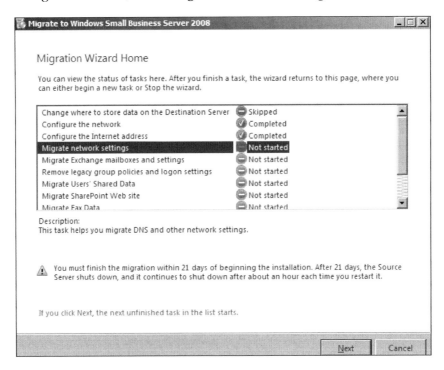

Click the first link, **Launch the DNS Forwarders Migration Task**, and the system will launch the tool.

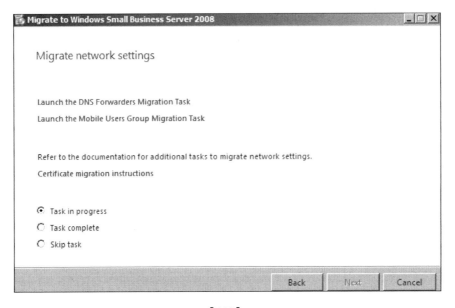

As you can see from the following screen, almost before you realized, the migration has happened and you simply need to click on **OK**.

 DNS forwarders are configured to forward DNS queries to your ISP or other DNS service when the Internet address that you are looking for cannot be found on your local network. While your network can work without these, forwarders can speed up DNS queries.

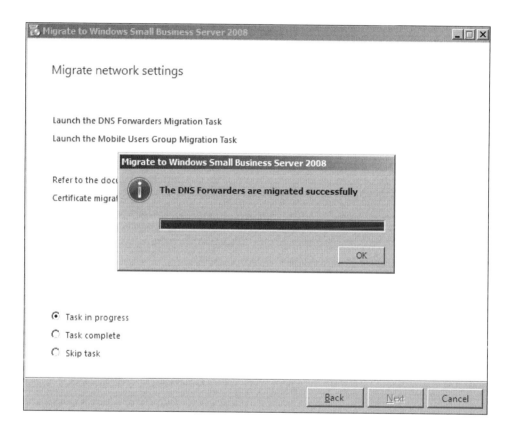

Now, click on the **Launch the Mobile Users Group Migration Task** and again you will very quickly see the **OK** button to click.

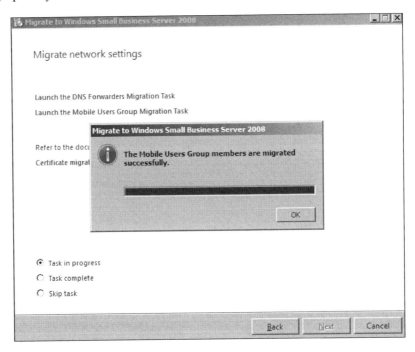

Move the task choice to **Task complete** and then click on **Next**.

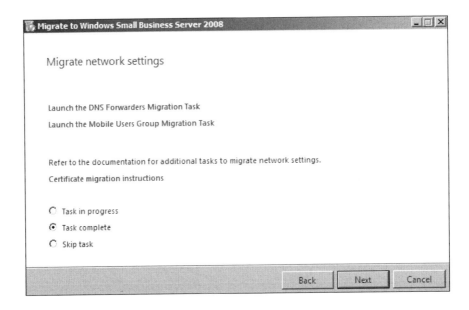

Other DNS information

Although much of the network configuration has been copied across, you should double-check any additional DHCP and DNS settings that you might have configured. If you had reserved IP addresses with DHCP, for example, these will need manually moving across.

Cleaning up the group policy settings

There are two things that need to be done to clean up the group policy. At the moment, policy objects and WMI filters have been set by both the SBS 2003 and 2008 servers and the SBS 2003 items need to be removed. If you have customized the SBS 2003 policies, you will need to re-customize the SBS 2008 policies.

If you don't remove the old items, your users may see unexpected error messages when they log on to the network as well as see security prompts if they are running Windows Vista.

Selecting **Remove legacy group policies and logon settings** in the Migration Wizard and clicking on **Next** on SBS 2008 provides you with three links to guidance on how to carry out this task. There is no automated assistance for this, so I'll walk you through the steps below.

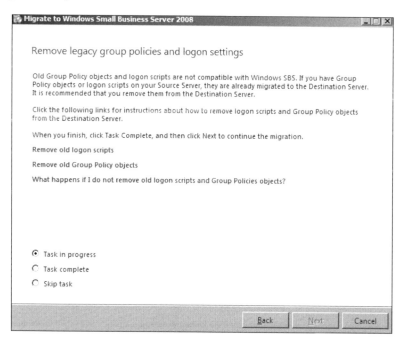

Removing old logon scripts

The first step is to remove the logon scripts from SBS 2003. While logged in as an administrator, select **Run** from the **Start** menu and type in **\\localhost\sysvol** and then navigate in the folder to **domainname.local** and then **scripts**.

Safety first

Before you delete this file, make a copy to a USB stick or other removable media so you can recover it or examine it even after the server has been decommissioned.

You should see a file called **SBS_LOGIN_SCRIPT** that you need to right-click on and delete.

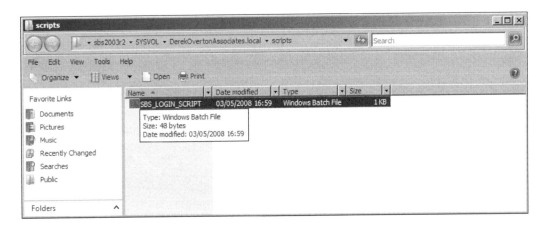

You will be asked if you want to permanently delete the file, to which the answer is **Yes**.

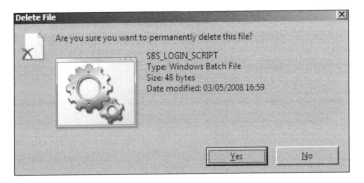

You now need to verify that the user profiles don't still have references to the login script. To do this, go to the **Start** menu and select **Active Directory Users and Computers** from the **Administrative Tools** menu. To find the users from SBS 2003, in the navigation pane expand the **<domain name>**, then **My Business, Users,** and finally **SBSUsers**. Now, right-click on your users and select **Properties**.

Move to the **Profile** tab and check to see if the logon script box is blank. If it is not, then clear it.

Check all the users and then close **Active Directory Users and Computers**.

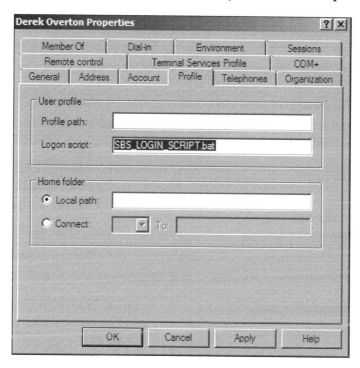

Removing old group policy objects

On the SBS 2003 system, open up Server Management, navigate to the **Advanced Management**, and then **Group Policy Management**. Continue expanding out your domain name and then click **Group Policy Objects**. On the righthand side of the screen, you will see all the **Group Policy Objects**.

Safety first—back up before you delete
Hopefully, you will not need these again, but just in case you remove a policy that you need later on, it is best to back it up first.

To perform the backup, right-click **Group Policy Objects** and select **Back Up All** from the menu. You must enter a **Location**, which is the folder that you wish to place the GPO backup files into and a description. Clicking **Back Up** will start the process.

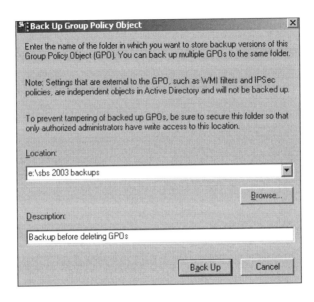

Once the backup is complete, you should see a message telling you how many GPO objects were backed up and more important, the text that **0 GPOs were not backed up**. You can then click on **OK** to continue.

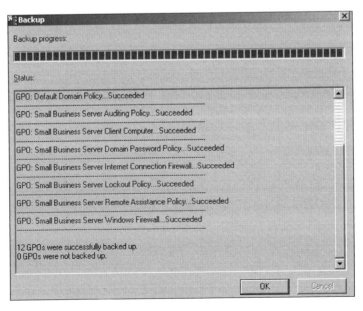

You need to select all the SBS 2003 objects. You can select multiple objects by holding the *Control* key down while you click the items to select. Select all entries that exactly match the items listed below, although you might not have them all on your SBS 2003 system.

- Small Business Server Auditing Policy
- Small Business Server Client Computer
- Small Business Server Domain Password Policy
- Small Business Server Internet Connection Firewall
- Small Business Server Lockout Policy
- Small Business Server Remote Assistance Policy
- Small Business Server Windows Firewall
- Small Business Server Windows Vista Policy
- Small Business Server Update services Client Computer Policy
- Small Business Server Update Services Common Settings Policy
- Small Business Server Update Services Server Computer Policy

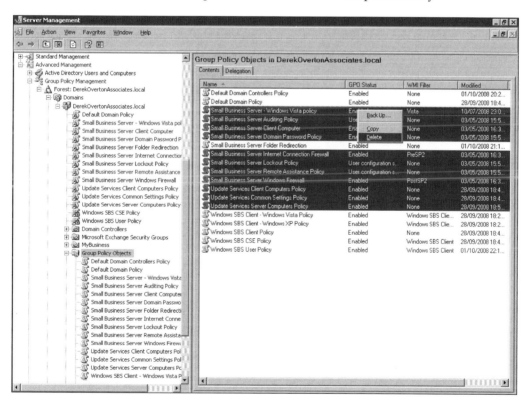

Right-click on the selected items and pick **Delete** from the menu.

You will be asked to confirm the deletion of the policy objects; simply click **OK** and the old SBS 2003 polices will be removed. You will see the results for each one in the summary window shown below. Again click **OK** to close the window.

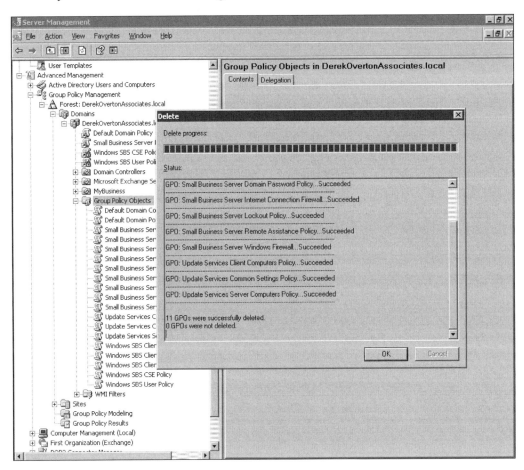

Removing WMI filters

Underneath the group policy objects are the **WMI filters** that also now have SBS 2003 and SBS 2008 items in them. Click on the **WMI Filters** and you will see the **PreSP2** and **PostSP2** filters. As is always the case before you delete hard-to-replace information, you should back it up. If you right-click on each of these and select **Export**, you can choose a location to save a MOF file. Once you have done this for both, you should select both of these using the *Control* key and right-click on them and select **Delete** again to remove these.

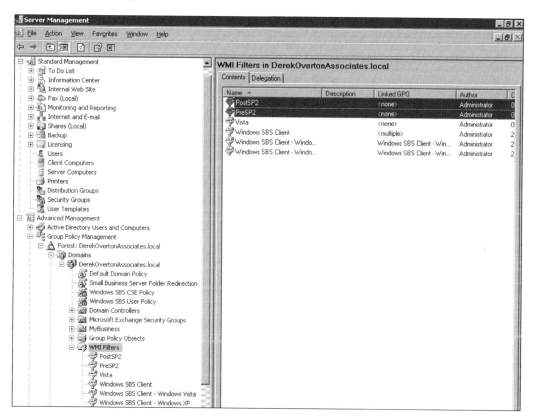

Click on **Yes** to confirm the deletion of the WMI filters.

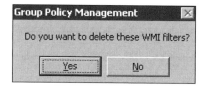

If this is successful, then you will see that the two items are removed from the list.

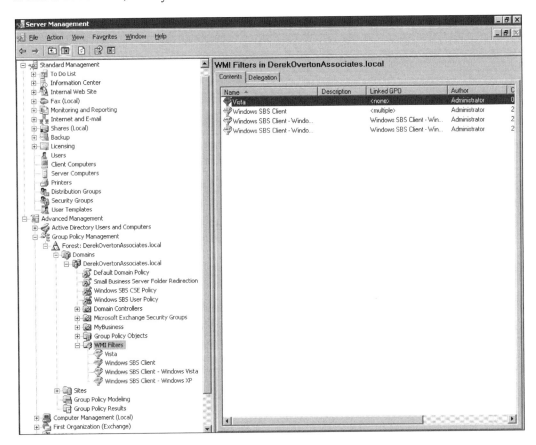

Close the Server Management Console on SBS 2003 and on SBS 2008 in the Migration Wizard, select **Task Complete** from the options and then click **Next**.

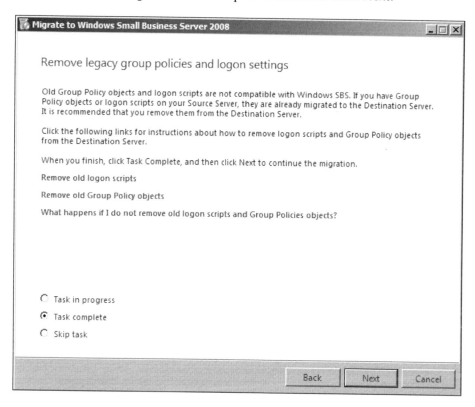

Summary

Following the successful completion of the migration tasks covered in this chapter, you should now have your SBS 2008 system on the network, and visible to local machines on the network. All your user data is still stored on the SBS 2003 system, but the management of your network has started to move to SBS 2008 with the provision of DHCP, DNS, Group Policy, and the web services that SBS 2008 will offer.

The next step in the migration is to start moving email, users' files, and CompanyWeb information from SBS 2003 to SBS 2008. After this is completed, SBS 2003 can be decommissioned.

6

Migrating Email from Exchange 2003 to Exchange 2007

This chapter covers the migration of email in Exchange 2003 on the SBS 2003 server to Exchange 2007 on SBS 2008. Completing this task this will again require activities on both servers.

Impact on users

This part of the migration will see users being impacted from the perspective of no access to email, so it should be conducted when this should not be an issue, such as during a weekend or evening and with the users knowing the situation. Migrating email can be very slow, sometimes taking hours to move individual mailboxes, so it is vital that users remove unnecessary email and empty their deleted items folder.

Migrating email from Exchange 2003 to Exchange 2007

Completion of this section will move all the mail from the SBS 2003 system to SBS 2008. It can take quite some time and includes a number of checks to try to ensure integrity between the systems. It is also the first of our tasks that once again requires activity on both the SBS 2003 and SBS 2008 systems.

Starting Migration on SBS 2008

On the SBS 2008 system, select **Migrate Exchange mailboxes and settings** and then click on **Next** from the main screen.

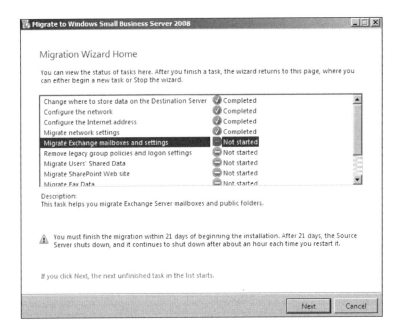

Clicking on the **Migrate Exchange Server mailboxes and public folders** link will provide you with advice and guidance on what to do. I've expanded on that in this section.

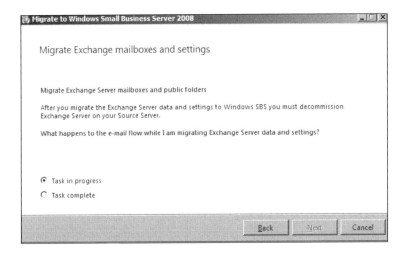

The second link **What happens to e-mail flow while I am migrating Exchange Server data and settings?** explains that mail should continue to flow while you are working on this task; however, I've experienced the server not receiving mail during a migration before. Rather than trusting mail will continue to arrive, I would set the expectation with users that no email can be sent or received during the migration.

> If you close the SMTP port on your firewall, then no mail will reach your SBS servers. Once the migration is complete, you can then open the port again, and external servers should re-send mail to be received. Providing the migration of email is less than 2 days, you are within the requirements for email redelivery. **Remember to re-open the port otherwise you'll be diagnosing email problems for a while!**

Backing up and validating Exchange database on SBS 2003 server

To be able to validate and backup Exchange, we are going to take it offline. This is done on the SBS 2003 server. Start by running the SBS 2003 **Server Management Console** and expanding the **Advanced Management** section followed by **Computer Management (Local)** and finally, **Services and Applications** before clicking on **Services**.

In the pane on the right, you should see a long list of services that are running on the system. Scroll down until you find the **Microsoft Exchange Information Store** and then right-click it and click on **Stop**.

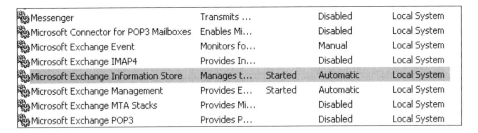

Messenger	Transmits ...		Disabled	Local System
Microsoft Connector for POP3 Mailboxes	Enables Mi...		Disabled	Local System
Microsoft Exchange Event	Monitors fo...		Manual	Local System
Microsoft Exchange IMAP4	Provides In...		Disabled	Local System
Microsoft Exchange Information Store	Manages t...	Started	Automatic	Local System
Microsoft Exchange Management	Provides E...	Started	Automatic	Local System
Microsoft Exchange MTA Stacks	Provides Mi...		Disabled	Local System
Microsoft Exchange POP3	Provides P...		Disabled	Local System

You will see a dialog box like the one shown in the following screenshot. It might take a few seconds before the box disappears. Do not click on the **Close** button as this may abort the service shutdown.

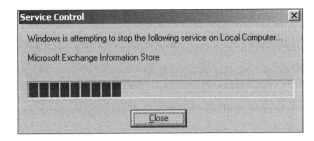

The Services list should no longer show **Started** against the information store.

We now need to identify where the Exchange database files are. They are normally found in c:\Program Files\Exchsrvr\MDBDATA and the four files are pub1.edb, pub1.stm, priv1.edb, and priv1.stm. It is possible that the files have been moved to another disk on your computer, so you may have to navigate to a different folder to find the store files.

Safety first—make a backup!
Either using Explorer or the Command Prompt copy command, you must make copies of the edb, stm, and log files before you begin.

The pub1 files contain your public folders and the priv1 files contain your email store, and they can be as large as 75 GB each!

We now need to run an integrity check against the files using the Exchange ESEUTIL tool.

ESEUTIL is the Exchange Server Database Utility tool that will verify, modify, and repair Exchange database files (also known as the store). When a database is corrupt or damaged, you can restore data from backup or repair it using ESEUTIL. It is normally installed in `C:\Program Files\Microsoft\ExchSrvr\Bin` on SBS 2003.

Open a command prompt by selecting **Run** from the **Start** menu and typing **CMD**. Then navigate to `c:\Program Files\Exchsrvr\bin` and run the ESEUTIL command using the following commands typed into the command prompt—changing the path with the edb files if your store databases have been moved.

```
Cd "c:\Program Files\Exchsrvr\bin"
eseutil /g  "c:\Program Files\Exchsrvr\MDBDATA\pub1.edb"
eseutil /g  "c:\Program Files\Exchsrvr\MDBDATA\priv1.edb"
```

If all is well, you should see two checks that execute without errors similar to the screen below. One thing to note is that the more email in the store the longer each check will take.

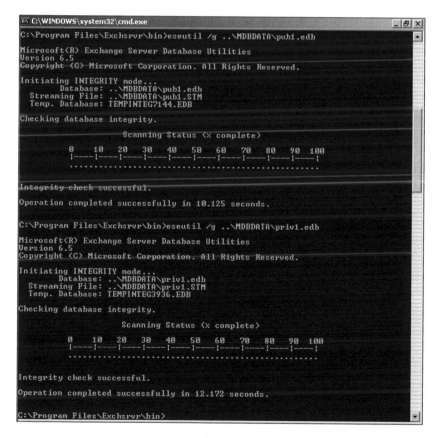

If you do have errors, then you will need to run the ESEUTIL with the /r command. Look at http://davidoverton.com/r.ashx?14 for information on the use of ESEUTIL to correct errors. All the errors should be checked and repaired until ESEUTIL no longer reports errors. More information on error messages can be found at http://davidoverton.com/r.ashx?15.

 ESEUTIL will repair faults that can be minor check-sum issues through to data corruption. It is possible that you will lose some data as the tool works, but if you have corruption, then there is little you can do to resolve this and have a successful migration. If users have copies of their mail store on their laptops, such as in Outlook, it is advised they export a PST file before reconnecting to the network to ensure that the maximum amount of data is retained.

You will need to restart the Exchange process by going back to the services screen where you right-clicked and stopped the **Information Store** and right-click on it again and select **Start**.

Removing Internet connectors from SBS 2003

On the SBS 2003 server, expand out the **Advanced Management** section and then the Exchange Server section, which is often the name of your domain and then Exchange in brackets. Continue expanding the **Administrative Groups**, then **first administrative group** and finally, the **Connectors**. Under here, you will see the **SmallBusiness SMTP connector**. Right-click on this and select **properties**.

Look at all the tabs and note the settings for future reference, but in particular, the **General** tab for the **Smart Host** routing or other rules that have been placed in the other tabs. Some of this will need to be entered by hand into the SBS 2008 Exchange 2007 settings.

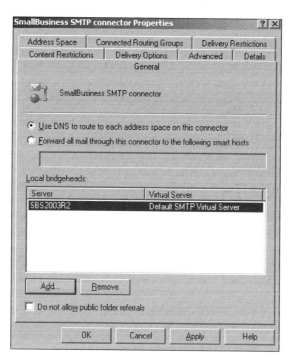

Now, click on **Cancel** and then right-click again on the **SmallBusiness SMTP connector** and this time select **Delete**. Click on **OK** when asked to confirm this.

Migrating POP3 connectors from SBS 2003

Underneath the **SmallBusiness SMTP connector**, there is the **POP3 Connector Manager**. While you could open the POP3 Connector Manager and note all of the accounts and settings, I believe you should take this opportunity to move from POP3 to Exchange 2007.

On the basis that you have had SBS 2003 for quite some time and are now moving to SBS 2008, it is time to contact your ISP and make the move so that: the email DNS MX record points to the SBS box, user accounts are created, and security information, such as the SPF mail ID is set correctly for your server.

To learn more about the Sender ID SPF Record and to create one, visit http://davidoverton.com/r.ashx?16.

Should you still be determined to use the POP3 connector, then you will need to note each of the mailbox accounts and their POP3 account information and then re-enter this on the SBS 2008 server under the **Network** tab. Click **Connectivity** and then right-click the **POP3 Connector** and select **View POP3 Connector properties**. Click **Add** on the **Mail** tab and re-enter all the information.

You will also need to disable the **Microsoft Connector for POP3 Mailboxes** service in the services section we used earlier to start and stop the Information Store. More help on this subject is included in the help in the Migration Wizard.

Moving the Offline Address Book from SBS 2003 to SBS 2008

Now, we continue on the SBS 2008 system. Start the **Exchange Management Console** from the **Start** menu and expand out **Organization Configuration** and click on **Mailbox**. If you click the **Offline Address Book** tab, you will notice that the text under **Generation Server** points to the SBS 2003 server and we need to move this to the SBS 2008 server. Right-click on the **Default Offline Address Book** and click **Move**.

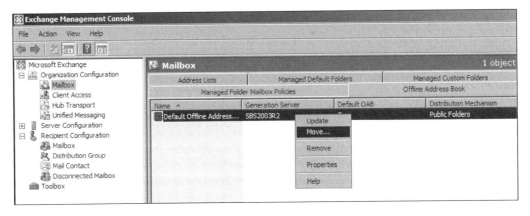

You will be presented with the **Move Offline Address Book** wizard and need to click on the **Browse** button.

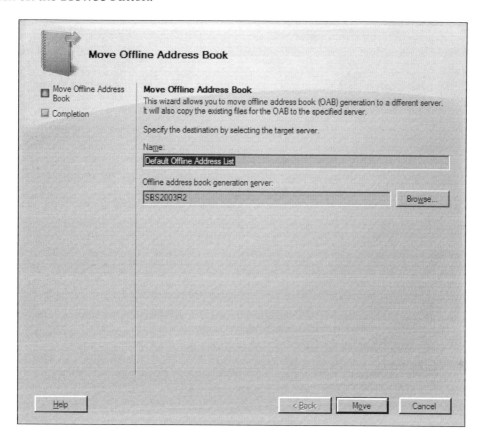

You will see a list of servers running Exchange, that is, the SBS 2003 and the SBS 2008 servers. Select the SBS 2008 server from the list. This is the one with a version number of **8.1** (or higher).

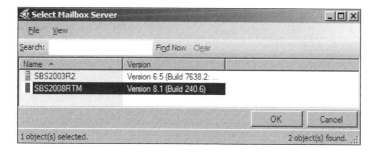

Click on **OK** and you should see the name of the SBS 2008 server in the **Offline address book generation server** box. Now, click **Move** to start the process.

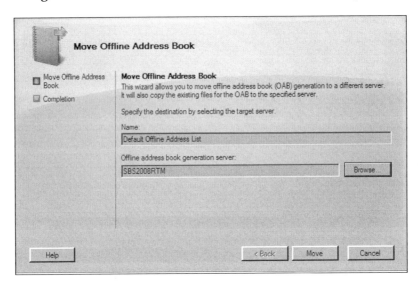

The process should be fairly quick and you should see a green check mark for the completed processes (as shown in the following screenshot).

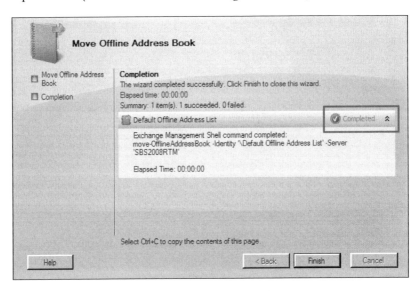

Click **Finish** to get back to the Exchange Management Console. Now, right-click on the **Offline Address Book** and select **Properties**.

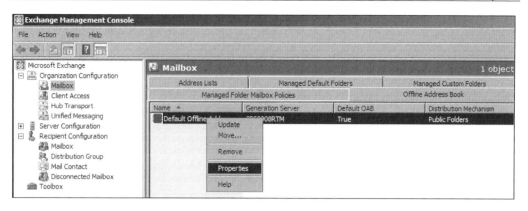

We now need to enable web-based distribution by clicking on the **Distribution** tab, putting a check mark in the **Enable Web-based distribution** check box, and clicking the **Add** button to add the SBS 2008 server to the list.

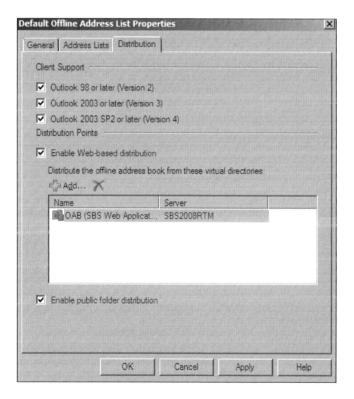

Click the **OK** button and this part is done.

Moving mailboxes from SBS 2003 to SBS 2008

Still in the Exchange Management Console, expand out the **Recipient Configuration** and then click on **Mailbox**. You will notice that some of the mailboxes have a type of **Legacy Mailbox**. These are the items that need migration. Select all the ones that need migrating using the *Control* key to select more than one at a time and right-click on them and select **Move Mailbox**.

 This can take more than 24 hours if the users have not removed unnecessary email and emptied their deleted items folder.

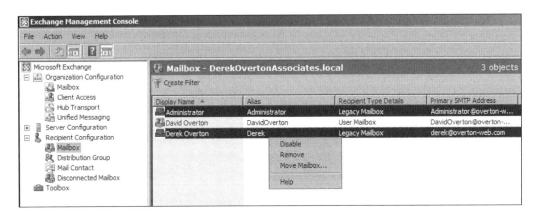

Select the SBS 2008 server from the list provided.

Then select **Next** to move on to the options for moving. Ensure that you select **Skip the corrupted messages** in the options and select a reasonably large number of messages to skip. Having run ESEUTIL, I would expect that there are no corruptions in the Exchange 2003 store, but rather than having the process stop should one have been introduced, I allow for them to be skipped as running ESEUTIL to fix these would result in them being skipped anyway. Then, select the **Global Catalog** and **Domain Controller** options by checking the boxes and clicking the **Browse** buttons. In each case, choose the SBS 2008 system.

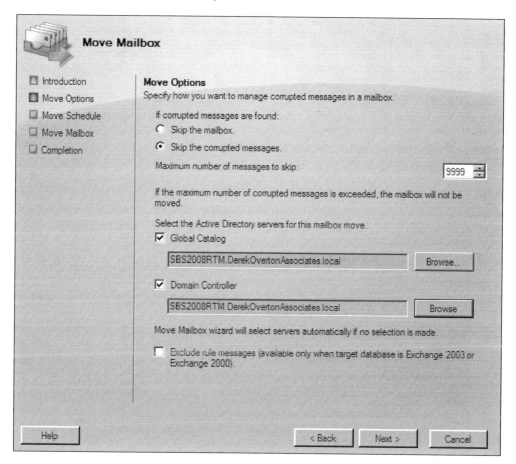

You can choose a time and date at which the accounts will start their migration. Because I like to if check things are working correctly, I always watch the process start and therefore, select **Immediately**. If you plan to set it running over night or early on a Saturday morning, then you can set a time and then click **Next**.

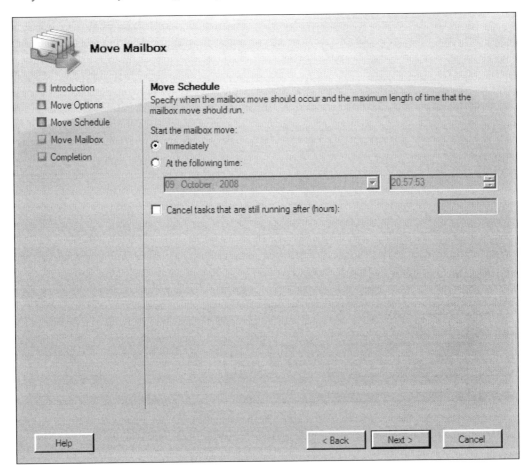

You will see a report telling you what is planned to be moved; simply click on **Move** to start the process off.

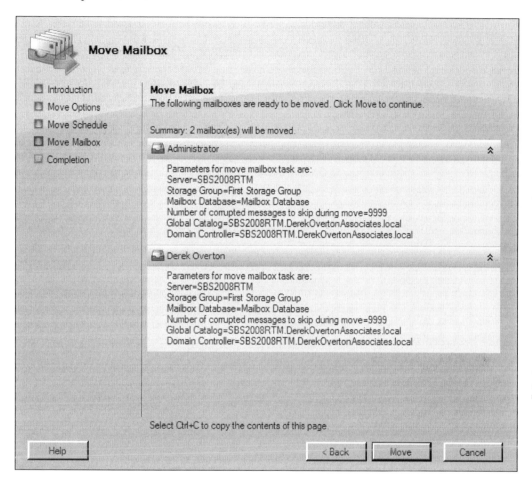

After the wizard runs, you get a summary screen confirming that everything went OK and you can click on **Finish** to exit this wizard. Obviously, if you had errors you need to explore those. Given the fact that you have already checked the integrity of your SBS 2003 mail store, network problems are the next most likely issue.

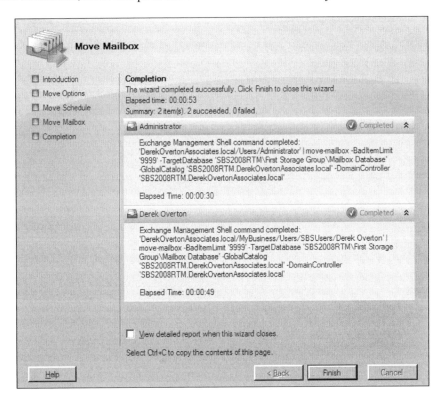

If you now look at the same list of mail accounts, you can see that they are simply **User Mailbox** and not Legacy anymore.

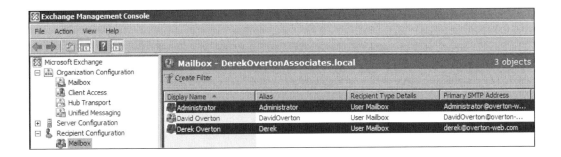

Moving Exchange Server public folders from SBS 2003 to SBS 2008

The last part of the Exchange migration is the move of the public folders.

> Even if you do not actively use public folders, this must be completed as Exchange uses Public Folders to store information such as calendars as well as the SBS 2003 default folders. Exchange 2007 will generate errors if the SBS 2003 system is removed and the public folders still reside on it.

To do this, go back to the SBS 2003 server and navigate under the **First Storage Group** to **Public Folder Store**. Right-click on this item and select **Move All Replicas**. Select the SBS 2008 server and click **OK**.

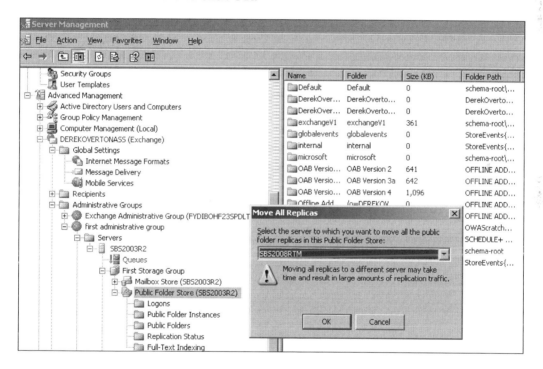

It will take a while, but if you keep refreshing the store, you will notice it gets more and more empty. It is important that you allow this to empty before removing the SBS 2003 system from the network.

Finishing the Exchange Migration task

When you finish migrating the mailboxes and public folders, close the **Exchange Management Console** and the **Server Management Console** on SBS 2003. In the Migration Wizard, click **Task Complete** and then click **Next**.

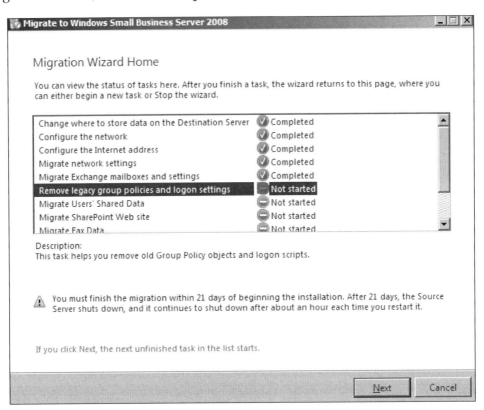

Finishing the Exchange 2007 migration and checking systems

Although you have moved your data across, it is worth checking that Exchange 2007 is accessible via the web and Microsoft Outlook.

Updating additional settings

Earlier in the migration task, you noted the settings in the SMTP Connector on your SBS 2003. If there were extra domains or other settings, besides Smart Relay routing, then you need to set those same settings in Exchange 2007. To do this, start the Exchange Management Console on the SBS 2008 system and navigate to **Hub Transport** under **Organization Configuration**. Here, you will see tabs for the settings you noted.

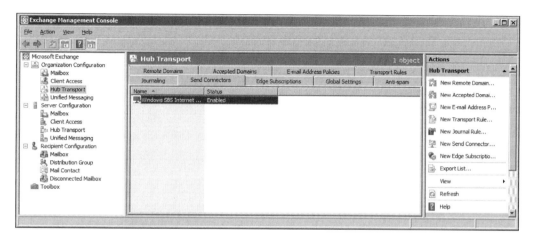

Network checks

You need to ensure that your firewall is configured to let SMTP traffic through (port 25) and is configured to send it to the IP address of your SBS 2008 server. You also need to check that SSL connections (port 443) are also configured to direct traffic to your SBS 2008 server.

To check that you have Internet access to Outlook, go to `http://remote.yourdomain.co.uk/OWA` where **yourdomain** is changed as appropriate. You should see the OWA screen as shown in the following screenshot if the Web connectivity is working. If you can log in and see email, then Exchange is correctly configured for remote access.

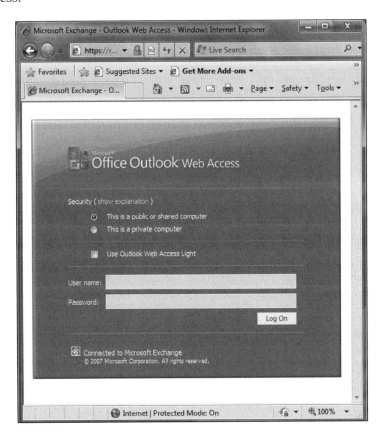

Configuring Outlook for the SBS 2008

When a user starts up Outlook, if the SBS 2003 system is still present with Exchange 2003 still running then their setting should be updated to point to the new server. If this is not the case, you will need to do this by hand. Start Outlook on a client PC and check that it connects to email.

If it does not, select **Account Settings** from the **Tools** menu. This will bring up the **Account Settings** window. If there is more than one account configured, you will see multiple accounts listed. If the SBS email is the only mail configured, you will just see one entry. Find the one that has a type of **Exchange**, click on it and then click on the **Change** button.

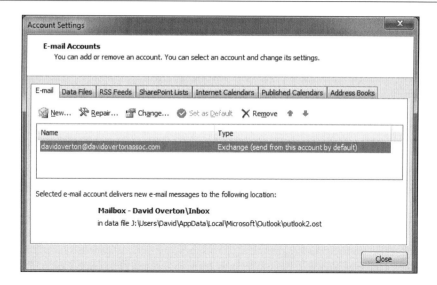

On the **Change E-mail Account** screen, check that the **Microsoft Exchange server** contains the path for the SBS 2008 system. If it does not, correct it to the right path for the server.

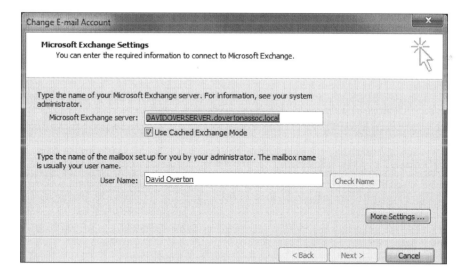

Once Outlook is connected, try sending and receiving mail to an address outside of your network, such as a MSN or Hotmail address and try sending to your SBS 2008 email domain.

Working around a known bug with Outlook Anywhere

Outlook 2003 and beyond and SBS 2008 provide a feature called Outlook Anywhere. This enables the full functionality of Outlook with access to colleagues' calendars and public folders, while only connected to the Internet. This relies on a secure web connection to function.

There is a known issue that can cause users to experience very slow connections when using Outlook Anywhere. To work around this, you need to **open Internet Information Services (IIS) Manager** from the **Start** menu. Then navigate to the **Sites** section and expand **the SBS Web Applications** and then click on the **RPC** folder. The screen will show a number of icons and you will need to double-click the **Modules** one.

When the modules are displayed, select the **HttptoHttpsRedir** module and then click on the **Remove** button in the **Actions** pane. Confirm the removal and close down the IIS Manager.

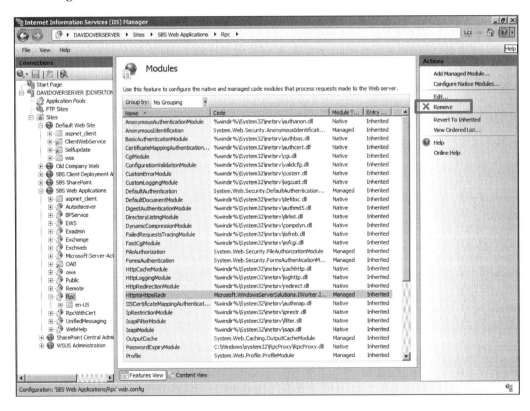

Summary

Your Exchange email will now be residing on the SBS 2008 system and once the firewall is correctly configured, email will be flowing into SBS 2008, and your Outlook users should be getting email without issue.

You will have removed the public folders and the GAL from SBS 2003 too, enabling Exchange 2003 to no longer be part of the solution. This also means that your users can now use the Exchange 2007 Outlook Web Access via the Remote Web Workplace should they need remote web-based access.

The next step is to continue the migration, moving the rest of the user data stored on the SBS 2003 server to SBS 2008.

7

Migrating the CompanyWeb SharePoint Site

This chapter covers the migration of data in the CompanyWeb—`http://CompanyWeb`, a Windows SharePoint Site from SBS 2003 to a site called OldCompanyWeb on SBS 2008. If you have no data stored in the SBS 2003 SharePoint site, then you do not need to carry out this task. If you have other SharePoint v2 sites on your SBS 2003 system, then the same process and procedure can be repeated for the other sites with care taken to identify the databases and site names.

SBS 2008 ships with Windows SharePoint v3, which is different enough to stop a simple import of data from the Windows SharePoint v2 site that is hosted on SBS 2003. For that reason, the recommended approach is to have two sites and to advise the users to utilize the new site going forward, but to retain data in the old site too. Should it be desired, the data and documents can be copied between the sites once the migration is completed.

This involves steps on both the SBS 2003 and SBS 2008 system to complete.

Impact on users

Once the migration process has been started, users will not be able to access the CompanyWeb site and will have to change the URL that they use to: `http://OldCompanyWeb` or you will need to change the name of the new CompanyWeb site that is part of SBS 2008. Depending on the amount of data, it will take between one and four hours to complete.

To start the migration task, select the **Migrate SharePoint Web site** task from the **Migration Wizard Home** list of tasks and click on **Next**.

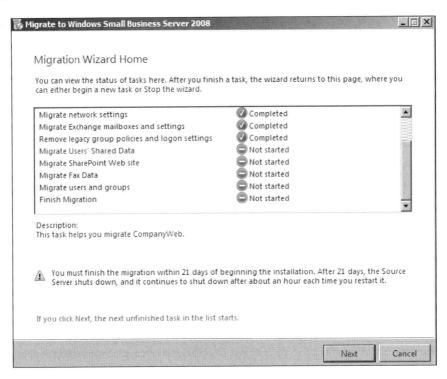

You are presented with links to the help file documenting how to complete the task on each server. There is no actual processing carried out by the wizard. I will walk you through the process and offer scripts wherever possible. Scripts help with when you don't want to use the user interface or will be performing more than one migration as they are often faster, reliable and consistently repeatable.

All the scripts can be found at `http://davidoverton.com/r.ashx?1B`.

After the migration, some of the links, such as the link to Outlook and the Help Desk will no longer work.

The task consists of the following steps:

- On the SBS 2003 server:
  - Prepare and check CompanyWeb on SBS 2003 for migration.
  - Back up the database.
  - Copy the files to a removable device or create a network share.

- On the SBS 2008 server:
  - ° Configure the DNS for the migrated site.
  - ° Import the data.
  - ° Create the OldCompanyWeb site.
  - ° Tidy up the site.

Extracting data from SBS 2003 server

To check and prepare the CompanyWeb, we will need to carry out three tasks:

- Run WSS v3 Pre-scan tool.
- Add extra users to CompanyWeb on SBS 2003.
- Stop web site.

All the tasks described below are carried out on the SBS 2003 system, although the Pre-scan tool must be copied from the SBS 2008 server.

The database can either be the original WSDE database or could have been upgraded to SQL 2000 or SQL 2005. Provided the database has not been moved to another server or had its name changed, the steps will perform as expected. If you have changed the database name, please change the name of the database in the steps in this chapter.

Running WSS v3 Pre-scan tool

The Pre-scan tool will check the CompanyWeb database to ensure no issues exist in the site before it is imported into SBS 2008. You will need to copy the Pre-scan tool from the SBS 2008 system to the SBS 2003 system. I did this by copying the file to the ClientApps directory on the SBS 2003 system over the network, but you can also copy the file onto removable media and move it between the two systems.

 If the Pre-scan tool is not run, then SBS 2008 will not be able to import the database.

The Pre-scan tool is found on SBS 2008 at `%Program Files%\Common Files\Microsoft Shared\Web Server Extensions\12\Bin`. If you navigate to this location and also open **\\<source server name>\ClientApps** by going to the **Start** menu and selecting **Run** then you can copy between the two.

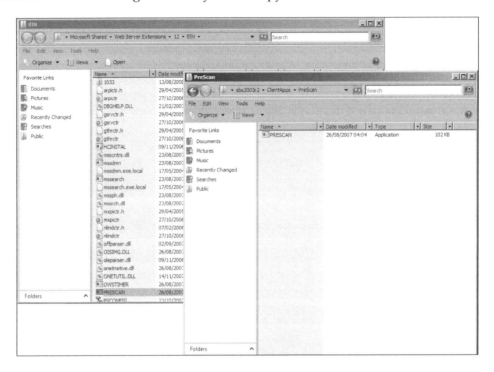

On the SBS 2003 system, you can open a command prompt from the **Start** menu and use the **CD** command, such as **CD \ClientApps\PreScan** and then type in **prescan.exe /V http://companyweb** to generate the report.

The output of the scan, as shown in the previous screenshot, provides the location of the log file. If you open this file, you should see a report similar to the one opposite. Note that **broken sites** and **broken webs** are equal to 0.

```
PreupgradeReport_633593603452094383_Log.txt - Notepad                    _ □ ×
File  Edit  Format  View  Help
10/11/2008 22:19:06 Querying SPSite quota and locks on 2d0fc688-079c-4163-9fbb-4d0de10ada79
10/11/2008 22:19:06 Scanning SPWeb: http://companyweb
10/11/2008 22:19:07   Updating list schema in web.
10/11/2008 22:19:10 Checking if
Server="SBS2003R2\SharePoint";Database="STS_SBS2003R2_1";Trusted_Connection=yes;App="prescan.exe" is a WSS V2 SP2
database.
10/11/2008 22:19:10 Checking if any site has not yet been scanned in
Server="SBS2003R2\SharePoint";Database="STS_SBS2003R2_1";Trusted_Connection=yes;App="prescan.exe".
10/11/2008 22:19:10 Checking if any list has not yet been scrubbed in
Server="SBS2003R2\SharePoint";Database="STS_SBS2003R2_1";Trusted_Connection=yes;App="prescan.exe".
10/11/2008 22:19:10 Scan finished without failure.
10/11/2008 22:19:10 ============================Logs============================
10/11/2008 22:19:10 Log file: C:\DOCUME~1\ADMINI~1\LOCALS~1\Temp\PreupgradeReport_633593603452094383_Log.txt
10/11/2008 22:19:10 Summary file:
C:\DOCUME~1\ADMINI~1\LOCALS~1\Temp\PreupgradeReport_633593603452094383_Summary.xml
10/11/2008 22:19:10 ============================Totals============================
10/11/2008 22:19:10 Number of sites skipped (already scanned):  0
10/11/2008 22:19:10 Number of sites scanned:   1
10/11/2008 22:19:10 Number of broken sites:   0
10/11/2008 22:19:10 Number of webs scanned:   1
10/11/2008 22:19:10 Number of broken webs:   0
10/11/2008 22:19:10 Number of webs using custom template:  0
10/11/2008 22:19:10 Number of pages scanned:  84
10/11/2008 22:19:10 Number of unghosted pages:  0
```

Adding extra users to CompanyWeb

We have to add three users to the SBS 2003 CompanyWeb site before it is migrated, to allow the upgrade processes to work on SBS 2008. You can do this one of two ways. If you are comfortable with command-line scripting, then use the following script. If you are not comfortable using scripts, follow the web administration pages. The end result will be that we have three new users added to the site:

User Name	Site Group Setting
Windows SBS SharePoint_OwnersGroup	**Administrator**
Windows SBS SharePoint_MembersGroup	**Contributor**
Windows SBS SharePoint_VisitorsGroup	**Reader**

Adding users by script

The advantage of script commands is that they can be put into a text file and run without fear of a setting being mis-typed. The disadvantage is that they do not interpret the results, so can go on blindly, even if a previous step has failed. Personally, I prefer scripts as they are so repeatable and often, much quicker than the non-script steps.

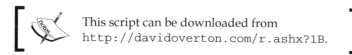 This script can be downloaded from http://davidoverton.com/r.ashx?1B.

To add the users, type the following into a command prompt:

```
cd "c:\Program Files\Common Files\Microsoft Shared\Web Server
Extentsions\60\bin"
```

```
stsadm -o adduser -url http://companyweb -userlogin "%%userdomain%%\
Windows SBS SharePoint_OwnersGroup" -useremail "administrator@%%use
rdnsdomain" -role Administrator -username "Windows SBS SharePoint_
OwnersGroup"
```

```
stsadm -o adduser -url http://companyweb -userlogin "%%userdomain%%\
Windows SBS SharePoint_MembersGroup" -useremail "administrator@%%u
serdnsdomain" -role Contributor -username "Windows SBS SharePoint_
MemberssGroup"
```

```
stsadm -o adduser -url http://companyweb -userlogin "%%userdomain%%\
Windows SBS SharePoint_VisitorsGroup" -useremail "administrator@
%%userdnsdomain" -role Reader -username "Windows SBS SharePoint_
VisitorsGroup"
```

If this is successful, you will see a screen similar to the one below:

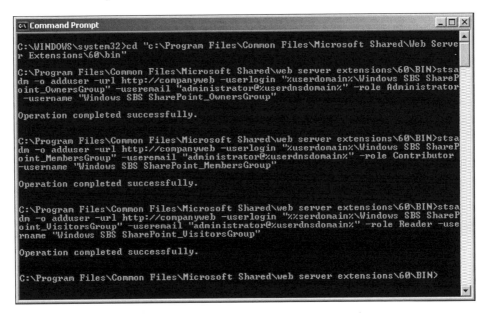

Adding users via the web administration pages

Open the existing site by typing `https://CompanyWeb` into the address bar in
Internet Explorer. It is important that you use `https` as this will redirect you to
`https://CompanyWeb:444` ensuring that you are connected to the right site, even
on the server.

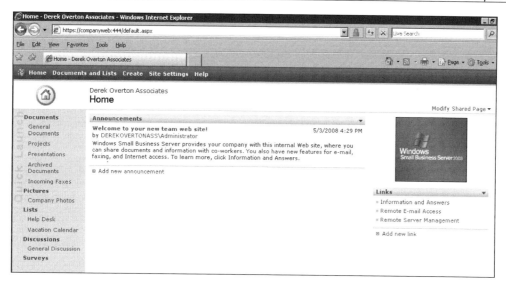

At the top of the screen is the **Site Settings** link that you need to click on to bring up the screen seen in the following screenshot.

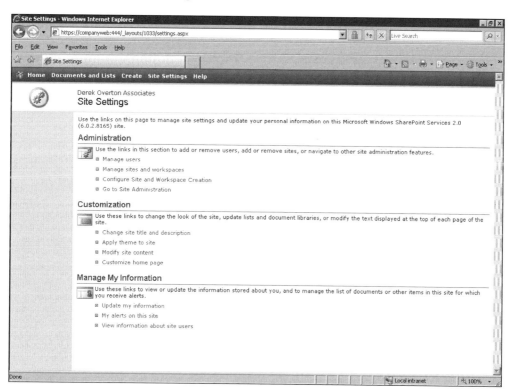

Under the **Administration section**, click the **Manage Users** link to enable us to see the existing users of the site.

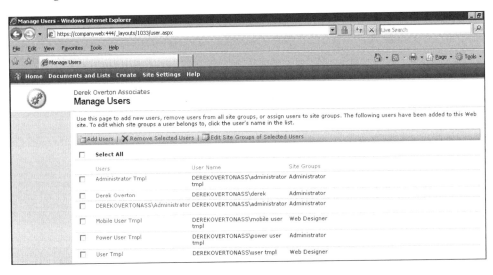

Now, click the **Add Users** button at the top of the screen as we need to add users to the system, each with different credentials.

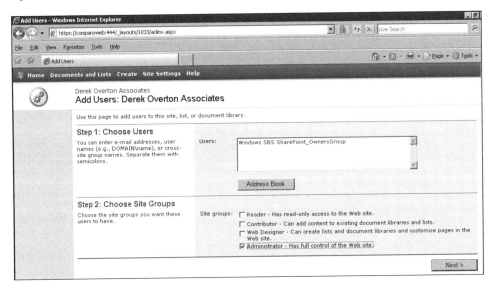

Type in **Windows SBS SharePoint_OwnersGroup** into the **Users** section and check the **Administrator** option in the **Site Groups** section and finally, click on the **Next** button.

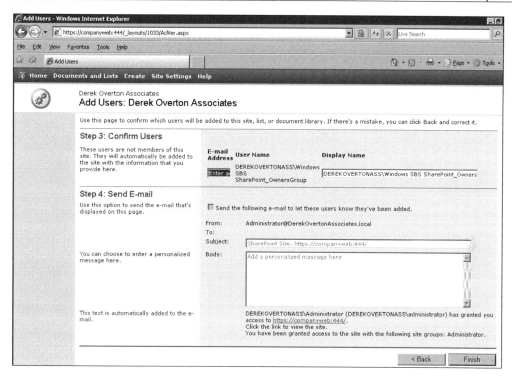

When this has completed, you will be back at the list of users. Repeat the task to add the two additional users with the permissions as below. Once finished, you will have added the three users as listed in the table.

User Name	Site Group Setting
Windows SBS SharePoint_OwnersGroup	Administrator
Windows SBS SharePoint_MembersGroup	Contributor
Windows SBS SharePoint_VisitorsGroup	Reader

Re-run the Pre-scan tool

Before you take the web site off-line you need to re-run the pre-scan tool so that it marks the database as checked. Having run the tool earlier it should run again without errors. If you do see errors, resolve them and re-run the tool.

Stopping the web site

To stop further activity on the web site, we need to stop the CompanyWeb site on the SBS 2003 server.

Stopping the web site using a script

As with all the scripts, this can be found at `http://davidoverton.com/r.ashx?1B`. Open a command prompt and enter the command: `cscript c:\windows\system32\iisweb /stop "Companyweb"` to stop the web site.

If you have not used the script, then you need to navigate to the web site that hosts CompanyWeb and stop the site. To do this, open **Server Managerment** on the SBS 2003 server and navigate to the **Advanced Management** section, then **Internet Information Service**, and click on the plus sign next to the name of your SBS 2003 server. This should expand out revealing **Web Sites** that you need to click on before you can right-click on **CompanyWeb** and select **Stop** from the menu.

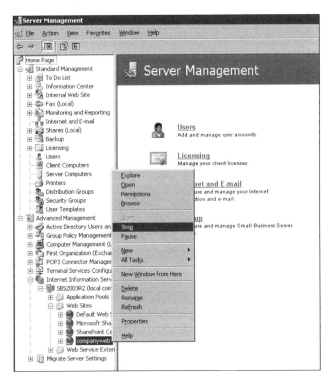

Backing up the database

Before we start making alterations to the CompanyWeb site in the migration, we need to make a backup using scripts or the SQL Management tools. If the SQL Management tool was not present on your system before, it was installed when you applied the SQL 2005 update as part of the preparation in Chapter 3. The SQL tools work no matter which version of SQL you have installed on your SBS 2003 server.

Backing up via script

Should you wish to back up via a command line, use this command to create a backup into the folder **C:\CompanyWeb_Backup**. To run the script, open a command window and type or paste the following:

```
md c:\companyweb_backup
osql -E -S %computername%\SharePoint -Q "backup database STS_
%Computername%_1 to disk = 'c:\companyweb_backup\sts_%computername%_
1.bak';"
```

You will see a response similar to the one shown below if the backup is successful.

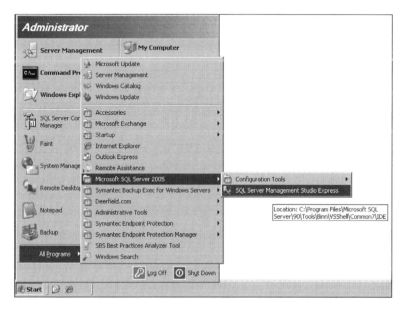

Backing up using the user interface

Go to the **Start** menu and find the **SQL Server Management Studio Express** tools in the group **Microsoft SQL Server 2005**.

You will be asked to choose a database Server name and you want to choose
<SBS 2003 server Name>\SHAREPOINT and then click on **Connect** to sign
in with your administrator credentials.

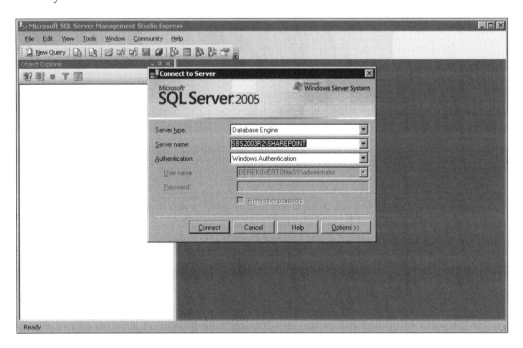

Once connected, expand out the database list to find the one called
STS_<SBS 2003 Server Name>_1. Right-click on the database and pick
Tasks and **Back Up** from the menu.

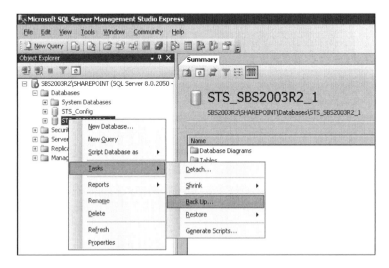

Leave all the settings at their default, but ensure **Back up to** is set to **Disk** and then click on the **Add** button.

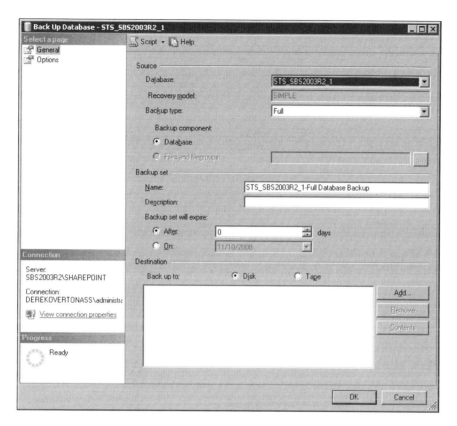

Type in the name of a place to back up to or click on the **dotted** button to browse for a location. This can be another disk in the SBS 2003 system or a USB removable disk, but it must have enough space to contain the full backup. Click **OK** to accept the filename you have typed or selected.

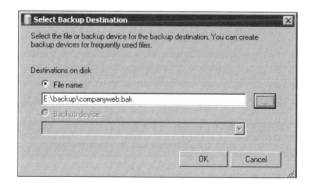

You will now see the backup destination listed in the **Destination** section and you can then click on **OK** to start the backup. This is normally quite a speedy process.

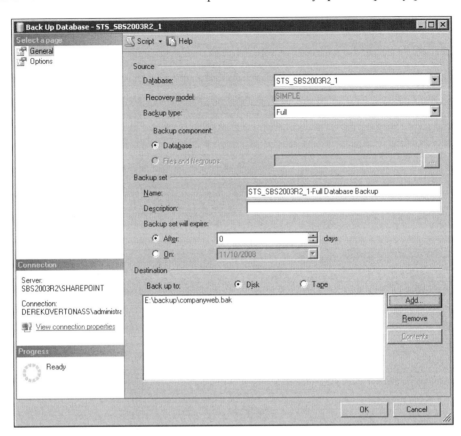

Once it has completed, you will see the message below indicating a successful backup.

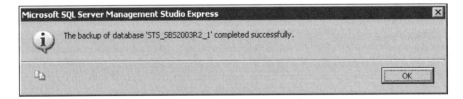

Detaching the database before moving

We now need to detach the database from SBS 2003 so we can move it to SBS 2008.

Detaching the database by script

To detach the database by script, open a command prompt and enter the following. This will also provide the location of the database files so you can copy them:

```
osql -E -S %computername%\SharePoint -h-1 -d sts_%computername%_1 -Q
"set nocount on;select filename from sysfiles;"
osql -E -S %computername%\SharePoint -Q "EXEC sp_detach_db 'STS_
%Computername%_1', 'true' "
```

Once this has been completed, you will see the following:

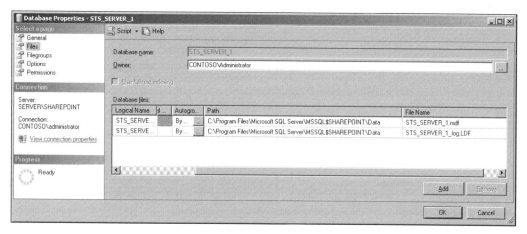

Detaching the database using the user interface

Before we detach the database, it is useful to know where the data files are stored so we can copy them later in the task. To do this, find the database name again (**STS_<SBS 2003 server name>_1**) and right-click on the name and select **Properties**. Select the page **Files** and expand the columns **Path** and **File Name** so you can clearly see where the files you need to move are stored.

Now, close the properties and right-click on the database name and select **Detach** from the **Tasks** menu.

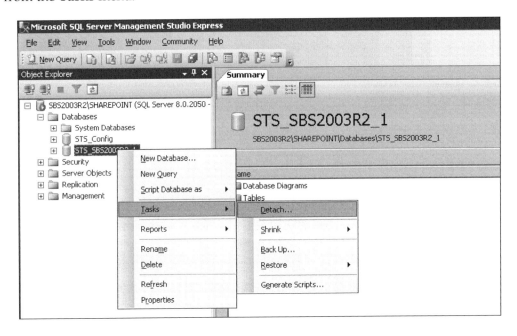

Put a check mark in the **Drop Connections** check box and make sure that there is no check mark in the **Update Statistics** option and then click **OK**.

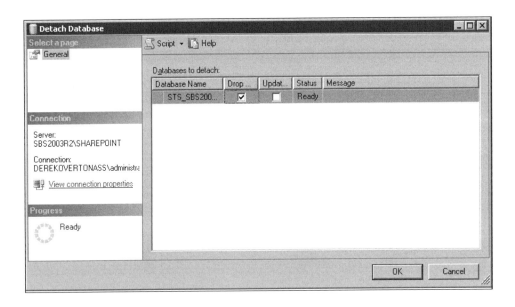

If the update is successful, the database will no longer appear in the list of databases in **Object Explore**. This is the end of the work we need to do in Microsoft SQL Server Management Studio Express, so close it.

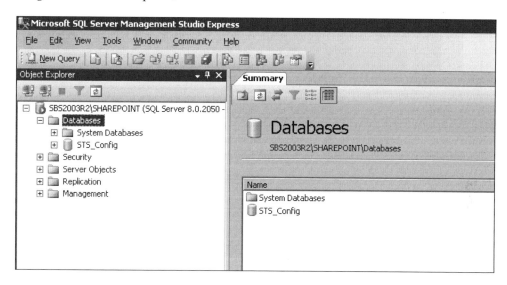

 If you wish to undo these operations, then you simply need to attach the database files and start the web site again. To do this via a script, see http://davidoverton.com/r.ashx?1B.

Copying the database files

You will need to copy the database files to the SBS 2008 Server. The actual filenames and paths were gathered in the detach database section; however, they are normally stored in the folder C:\Program Files\Microsoft SQL Server\MSSQL$SharePoint\ Data in SBS 2003 and these are the filenames you will need to copy to the SBS 2008 server:

*   STS_<SBS 2003 Server Name>_1.mdf

- STS__< SBS 2003 Server Name>_1_Log.ldf

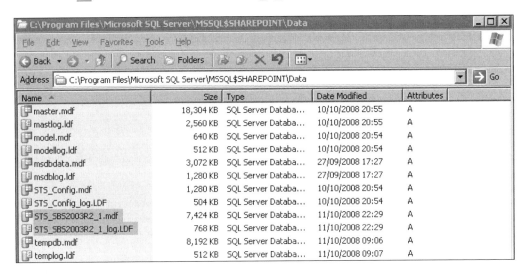

Once you have made a copy of these files, you are now ready to continue the process on the SBS 2008 system.

Adding OldCompanyWeb to SBS 2008

To create the site on SBS 2008, we need to carry out a number of steps:

- Configure the DNS for the migrated site.
- Import the data in SQL.
- Create the OldCompanyWeb site.
- Create the SharePoint Installation.

These steps are all carried out on the SBS 2008 server. All the scripts used in this section can be found at http://davidoverton.com/r.ashx?1B.

Configuring the DNS for the migrated site

We need to make `http://CompanyWeb` point to the SBS 2008 web site and `http://OldCompanyWeb` point to the copy of the old SBS 2003 site.

Updating DNS via the command line

To carry out the tasks required on DNS, open an elevated (administrative) command prompt and type the following:

```
dnscmd /recordadd %userdnsdomain% OldCompanyWeb CNAME %computername%.%
userdnsdomain%
```

```
dnscmd /recorddelete %userdnsdomain% CompanyWeb CNAME /f
```

```
dnscmd /recordadd %userdnsdomain% CompanyWeb CNAME %computername%.%us
erdnsdomain%
```

These commands will create a new DNS entry for OldCompanyWeb, while deleting the entry that referenced the SBS 2003 server, and create a new reference for SBS 2008. Once complete, you will see a screen as below:

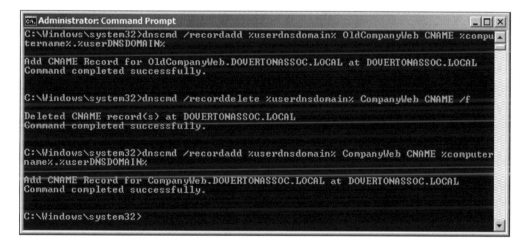

Updating DNS information through the user interfaces

This is done in the DNS settings, so click **Administrative Tools** on the **Start** menu and select **DNS**.

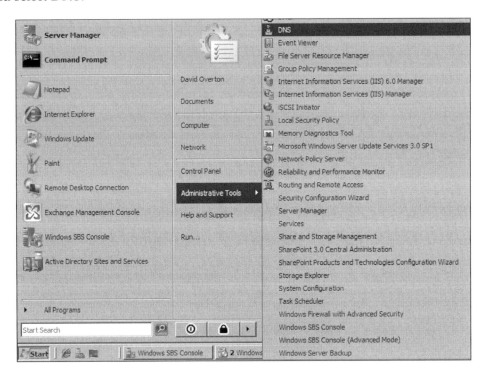

You will need to navigate down the DNS tree clicking the plus signs to expand **<SBS 2008 Server>** and **Forward Lookup Zones** and then clicking on **<Your Domain>**. Now, find **companyweb** in the righthand pane. You will notice that the DNS entry points to the SBS 2003 server. Right-click on it and select **Properties** and you can change the **FQDN** to be correct for the new server. If you are not sure of this, use the browse button to pick an item.

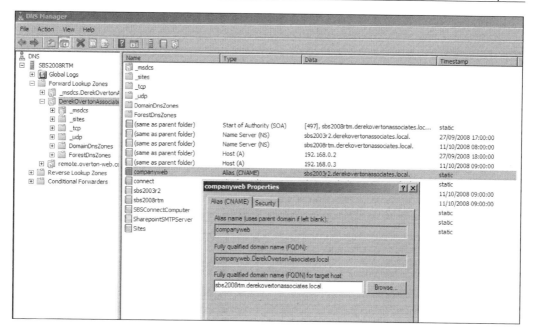

Now, right-click the **<Your domain name>** and click **New Alias (CName)**.

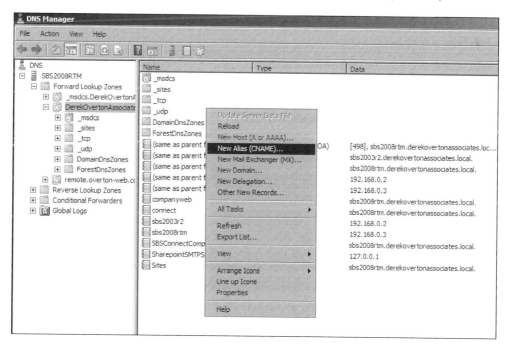

In the dialog that pops up, type in **OldCompanyWeb** into the **Alias Name** box and again type or browse for the SBS 2008 server in the **FQDN** item.

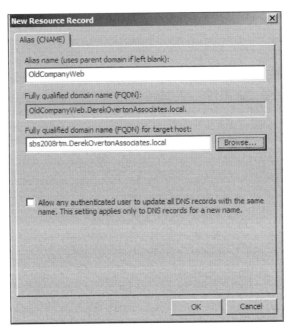

Click **OK** and check in the DNS settings to ensure that both **companyweb** and **oldcompanyweb** now are set to point to the SBS 2008 server.

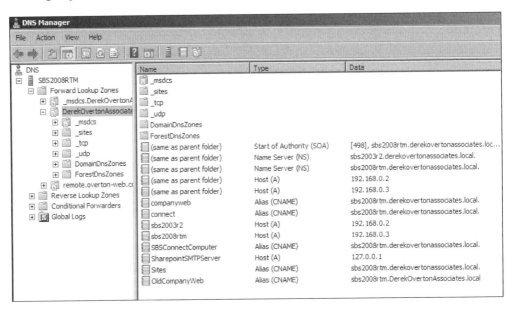

Importing the data

The next step is to add the SBS 2003 CompanyWeb data into the SBS 2008 database for SharePoint V3.

It is important that you have located the databases into a permanent location on the SBS 2008 server. I created a folder called `migrated_files` and then another within it called **OldCompanyWeb** on the C-drive of the SBS 2008 server and copied the data files there.

 Choose the location where the data will be stored with care—it should reflect your data storage plans. If you store all your data on a different disk from the system disk, place these files on that same disk.

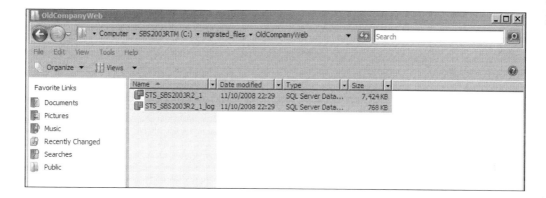

Re-attaching the database by command line

To re-attach the database via a command line, open a command prompt with administrative privileges and enter this command, changing the database from `STS_SERVER_1` to match the name of the database from your SBS 2003 system:

```
osql -E -S \\.\pipe\mssql$microsoft##ssee\sql\query -Q "EXEC sp_
attach_db 'STS_SERVER_1', 'c:\Migrated Files\OldCompanyWeb\STS_Server_
1.mdf','c:\Migrated Files\OldCompanyWeb\STS_Server_1_log.LDF'"
```

This will attach the database using the original name, upgrade it, if relevant, for the version of SQL it is attaching to and make it ready for use by SharePoint. Once this is done, you should see confirmation similar to that shown in the following screenshot:

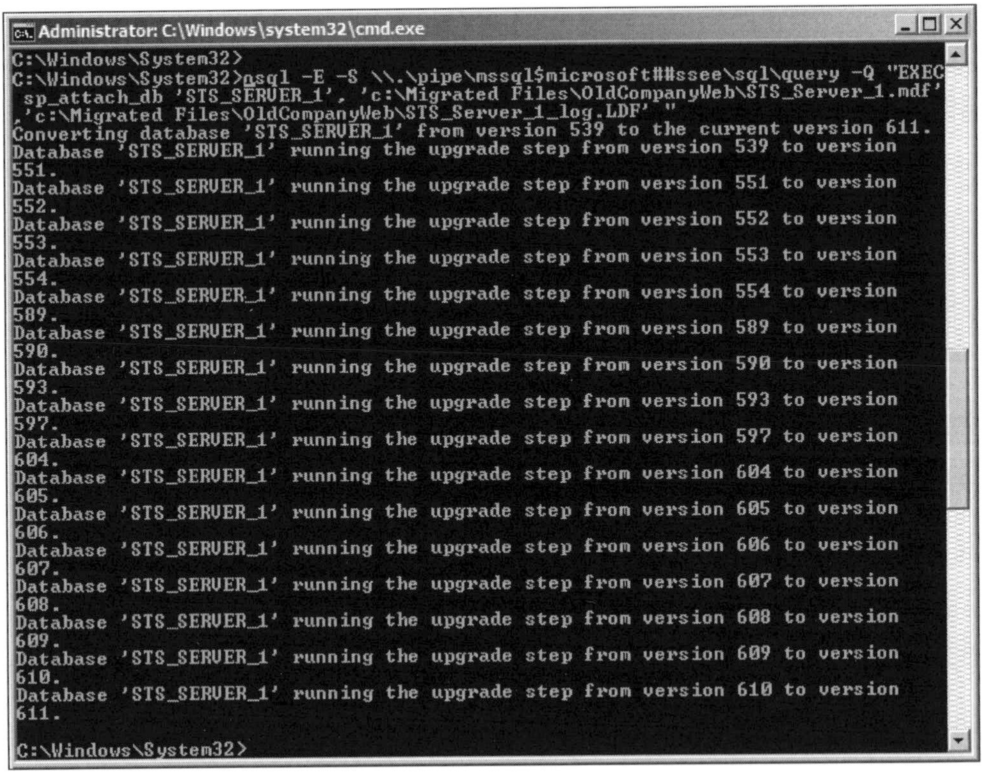

Re-attaching the database through the user interface

It is very important that you run the SQL tools by finding **SQL Server Management Studio Express** in the **Start** menu, right-clicking on it and selecting **Run as administrator**, otherwise you will not be able to log in.

On the connection screen, type **\\.\pipe\mssql$microsoft##ssee\sql\query** into the Server name text box and click connect.

Once you are logged in, right-click on **Databases** and select **Attach**.

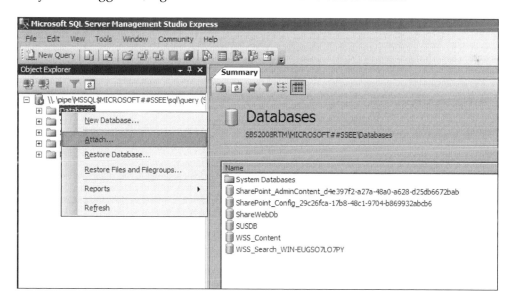

Click on the **Add** button and locate the database files you copied to the SBS 2008 server. You should see in the **<DatabaseName> database details** section that two files have appeared, namely **STS_<SourceServerName>_1.mdf** and **STS_<SourceServerName>_1_Log.ldf**.

Now, click **OK** to confirm the re-attachment, which should take just a few seconds. You may see an error message regarding locating the **full text catalogs**, but you can simply click **No** to this if it shows.

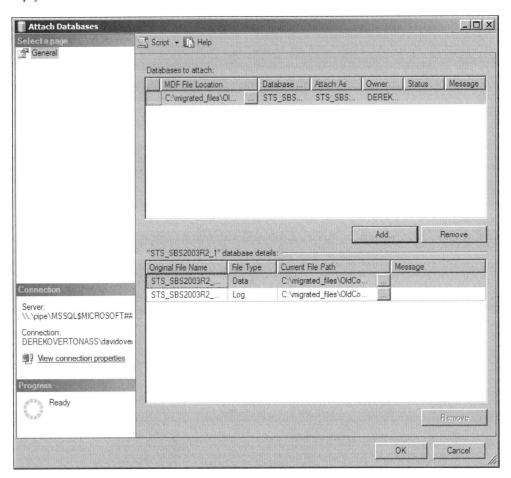

The database **STS_<SourceServerName>_1** should now be listed in the databases section meaning the attachment worked and you can now close **SQL Server Management Studio Express**.

Creating the new site to host the SBS 2003 data

The next stage is to create and provision the site that the SBS 2003 CompanyWeb site will sit in. For simplicity, we will now refer to it simply as OldCompanyWeb. There are four things we need to do to create the site:

- Create a new IIS site to host the site.
- Change the Administrator settings for the site.
- Create and configure a WSS v3 site for OldCompanyWeb.
- Restart IIS.

Creating a new IIS site to host the site

We need to create the place holder site for the OldCompanyWeb site. This can be done using scripts or the user interface.

Creating the web site using scripting

To create the site by script, use these commands from a command prompt run with Administrator privileges:

```
MD C:\INetPub\OldCompanyWeb

%systemroot%\system32\inetsrv\APPCMD add site /name:OldCompanyWeb
/bindings:"http/OldCompanyWeb:80:" /physicalPath:"C:\INetPub\
OldCompanyWeb"
```

Creating the web site using the user interface

On the **Start** menu, click on **Administrative tools** and then select **Information Internet Services (IIS) Manager**. Ensure you do not click the **6.0** version.

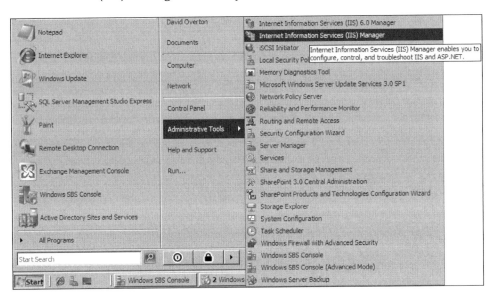

Expand out the navigation pane until you can see **Sites** and then click **Add Web Site**.

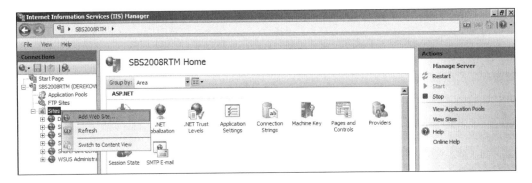

You will see a blank **Add Web Site** dialog appear.

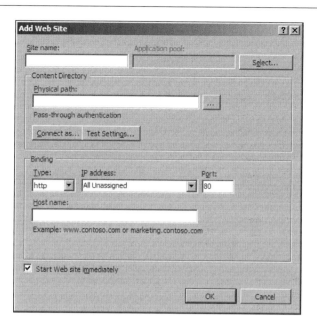

You will need to type in the name of **OldCompanyWeb** into the **Site name** text box. The Application Pool should default to **OldCompanyWeb** too.

You will need to select a place where this site will be stored on the hard disk. In the dialog box, navigate to **C:\inetpub** and then click **Make New Folder** and type **OldCompanyWeb** where the text **New Folder** appears.

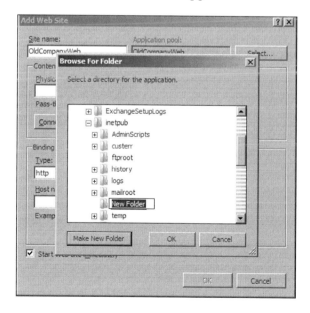

In the **Host name** in the **Binding** section, type in **OldCompanyWeb**. This should give you a completed form as shown in the following screenshot.

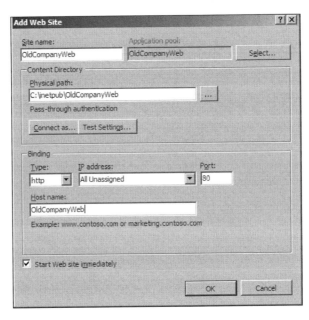

If you now click on **OK**, the web site is created, and we now need to configure it as a SharePoint site. Close the **Information Internet Services (IIS) Manager**.

Creating and configuring a WSS v3 site for OldCompanyWeb

While we have IIS holding a web page for OldCompanyWeb, we don't have the code behind the page to make it display as a SharePoint site, which is required to connect the database that you have migrated to the web site.

Go to the **Administrative Tools** menu on the **Start** menu and then select **SharePoint 3.0 Central Administration**.

Click **Create or extend Web Application** in the **SharePoint Web Application Management** section of the page.

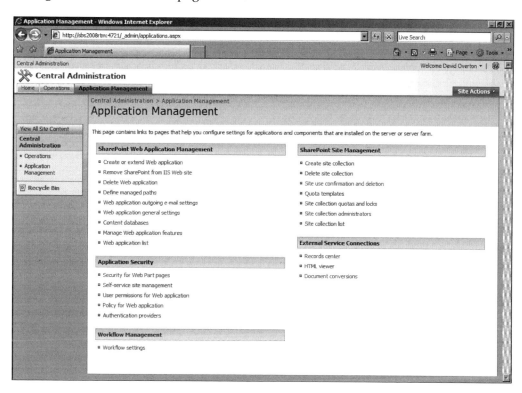

Click the **Application Management** tab under **Central Administration** and then, to create the OldCompanyWeb page, click **Create a new Web application**.

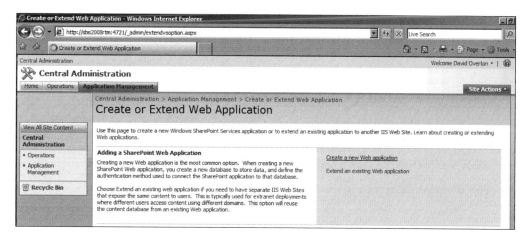

In the **IIS Web Site** section, click the option for **Use an existing IIS web site** and pick **OldCompanyWeb** from the drop-down list. This should update the other items **Port**, **Host Header**, and **Path** automatically.

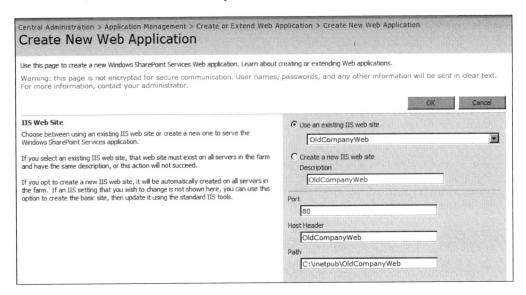

In the Security Configuration, you should be able to accept the default settings of **NTLM** authentication, **No** anonymous access, and **No** to SSL.

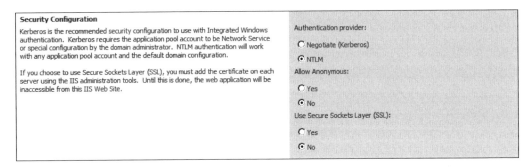

The load balancing section should have the **URL** as **http://OldCompanyWeb:80/** and the **Zone** as **Default**.

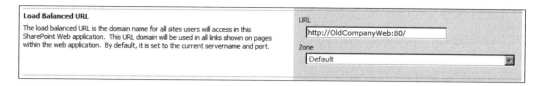

In the **Application Pool** section, click **Use existing application pool** and select the **OldCompanyWeb** application pool.

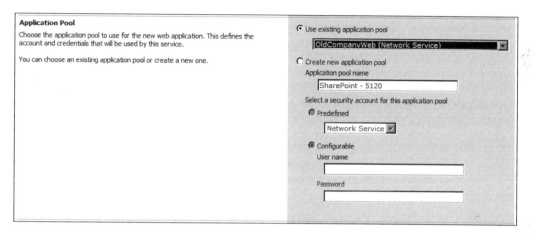

The **Reset Internet Information Services** setting should be set to **Restart IIS Manually**.

The database section has a bit of a split brain thing going on as we reference a name from your old server and the location on the new server. It also has a complex database name, but you should not have to type that in.

Ensure the **Database Server** is **<SBS 2008 Server>\Microsoft##SSEE**. Type **STS_<SBS 2003 Server Name>_1** into the **Database Name** box and select **Windows authentication (recommended)** for the **Database authentication**. Double-check the database name as it should refer to your SBS 2003 server name.

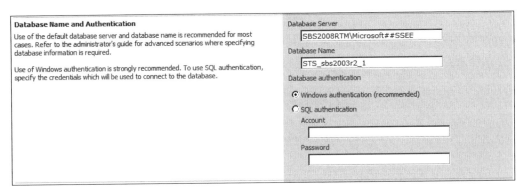

In the **Search Server** section, check that your SBS 2008 server is selected and click on **OK**.

You may well receive a warning about NTLM authentication to which you can simply click **OK**.

You will see the status change to **Operation in Progress**. This page will be present for a reasonable amount of time. For me, it was about 15 minutes, but it has been known to take longer if you have lots of data to be converted to Windows SharePoint Services 3.0.

Once it is complete, you will see the message stating **Application Created** to tell you all is well. If it fails, resolve the issue and restart this process.

This message also tells you that you need to run **iisreset /noforce**, which we will do later in the migration process.

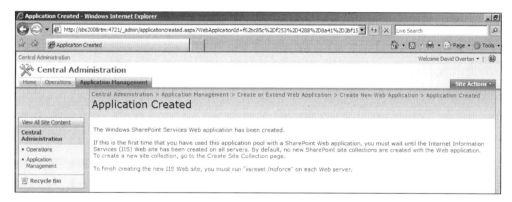

Changing the Administrator settings for the site

We now need to change the administrators to the SBS 2008 administrators. I would recommend using the administrator you created to start the Migration Wizard in Chapter 4.

Click the **Application Management** link on the breadcrumb bar underneath the **Application Management** tab.

You can now click on the **Site collection administrators** link to start the process to change the administrator for OldCompanyWeb.

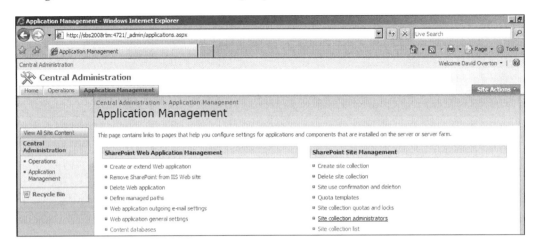

If the **Site Collection** does not state **http://OldCompanyWeb** then click the drop-down arrow and select **Change Site Collection**. If it does, skip to the items below on changing the site collection.

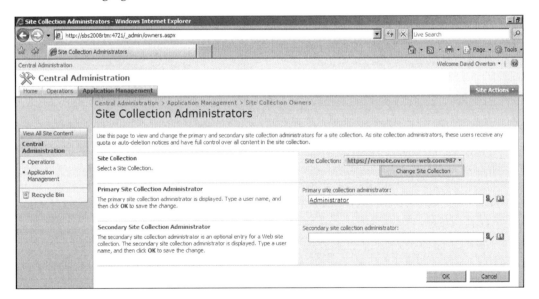

On the **Select Site Collection** page, click the **Web Application** drop-down arrow and select **Change Web Application** as shown in the following screenshot.

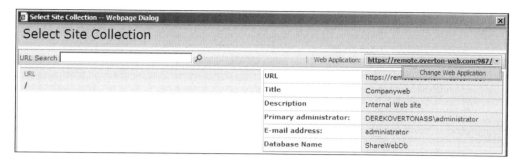

Now, select OldCompanyWeb from the list and it should return to the previous screen again.

In the **Primary site collection administrator**, you can now type in the name of the administrator or click the picture of a book. You can then type in part of their name and click on the magnifying glass to search for them. Pick them from the list and click **OK**.

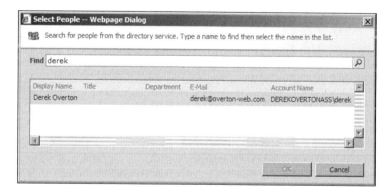

Do the same for a secondary administrator if desired and then click **OK**. This will have changed the administrators.

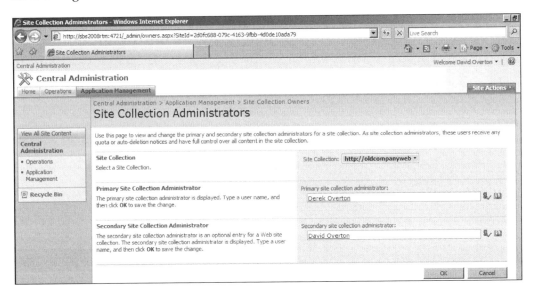

Restarting IIS

The time has come to restart IIS to enable the site to start and work correctly. You need to start an administrative copy of a command prompt. To do this, right-click on **Command Prompt** on the **start** menu and select **Run as Administrator**.

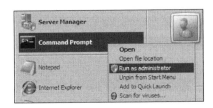

In the window that appears, simply type `iisreset` and it will stop and start the services as required.

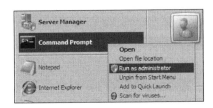

Tidying up

You should now be able to start the OldCompanyWeb in a browser, but we need to ensure things are good with it. The first step is to make it a trusted site on the server.

 There are those who would rightly tell you this is a security risk as browsing the web from the server is to be avoided. However, since this site is internal to your network and on the server, I believe this is a reasonable and a safe change to make.

To do this, browse to `http://OldCompanyWeb` on the server and double-click the **Internet logo** at the bottom of the browser.

You will see the **Internet Security** dialog appear. Select **Trusted Sites** and then click the **Sites** button. The Trusted sites list will appear. Type in here: **http://OldCompanyWeb** and click on **Add** followed by **Close** and **OK** in the Internet Security dialog.

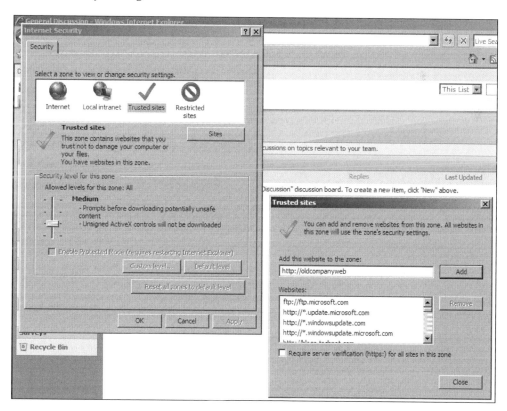

Ensuring all graphics files are copied across

Now, navigate around the site to check that things are OK. The most likely issue will be the fact that some of the SBS 2003 graphics are missing, such as this default image above the **Links** section. If you right-click on the red cross and select **Properties,** you will see a path to the place it is expecting to find the image. In the example below, it is **http://oldcompanyweb/_layouts/images/homepage_sbs.gif**. These images are provided by Windows SharePoint Services v2 and SBS 2003. Not all of these are automatically provided on SBS 2008.

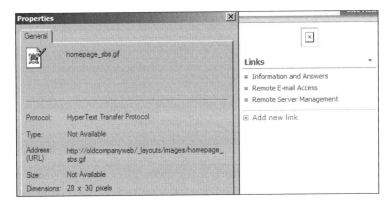

The **_layouts** part of this path tells us that this is one of the Windows SharePoint Services V2.0 images that are still present on the SBS 2003 server. You can either change the image or you can copy across the old image file. You can access these files from you SBS 2008 server by selecting **Run** from the **Start** menu and typing in **\\<SBS 2008 Server Name>\c$\program files\Common Files\Microsoft Shared\ web server extensions\60\TEMPLATE\IMAGES**.

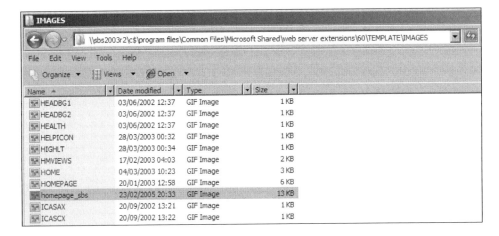

To make them appear in the **_layouts** directory on the SBS 2008 server, you need to copy any missing images to **\Program Files\Common Files\Microsoft Shared\ Web Server Extensions\12\template\images**.

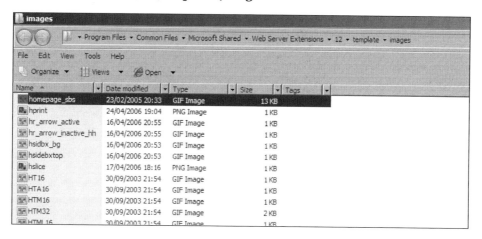

Now, reload the page and the image should appear as expected, such as the example below.

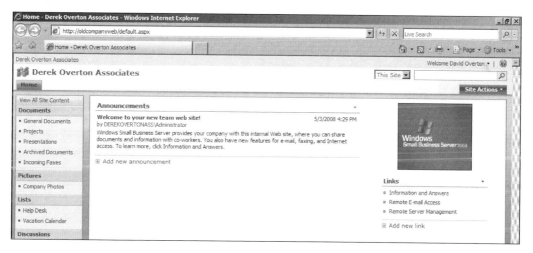

Changing web site names

It is possible that you wish your users to continue to access the OldCompanyWeb site via the URL they always knew — http://CompanyWeb — and for the new site provided in SBS 2008 to be known by another name, such as http://CompanyWebV3. Some of the features of the site, such as it being a repository for faxes as they arrive will no longer function, but any linked documents or other links to the document stores will continue to work if this is carried out.

To do this, find **SharePoint 3.0 Central Administration** under the **Administrative Tools** on the **Start** menu. Once the web-based tool has loaded, navigate to the **operations** tab and click on the **Alternative access mappings** link.

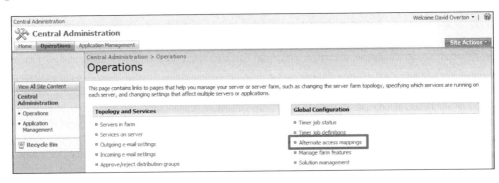

Now, pick the web site such as **http://CompanyWeb** you wish to rename and click it.

 You must perform this task twice: first to rename **CompanyWeb** to, for example, **CompanyWebV3** and then **OldCompanyWeb** to **CompanyWeb**.

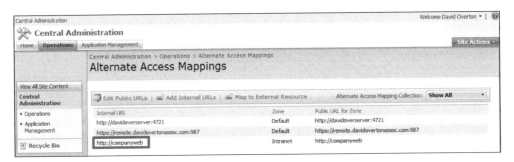

Change the URL once it is displayed to your chosen value and then click on **OK**.

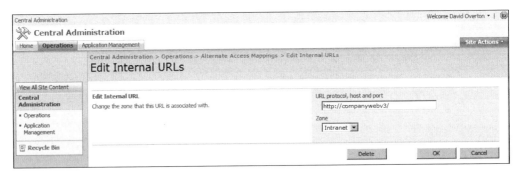

Before the web sites start working, check that the DNS names are correct. This can be achieved by following the instructions in *Configure the DNS for migrated site*, but replacing OldCompanyWeb in the instructions with the new name you have chosen for the new site. This will give you DNS settings that point `http://CompanyWeb` and `http://CompanyWebV3` both to your server.

Completing the task

Select **Task Complete** in the Migration Wizard and click on **Next**.

Summary

The intranet web site now known as `http://OldCompanyWeb` will now be running on your SBS 2008 server. The DNS entries will have been updated to enable connection to this site as well as enabling access via `http://CompanyWeb` to the new site.

All data will be available for access, but the recommendation is that users start customizing and using the SBS 2008 pre-installed site going forward.

The final items of user files that need to be migrated are the files in shared folders and this is covered in the next chapter.

8

Migrating Users and Data from SBS 2003

This chapter covers the finalizing of the migration tasks with the migration of the users and the remaining data from the SBS 2003 system to SBS 2008. Once again, tasks will need to be completed on both systems meaning that the SBS 2003 server must still be in use until these tasks are completed. Once all tasks are completed, you can recycle the hardware either by installing another licensed copy of Windows on the server or by asking your local recycling centre to recover the metals from the server.

We will cover the following tasks in this chapter:

- Migrating file shares
- Migrating the fax data
- Migrating users and groups
- Migrating LOB applications
- Finishing the migration

Impact on users

These tasks will have significant impact on users and should be carried out without users being attached to either server. Email may continue to be used without an issue. I would expect this section to take between four and eight hours to complete.

If you have closed the Migration Wizard from the previous chapter, re-open the **Windows SBS Console** and select the **Migrate to Windows SBS 2008** task.

Migrating file shares

One of the functions that is critical for users that SBS carries out is managing and protecting users' files. This can be a complex area with a number of file shares and folders, each with different security controls in place relying on you noting down these settings by hand. To ease this, I have assembled a set of tools to make this process predictable and reliable. The scripts and information about the Microsoft tool required can be downloaded from `http://davidoverton.com/r.ashx?1C`.

As I am keen to see a successful migration, you can use the tools I describe here to automate the process or follow the instructions provided as part of the migration process within the wizard.

Instructions for migration

Select the **Migrate Users' Shared Data** option from the wizard and click on **Next**.

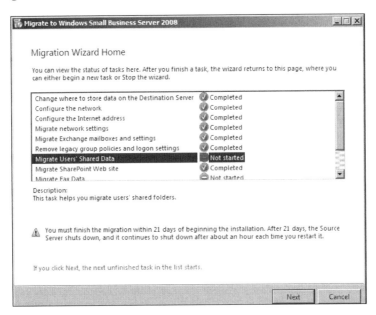

You can then read the instructions by clicking on the link **How do I migrate users' shared data**. I believe these instructions are good, but there is lots of manual work and opportunity for steps to be missed resulting in missing or insecure data. If you have many shared folders to migrate, I strongly recommend the scripted process described in this chapter. Even if you only have one file share to migrate, the user files share, due to the security permissions these scripts will make it easier. These scripts follow the steps of the process described in the wizard documentation, but do not rely on you having to note things down or create new file shares by hand.

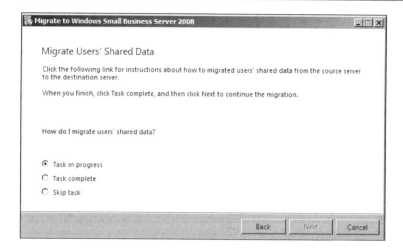

Preparing on the SBS 2003 system

We need to recreate the shares, all their security permissions, and the files with the appropriate NTFS permissions on the new system.

Go to `http://davidoverton.com/r.ashx?1D`, which will download the **RMTSHAR.EXE** tool from the Microsoft site: `ftp://ftp.microsoft.com/bussys/winnt/winnt-public/reskit/nt40/i386`. If you navigate to the site, download the file as shown below.

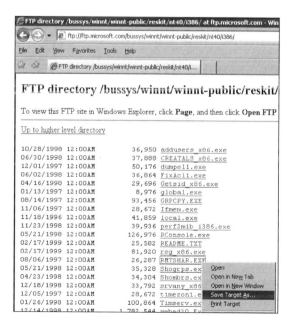

Once you have downloaded the file, run it to extract the program **RMTSHARE.EXE**, which needs to be put in the same folder as the scripts you downloaded from my site.

I created a folder on my SBS 2003 desktop called **David** and then **Script** underneath that and placed the files all in there. Open a **Command Prompt** from the **Start** menu and move to that directory by typing CD %HomePath%\desktop\david\script. Obviously, type in the folder names that you have used.

You then need to run the migration program, which will present a list of shares that you edit and then create a script to run on the SBS 2008 system. The RMTSHARE. EXE program is used by the scripts to extract all the folder permissions.

To start the script off, type in share_migration <sbs2003 server name> <sbs 2008 server name> into the **Command Prompt** window where the two server names are entered. These are the names you would type to network connect to the servers. You will initially see a warning that some of the files used by the script will be deleted and you will need to press a key to continue.

```
Command Prompt - share_migration.cmd sbs2003r2 sbs2008rtm

C:\DOCUME~1\ADMINI~1\Desktop\David\script>dir
 Volume in drive C has no label.
 Volume Serial Number is 8CE8-5A32

 Directory of C:\DOCUME~1\ADMINI~1\Desktop\David\script

11/10/2008  19:40    <DIR>          .
11/10/2008  19:40    <DIR>          ..
11/10/2008  19:37             2,426 process_rmt_output.vbs
04/08/1997  16:37            30,208 RMTSHARE.EXE
11/10/2008  19:39             1,934 share_migration.cmd
               3 File(s)         34,568 bytes
               2 Dir(s)   3,914,207,232 bytes free

C:\DOCUME~1\ADMINI~1\Desktop\David\script>share_migration.cmd sbs2003r2 sbs2008r
tm
This will delete and re-create the following files:
- ShareList.txt
- Shares_Permissions.txt
- Migrate_Shares_from_sbs2003_to_2008.cmd
THIS WILL CREATE THE MIGRATION SCRIPT TO MOVE SHARES FROM THE SBS 2003 SERVER 's
bs2003r2' TO THE SBS 2008 SERVER 'sbs2008rtm'
This script must be run on the SBS 2003 system
press a key to continue or CTRL-C to abort
Press any key to continue . . . _
```

The script will open up a Notepad window with all the shares available on the SBS 2003 system including those that cannot be migrated, such as printers, policy shares, or tools from SBS 2003 that are not relevant or are already provided with SBS 2008 such as the fax client. Delete all the shares from the list that you do not wish to migrate to the new server. This would normally include the following:

- SYSVOL
- clients
- tsclient
- tsweb
- faxclient
- clientapps
- NETLOGON

Some file shares are shared with a $ sign at the end to stop them appearing on a network list, while applications and users can still access them. You need to evaluate if these should be moved across. Also, disks are shared as the drive letter followed by a $ sign. You normally do not want to migrate a whole disk, so these would normally also be removed.

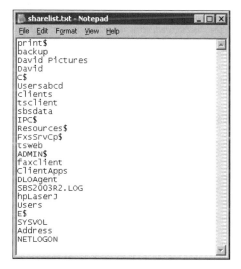

Once you have trimmed down the list, you will see something more like my list shown in the following screenshot. In the example, I have included the SBS 2003 ClientApps file share as I have a number of applications that I had added to SBS 2003 for installation on PCs. I want to continue to install these third-party applications with SBS 2008 and by migrating the share from SBS 2003 to SBS 2008, I can configure them to still be available once the SBS 2003 server is removed. Chapter 11 covers briefly using applications distribution.

Now, save the file and close the window. This will continue the scripted process. You may see some error messages stating **Could not find ....** where the filenames are the ones used by the scripting process. The script routine is, however, gathering security details about each share and creating a script that will create those on the new server and copy the files across.

```
Command Prompt
Processing Shares
Could Not Find C:\DOCUME~1\ADMINI~1\Desktop\David\script\shares_permissions.txt
Processing backup
Processing David
Processing David
Processing Usersabcd
Processing sbsdata
Processing ClientApps
Processing DLOAgent
Processing SBS2003R2.LOG
Processing Users
Done gathering information
Could Not Find C:\DOCUME~1\ADMINI~1\Desktop\David\script\Migrate_Shares_from_sbs
2003_to_2008.cmd
Processing file to create migration script to be run on the SBS 2008 server - sb
s2008rtm
Output processed
the Output file Migrate_Shares_from_sbs2003_to_2008.cmd must
press a key to continue or CTRL-C to abort
C:\DOCUME~1\ADMINI~1\Desktop\David\script>_
```

Completing migration on the SBS 2008 system

The next stage in the file migration should be carried out on the SBS 2008 system. You will need to open an administrative command prompt to run the script. To do this, right-click on **Command Prompt** on the **Start** menu and select **Run as Administrator**.

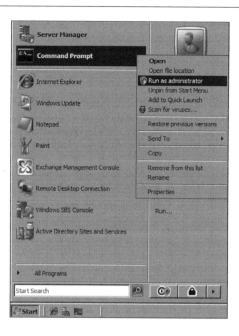

The script produced the file **Migrate_Shares_from_sbs2003_to_2008.cmd** on the SBS 2003 server that needs to be run on the SBS 2008 server. To do this, you can either copy across on removable media or create a file share that can be accessed by the SBS 2008 administrator. In the following screenshot, you can see that I created a file share and then accessed it from SBS 2008 to copy the file across.

Once the file is copied across, you will need to edit it by typing **notepad Migrate_Shares_from_sbs2003_to_2008.cmd**.

```
C:\Windows\System32>net use * \\sbs2003r2\david\script
Drive Z: is now connected to \\sbs2003r2\david\script.

The command completed successfully.

C:\Windows\System32>z:

Z:\>dir
 Volume in drive Z has no label.
 Volume Serial Number is 8CE8-5A32

 Directory of Z:\

11/10/2008  19:44    <DIR>          .
11/10/2008  19:44    <DIR>          ..
11/10/2008  19:44             2,286 Migrate_Shares_from_sbs2003_to_2008.cmd
11/10/2008  19:37             2,426 process_rmt_output.vbs
04/08/1997  16:37            30,208 RMTSHARE.EXE
11/10/2008  19:43               104 sharelist.txt
11/10/2008  19:44             2,696 shares_permissions.txt
11/10/2008  19:53             1,930 share_migration.cmd
               6 File(s)         39,650 bytes
               2 Dir(s)  3,899,285,504 bytes free

Z:\>notepad Migrate_Shares_from_sbs2003_to_2008.cmd

Z:\>
```

For each share in the Notepad file, you will notice a section similar to the one shown in the following screenshot. You will need to change the destination folder setting to the location where you want a directory created, shared, and then the files copied into it.

```
REM MIGRATING backup
REM ===================================
SET Dest_Folder="c:\migrated_files\backup"
```

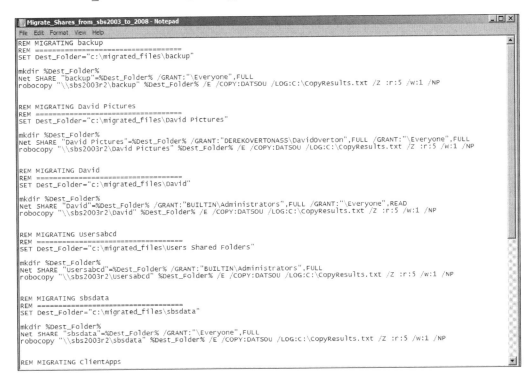

Change the destination folder for each share in the Notepad file. Run the script **Migrate_Shares_from_sbs2003_to_2008.cmd** and the process will start. The length of time is dictated by the speed of the network and the amount of data, but it may run for a few hours. A log file is created for each shared folder copied and placed in the root of the C drive as `C:\CopyResults<n>.txt`.

> The script is non-destructive to the SBS 2003 server, so in the worst case, you can delete the newly created folders and start again.

Once the script has completed, you should check the end of the log file to ensure all files were copied. As this uses robocopy, a summary is produced that includes how many files were and were not copied. If a file copy failed, investigate the cause and re-run the script or the section of the script.

Migrating the fax data

If you did not use a fax on your SBS 2003 system, then you can skip this section; however, if you did, or you want to add a fax, follow these instructions:

- Install the modem.
- Install and start the Fax Service.
- Migrate the fax data across.
- Configure the Fax Service.

 If you are running as a Hyper-V virtualized machine, you will not be able to add a normal serial modem, but would be required to have a software modem, which is far less common. For that reason, you may not be able to complete this section if you are running with Hyper-V.

Installing the modem

Open up **Control Panel** and double-click on **Phone and Modem Options**.

It is probable that your modem will not be listed, so you will need to add the modem by clicking on the **Add** button. You should then be able to click on **Next** to start the detection process and SBS 2008 will find your modem.

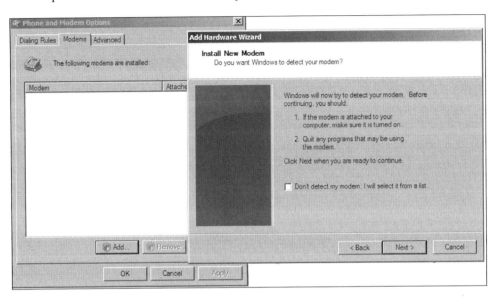

If your modem is found, click on **Finish**. If it is not, check that your modem is powered on and that the connections to your server are OK. If the modem is a card inside your computer, check that the drivers are loaded and that it is supported on Windows Server 2008.

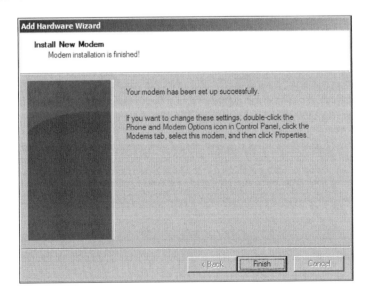

The modem should now be listed in the **Phone and Modem Options** and you can click on **OK** and close **Control Panel**.

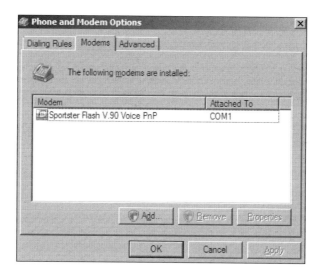

Installing and starting the Fax Service

Now, we have the device added for the Fax Service and we need to install it. Select **Windows SBS Console** from the **Start** menu. Click on the **Network** tab and then the **Device** tab underneath it. You should see a message stating **The Fax Service is not installed. To install it, click "Start the Fax service."**

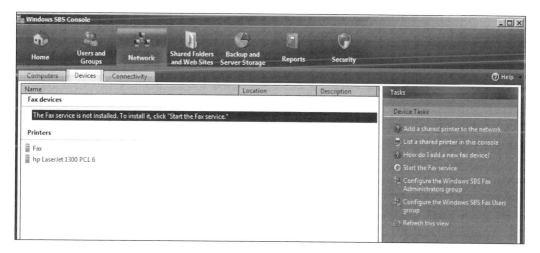

Click on the **Start the Fax Service** task and when asked if you want to install the service, click **Yes**.

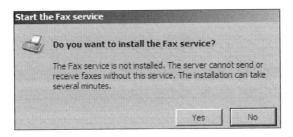

The component will install itself and will finish by telling you that you need to restart the computer. Click on the **Close** button and restart the server.

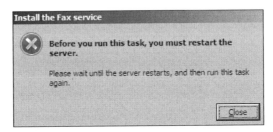

Once the Server has restarted, go back to the **Windows SBS Console** to the **Network** tab and **Devices** and click on the **Start the Fax service** task again and you should be informed the service has started.

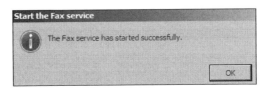

You will then be asked to configure the Fax Service, but this can be done later, so click on the **No** button.

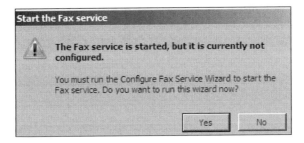

Go back to the **Home** tab in the **Windows SBS Console** and re-start the Migration Wizard. Go to the **Migrate fax data** task. Check one or both of the check boxes for a location where fax data will be stored and then click on the **Click to start migrating your fax data** link. The migrated data will be stored in the locations you select here, although you can then define where new faxes are delivered to later in the process.

Migrating the fax data

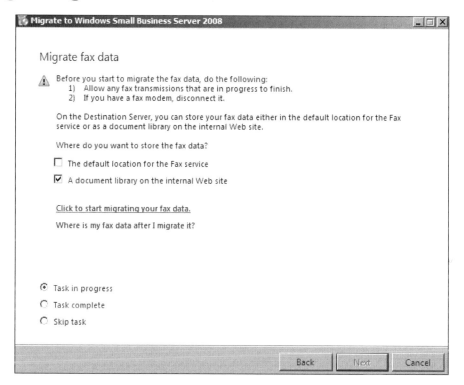

This will start the migration process and once it is completed, you will be able to click the **OK** button to configure the Fax Service itself.

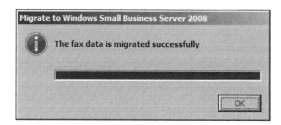

To find the fax data, look in the following locations of SBS 2008:

Location Title	Folder on SBS 2008
Inbox	`%ALLUSERSPROFILE%\Microsoft\Windows NT\MSFax\Inbox`
Sent items	`%ALLUSERSPROFILE%\Microsoft\Windows NT\MSFax\SentItems`
Cover pages	`%ALLUSERSPROFILE%\Microsoft\Windows NT\MSFax\Common Coverpages`

Location Title	Folder in Windows SharePoint Services on SBS 2008
Inbox	`Fax Center\Saved Faxes`
Sent items	`Fax Center\Sent Faxes`
Cover pages	`Fax Center\Send a Fax`

Configuring the Fax Service

You will now be asked to configure the Fax Service with information about your business. How complete your information was in the migration answer file determines how much you need to type into these forms. The first screen is information that will pre-populate a fax cover page.

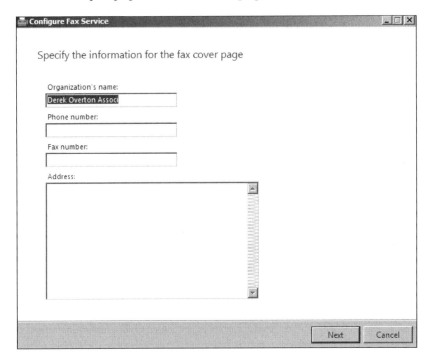

The next screen configures the text that appears as a short line of text at the top of a fax transmission identifying your company.

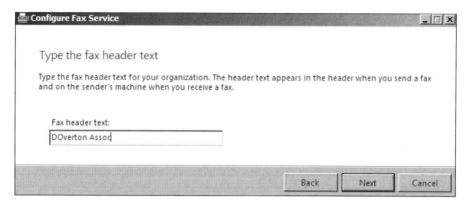

On the next screen, put a check mark against the modem you configured earlier on. Assuming you only have one modem and you use it for both sending and receiving, you will need to check the same modem for this and the next screen. If you have a specific modem for receiving and one for sending, then first screen is the modem that will be used for sending and the second for receiving.

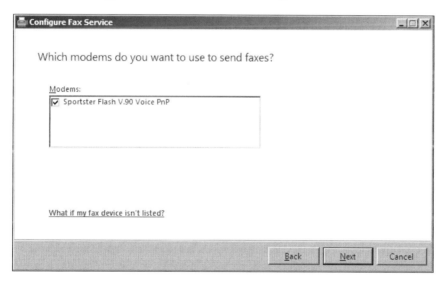

A single fax can be sent or routed to up to four locations. If you would like an email to be sent with the fax attached as a TIFF file, then put a check mark in the **Route through e-mail** box and enter a list of one or more email addresses in the text box beneath the check box.

If you would like to see the faxes appear in a SharePoint Services site, then check **Store in a document library** and select the desired location from the drop-down list. By default, the location is the **Internal Web Site – Fax Center**.

If you want them to print out, similar to from a traditional fax machine then put a check mark in the **Print** check box, but be aware that the printer must already be installed to be able to select this. You will be able to change this later should you desire.

The final option is to choose **Store in a folder**. If you want the files to be placed on the hard disk, then check this option and then type or browse to the folder you want to use.

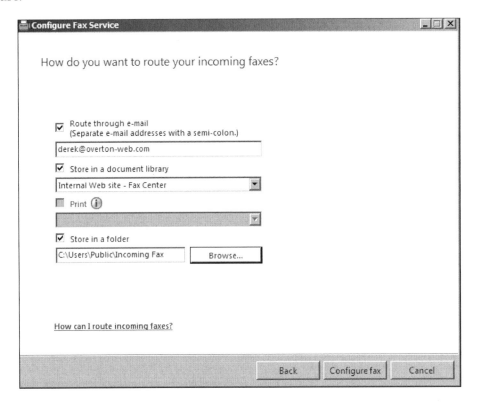

After you click on **Configure fax**, the system will process the options and then you will be told that you have configured your fax.

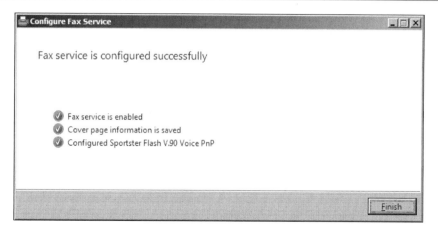

Click on the **Finish** button and you will be back at the Migration Wizard. Select the **Task Complete** option and then click on **Next**.

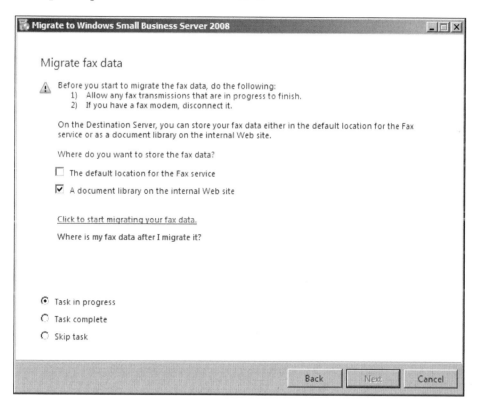

Migrating users and groups

The final part of moving data between the two systems is to change the users' accounts to conform to the SBS 2008 roles. While Active Directory will have shared all the user and logon information between the two servers, the accounts will not yet show up in the Windows SBS Console as it does not show the users with non-SBS 2008 roles.

The procedure we will follow has the following steps:

- Enable any SBS 2003 groups to appear in SBS 2008.
- Create user roles.
- Migrate users by role.
- Enable users to connect to a computer through remote web workplace.
- Remove SBS 2003 system accounts that are no longer required.

To start the process, select **Migrate users and groups** in the Migration Wizard and click on the **Next** button.

While the screen offers some help and a wizard, if you read the help there are a number of steps you need to do before continuing the wizard.

Modifying SBS 2003 groups so they work with SBS 2008

On SBS 2008, the Windows SBS Console only displays a specific selection of groups in the console and other tools. This is because SBS 2008 and Windows 2008 create and use a number of groups for system management that would potentially confuse users if they were shown in the console. It adds information to the groups to enable them to appear in the console; however, the groups from SBS 2003 do not yet have that information. To enable those groups you wish to appear, you need to modify them in Active Directory. Basically, they don't have a SBS 2008 role assigned to them and this is the information that needs to be added.

If you did not create any custom groups or are happy to use the existing SBS 2008 groups, skip this section.

Open the **Start** menu and select **Administrative Tools** and then **ADSI Edit** from the menu to start the editor we will use.

 ADSI Edit is an incredibly powerful tool that can enable deep changes within Active Directory. You should only use it following detailed instructions otherwise there is a real chance you can destroy your system.

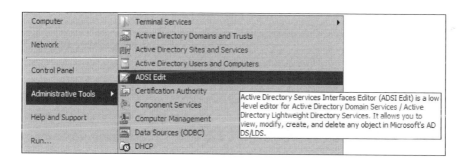

When the **ADSI Edit** window appears, right-click on **ADSI Edit** in the left navigation pane and select **Connect to**.

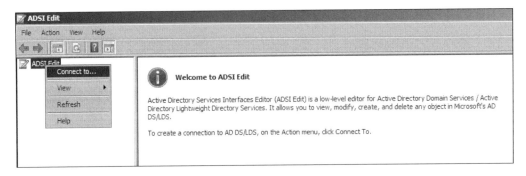

Accept the default connection options and click on **OK**.

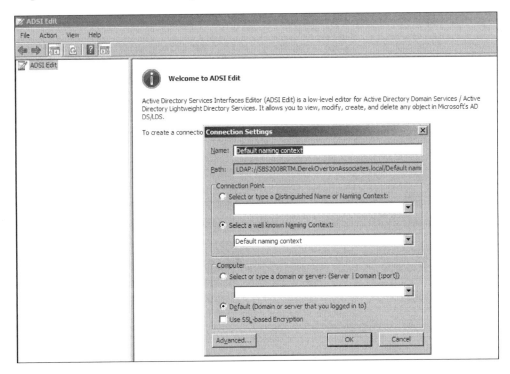

You now need to navigate the expanding the sections **DC=<Domain>,DC=local** followed by **OU=MyBusiness** and **OU=Security Groups**. Find a group you wish to make visible and right-click on it and select **Properties**.

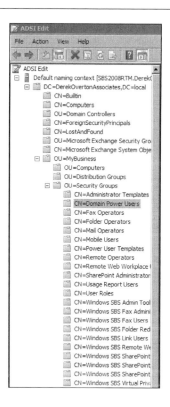

Navigate down the **Attribute** list until you find **msSBSCreationState**, which should have a **Value** of **<not set>**.

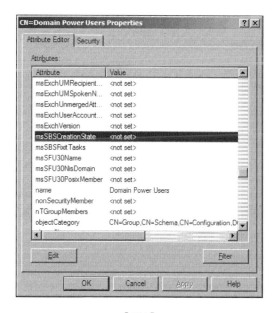

Click on the **Edit** button and change the **Value** to **Created**, noting the fact that the capital **C** is important as is the fact that the rest of the word is in lower case. If this is not entered like this, then it will fail to have the desired effect.

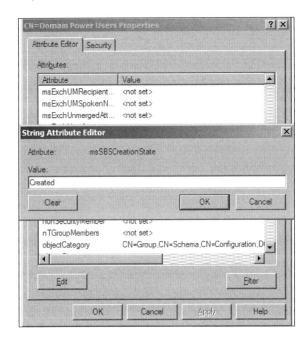

Click on **OK** in the **String Attribute Editor** and then **OK** to the **Properties** window. You should now repeat this exercise for all other groups you wish to make available in the SBS 2008 console and user settings.

Once you have finished, close ADSI Edit and return to the **Windows SBS Console**. If you refresh the page, you will see that the modified groups, such as the **Power Users** that I modified are now listed in the **Groups** tab.

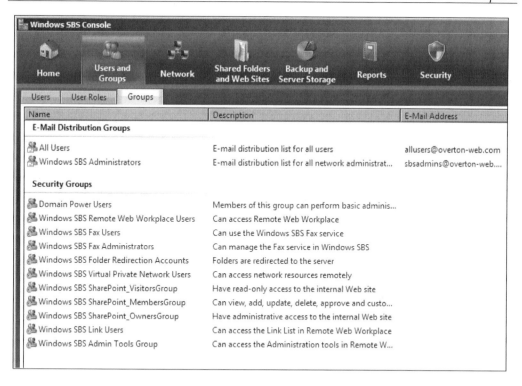

Creating new account roles

The next optional item is to create new user roles. A role defines a number of aspects of a user, such as:

- Which groups they belong to
- Their email quota
- Whether they have remote access
- Their file quota
- Server redirection policy

The granularity in SBS 2008 means that all users are put together in the Standard User role and there are two administrative roles. If you wish to control some of the aspects above for a subset of users, then you will need to add custom roles so you can assign them to users.

If you are happy to accept and use the SBS user roles, then you do not need to complete this step and can skip ahead to the *Migrating users by role* section.

In the **Windows SBS Console,** go to the **Users** tab and then the **User Roles** tab and click on **Add a new user role** on the task list.

There are a number of options here that enable you to customize the role. Obviously, the **User role name** cannot be the name of a user or an existing role.

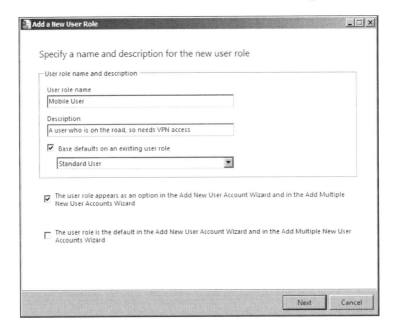

Continue through the wizard selecting the information that is appropriate for your desired role until the **Adding the new user role** screen appears.

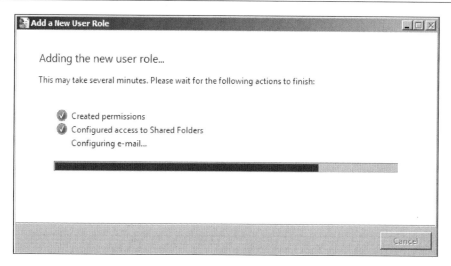

When the process is complete, click on the **Finish** button and repeat the process for any roles you wish to add.

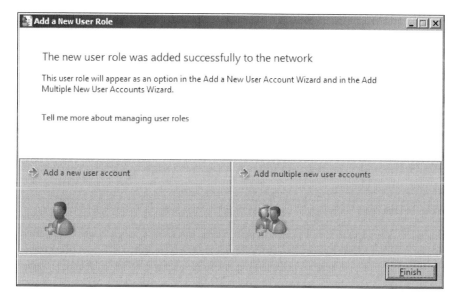

Migrating users by role

We are now able to actually finish migrating the users. To do this, click on the **Run the Change User Role Wizard** link in the Migration Wizard.

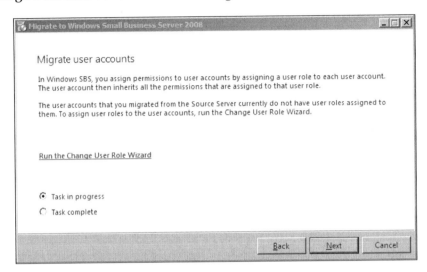

Now, select the **Role Name** for the group of users you wish to migrate and then choose to either **Replace user permissions or settings** if you suspect they are not ideal or wish to start from a known quantity, or **Add user permissions or settings** if you believe the roles on SBS 2003 were customized or are complex. Click on **Next** to continue the process.

By default there are three standard roles:

Standard user who can use the system and access their files

Network Administrators who have full access to the system

Standard Users with Administrator Tools who are standard users, who can see the administration tools links, but are prompted for an administrator's username and password to access them.

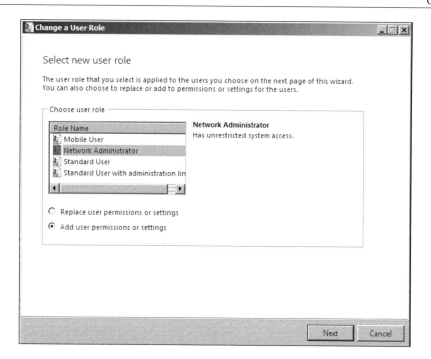

Now, pick the users you wish to apply this role to by selecting from the **All user accounts** list and click **Add**.

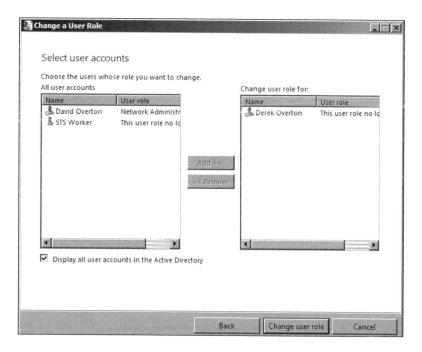

Now, click on **Change User Role** and the process will apply the settings to the chosen users.

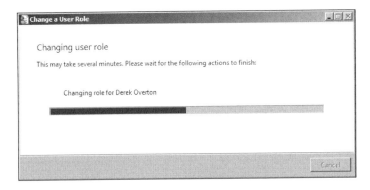

Once the process has finished, click on **Finish** to complete the changes.

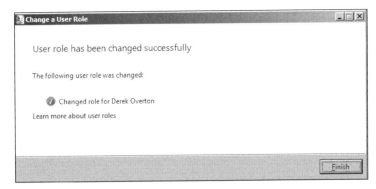

Enabling remote access to the computer

If some of the users you have migrated should have remote access to their physical computer in the office, then this will need to be modified in the **Windows SBS Console**. Select the **Users and Groups** tab and then double-click on the user.

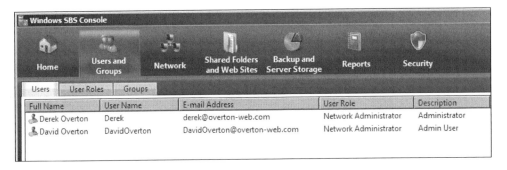

You can then add a computer to the user's list on the computers tab. I'll run through this more thoroughly in Chapter 11.

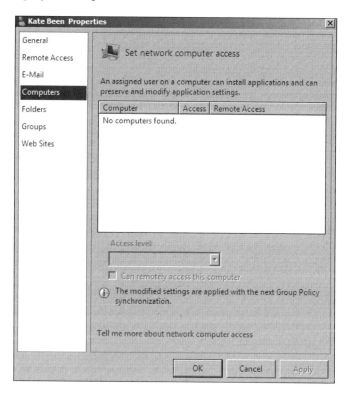

Removing unwanted users

There are a number of accounts that were created for SBS 2003 that can now be removed from Active Directory to help maintain the security of the system. Start by selecting **Administrative Tools** from the **Start** menu and then **Active Directory Users and Computers**.

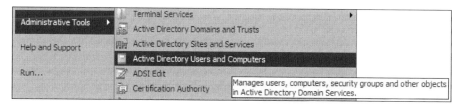

Navigate to **<Domain.local>** followed by **Users** and you will find users by the name of **IUSR_<SBS 2003 server>** and **IWAM_<SBS 2003 server>**. Right-click on them and select **Delete**.

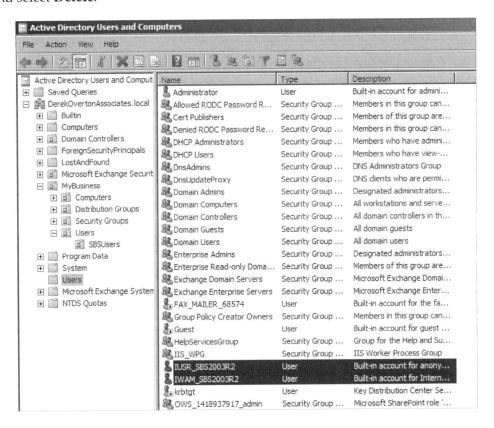

If you then navigate to the **MyBusiness** organizational unit, followed by **Users** and then **SBSUsers**, you will see **STS Worker** and **SBSBackup** which also need deleting.

SBS 2008 stores computers and users under the Organizational Unit of MyBusiness. This enables SBS 2008 to apply and manage policy and security as well as to only display a limited subset of Active Directory information that is relevant to the SBS 2008 administrator. Traditional Windows Server 2008 Active Directory information is kept in its normal locations so as to avoid confusion in the SBS 2008 interfaces.

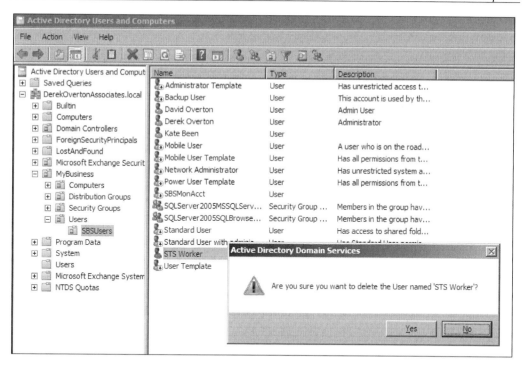

Click **Yes** to each question asking if you want to delete those users. Now, close the window, mark **Task complete** in the Migration Wizard, and click **Next**.

Migrating Line of Business (LOB) applications

The additional third-party applications that you have installed on SBS 2003 will need to be moved over to SBS 2008 too. Unfortunately, I can't tell you how to do that and a call to your provider for those applications will be required. If you have been paying maintenance to these organizations, then upgrades and support for Windows Server 2008 are likely to be covered.

It is important that all applications and data that you want have been migrated before you finish the migration. Once the migration is finished and the SBS 2003 server is removed, recovering information from a backup is significantly harder than from a live system.

While I cannot tell you how to migrate these applications, I can share the following areas to double-check from the vendor.

Platform compatibility

SBS 2008 is based on Windows 2008 x64. Your ISV will need to support the move from a 32-bit Windows 2003 server to a 64-bit Windows 2008 server.

They will need to support SBS 2008. While it is built on Windows Server 2008 Standard Edition, if they will not support the application then you have no recourse in the issue of an application failure.

If either of the above presents a problem, you have two options available to you:

- Change ISV application vendor.
- Use SBS 2008 Premium Edition and install 32-bit Windows Server 2003 on a second server.

Common file and data locations

Most ISV applications will require re-installing on the SBS 2008 server, so it is often not possible to simply copy some file locations and be completely migrated for an application. Below are a list of common places to check for data that could be useful.

Data Location	Reason
C:\InetPub	This is the default location for web-based applications to place their content. It is not the only place. A check in IIS Administration tool on SBS 2003 will allow you to learn more.
C:\Program Files	Programs frequently install to this location and some also put important data and settings in their directories in this location.
SQL Server	Use the **SQL Server Management Studio Express** tool from the **Administrative Tools** menu on the **Start** menu to explore which databases exist and ensure they are backed up.

Naming dependencies

Your applications may rely on the network name of your SBS 2003 server, which will be disappearing. In the last section of this chapter, I briefly cover how you can create a name in the DNS settings so that when someone refers to the SBS 2003 server, they are connected with the SBS 2008 server. This does require a slight lowering of the security settings for SBS 2008, so should only be used as a medium-term fix before the applications can be changed.

Finishing the migration

This is the final task in the Migration Wizard. The result of this task is that the SBS 2003 system will be decommissioned and can be recycled either as an additional server with a new operating system loaded, such as Windows Server 2008 as provided with SBS 2008 Premium, or as per your local government recycling requirements.

To start the process, select **Finish Migration** in the Migration Wizard and click **Next**.

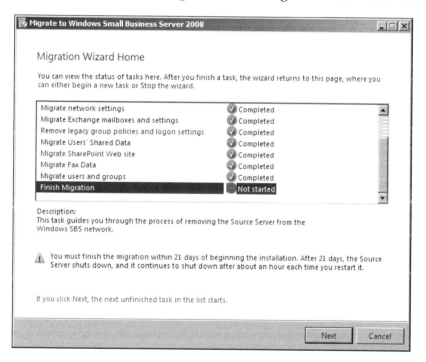

The Migration Wizard will next check that you have completed all the migration tasks. Select **Finish the migration** and again click on the **Next** button.

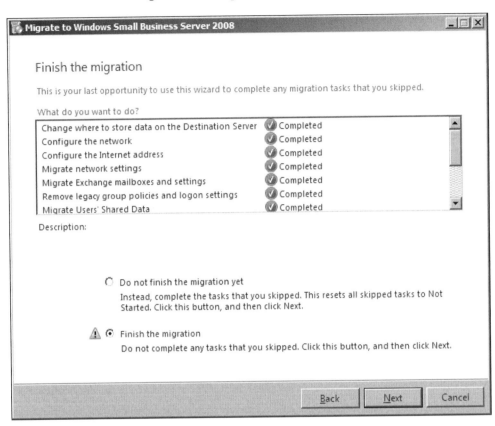

The Migration Wizard provides a link to documentation telling you how to demote the SBS 2003 server. In doing so, the SBS 2003 server will no longer function and will need to be turned off. You should ensure that all the data you require is present on the SBS 2008 system before following this last step. One option is to shut down the SBS 2003 server and check that your applications and data can still be found as expected.

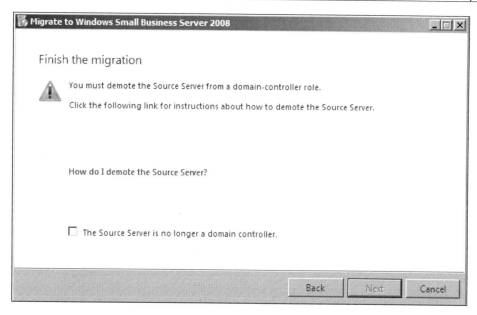

On the SBS 2003 server, select **Run** from the **Start** menu and type **dcpromo** and click on **Run** to start the Active Directory tool. Then click **Next** to move beyond the introduction page.

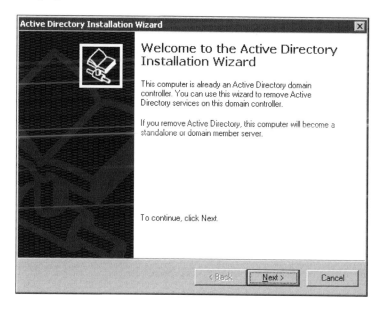

You will receive a warning about the SBS 2003 system being a **Global Catalog server**. Simply click on **OK** to move past this.

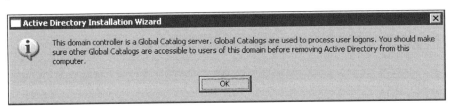

It is important that the check box for **This server is the last domain controller in the domain** does not have a check mark in it. This will enable the migration of various roles and responsibilities to the SBS 2008 system.

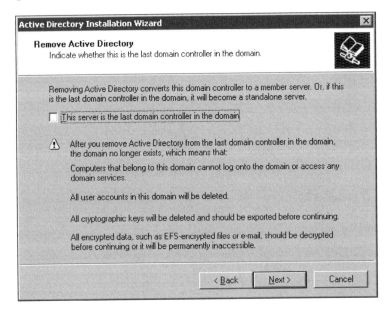

Since the machine will no longer be a domain controller, you will need to supply a password for the local administrator account on the system.

The summary screen will be shown to confirm the actions and then you can click on **Next**.

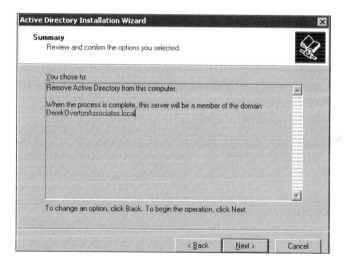

The process will continue and finally prompt you to reboot the SBS 2003 system. I would personally not perform the reboot, but instead shut down the server and not restart it.

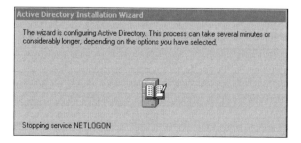

Back on the SBS 2008 system, put a check mark in the box **The Source Server is no longer a domain controller**. Now, click on **Next** to finish the migration.

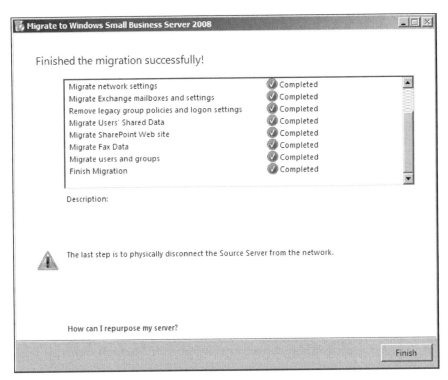

Making your SBS 2008 appear to also be the SBS 2003 server on the network

Some applications, and often users too, expect the server to exist at a specific network address. SBS 2003 would have had one name and SBS 2008 would have had to have a different name. Once the SBS 2003 server is removed from the network, it is possible to make the SBS 2008 server respond to a network request for the SBS 2003 server. Provided that the database or file share has been configured with the same name, it will be able to respond to the request as if it was the SBS 2003 server responding.

To do this, we need to update the DNS and NetBIOS settings and change a security setting in the registry.

Making changes to the DNS and NetBIOS settings

To update the DNS and NetBIOS settings, enter the following commands into a command prompt that has Administrative privileges.

```
netdom computername %computername% /add:<SBS2003 computer
name>.%userdnsdomain%

dnscmd /recordadd %userdnsdomain% <sbs 2003 computer name> CNAME %comp
utername%.%userdnsdomain%
```

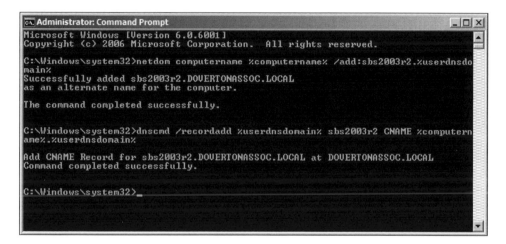

Updating the registry

While we now have the network pointers in place, we need to ensure that the security controls of SBS 2008 do not stop this from working correctly. To do that, enter the following command (note it is all one command so only press *Enter* once you have entered it all). Note that it will not be effective until the SBS 2008 server has been rebooted.

```
REG Add HKLM\SYSTEM\CurrentControlSet\Services\lanmanserver\parameters
/v DisableStrictNameChecking /t REG_DWORD  /v 1
```

When this is completed, it will return as shown in the following screenshot:

Following a reboot, you will now be able to access the SBS 2008 server via commands like **\\<SBS2003 Server Name>**.

Summary

You now have an SBS 2008 system on the network with SBS 2003 turned off and either plan to have it removed or reused as another server on the network.

You should retain the SBS 2003 backup as there may be files you need in the future that were somehow missed in the process and it is always better to be safe rather than sorry.

Your users' files should be accessible and the users should appear in the **Windows SBS Console** against a set of groups that you defined, enabling management of your IT within the business.

The next step is to enable the new services and understand how to securely utilize SBS 2008 for your business.

9

Configuring your Services

This chapter covers the process of finalizing the network setup—moving all the network services to be served from the SBS 2008 server.

To do this, we are essentially completing the tasks in the home screen of the Windows SBS Console, which should look like the screenshot below:

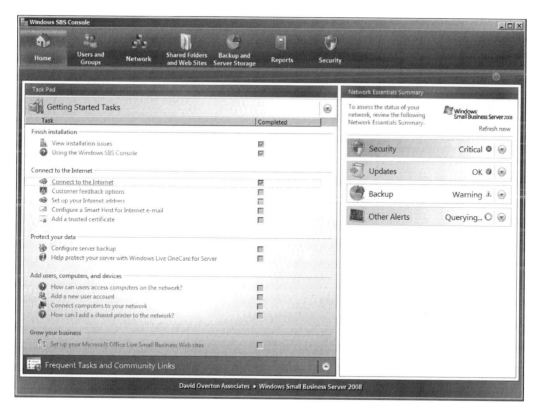

In this chapter, we will carry out the following tasks, some of which are optional:

- Accept the customer feedback option (as it is in this section of the console)
- Configure your Internet domain name for remote access and email
- Check your Internet network settings
- Enable email routing via your ISP (smart hosts) if required
- Install a paid-for SSL certificate (optional)
- Configure Office Live for Small Business for SBS 2008 (optional)
- Configure a VPN (also known as RAS) for external access (optional)

Assumptions

I'm assuming that you understand the concepts of Internet domain name, IP addresses, firewalls, and ports; otherwise, you will struggle to safely configure your network.

Accepting the customer feedback option

The first uncompleted task is to decide if you wish to share your system usage and interactions with Microsoft. This feedback collects no personal or contact information and is not used for directed marketing, but is used to gain a better understanding of SBS 2008 and how it could be improved in the future.

Select the **Customer Feedback Options** task from the **Home** tab in the **Windows SBS Console** and you will be given the opportunity to participate in the **Customer Experience Improvement Program**. I generally join the program, but if you are not sure, click on the **Read more about the program online** link and make your own judgement call. It will in no way impact your SBS 2008 installation whichever option you choose.

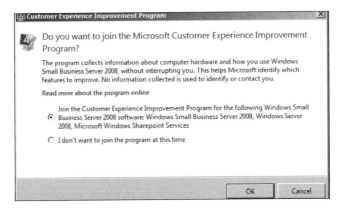

Configuring your Internet domain name for remote access and email

In this section, we will configure the Internet domain name that you will use to access your server. If you carried out a migration, then you will have already been through this task as part of the migration. I've decided to cover the task in more detail in this section in case you are performing your first installation of a server and the options may well be new to you. In this chapter, I will discuss the options to buy an Internet domain name online.

Start from the **Home** tab in the Windows SBS Console and select **Set up you Internet address**.

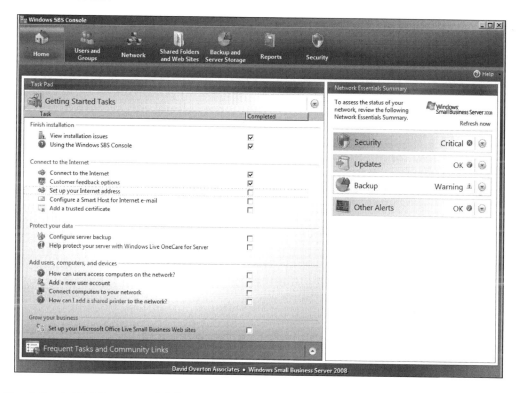

Read the initial **Internet Address Management** screen that states that you need the items listed below. If you do not have an Internet domain, we will run through purchasing a domain via the SBS tools or you can purchase one outside of the tool. Once you are sure, you can continue by clicking on **Next**.

- The name of your Internet domain
- The name of your domain provider
- The logon information for your domain provider

There are three routes you can take in the wizard, each similar, but different and governed by your answers to the first two questions asked in the wizard. They are in essence: will you use an existing domain or buy a new one and if you use an existing domain, will you manually configure the DNS entries or will SBS do it for you?

Step in Process	Buy a new domain	Use existing domain, SBS manages DNS	Use existing domain, you manage DNS
Do you wish to buy a domain?	Yes	No	No
Should SBS manage your DNS settings?	Skipped and set to yes	Yes	No
Choose domain name	Name desired domain	Enter domain name	Enter domain name and SSL name
Registrar	Pick registrar	Pick registrar	
Confirm and/or buy domain registrar detail	Register and purchase domain	Visit registrar to confirm settings	
Configure SBS with DNS login details	Confirm domain, SSL name, and registrar details	Confirm domain, SSL name, and registrar details	
Finalize process	SBS configured	SBS configured	SBS configured

Do you wish to buy a new Internet domain name?

The next page in the wizard asks if you own an Internet domain already. This domain will be used in several places and I've used yourdomain.co.uk in the examples below, but it could obviously have one of many top level domains, such as .com:

- Email addresses (someone@yourdomain.co.uk)
- Remote access via Remote Web Workplace at https://remote.yourdomain.co.uk/remote
- Remote access using a VPN at remote.yourdomain.co.uk
- Your public web site at http://www.yourdomain.co.uk

If you do not have a domain, or perhaps if your email today has an address like `davidmycompany@ispmail.net`, or because you have not had to worry in the past, then now would be the time to purchase a new domain. This can be processed outside SBS 2008, but I will describe the simple process to do it within SBS 2008.

 From a business impression point of view, using your ISP's email domain generally gives the impression of a very small and simple business, so choosing a domain name that is easy to remember and represents your company well is a critical step to success.

To purchase a new domain name, select **I want to purchase a new domain name** and click **Next**; otherwise, select **I already have a domain name that I want to use**.

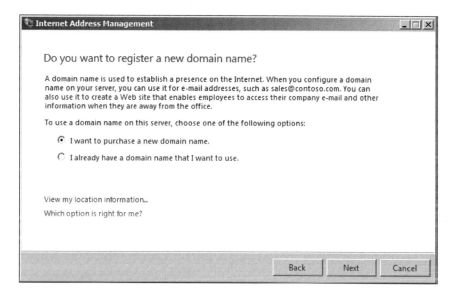

If you choose to buy a new domain name, then the next screen will not be presented to you.

Should SBS 2008 manage your DNS settings?

There are normally at least five DNS records created in a DNS table for SBS 2008. You can either set these by hand or SBS 2008 can manage these for you. If you are purchasing a domain name through SBS 2008, this will automatically be configured for you, if not, you need to choose an option from the following screen:

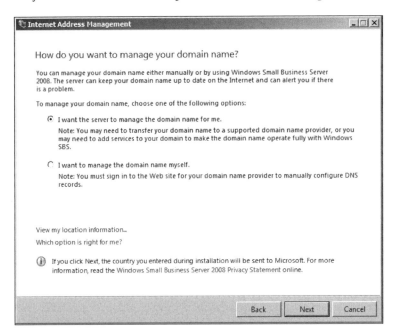

If you select **I want to manage the domain name myself** and click on **Next**, then you will be asked to confirm the **Domain name and extension** to use.

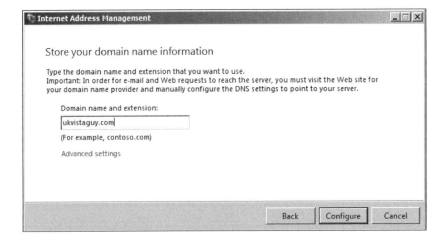

If you click on the **Advanced settings** link, then you can set up an alternative word to **remote** to appear in front on your domain name for remote access. By default, as shown in the list earlier, all remote access is provided via remote.yourdomain. co.uk. You can change the word **remote**, perhaps to *work* or *internal* if desired.

You could also choose to not have a prefix for remote access so that access to SBS 2008 is via http://yourdomain.co.uk; however, many web hosting providers, such as Office Live for Small Business do not currently support this configuration.

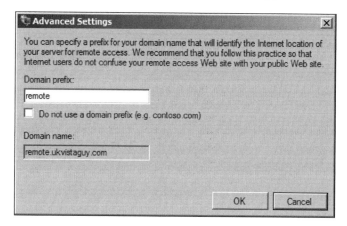

If you opened the advanced window, click on **OK** to continue and then click on **Configure** to start the configuration process.

You will need to have set the following DNS entries:

Resource Record Name	Record Type	Record Setting	Description
WWW	A	xxx.xxx.xxx.xxx	Static IP address of your web site or Office Live
Remote	A	xxx.xxx.xxx.xxx	IP address of your router that connects to your SBS 2008 system
MX	Alias (CNAME)	Remote.*yourdomain.co.uk*	Provides email routing so that mail sent to *someone@yourdomain.co.uk* will arrive on your SBS 2008 system

Resource Record Name	Record Type	Record Setting	Description
SPF	TXT	v=spf1 a mx ~all	Anti-spam feature. You should use a tool to configure this. If you send email via a smart host, the details will need to be entered here.
_autodiscover._tcp	SRV	Service: _autodiscover Protocol: _tcp Priority: 0 Weight: 0 Port: 443 Target host: remote.yourdomain.co.uk	Enables Office Outlook 2007 with Service Pack 1 and Windows Mobile 6.1 email clients to automatically detect and configure email settings

Buying a domain name or configuring Internet domain name information

The steps through the wizard are almost identical whether you are purchasing a domain using SBS 2008 to manage the DNS settings or just configuring the domain name. Rather than having two screenshots for each step that are only slightly different, I will only show the "buying a domain" set of screens. The buttons and input required for each step are identical, but the descriptive text is slightly different. I will describe the differences wherever necessary.

Start the process by typing the domain name you want and the extension that you wish to use. If, for example, you wanted yourdomain.co.uk to be your Internet domain name, then you would type **yourdomain** into the **Domain name** box and chose **.co.uk** in the **Extension** drop down. If you are purchasing a domain, this will be used to see what is available, while if you are planning on using it, it will be used to gather domain information. Once you have done this, click on **Next**.

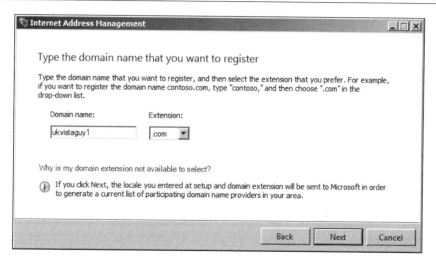

You now need to choose the domain registrar that you will use. Since SBS 2008 is managing the DNS for you, there is a limited set of providers. This list is growing over time, but I've found most DNS providers to be people I talk to infrequently, about every two years when I renew my domain, so they need to be reliable. SBS 2008 will take care of all the settings, so other considerations, such as the quality of their user interface do not influence my decision, while their reliability is very important to me.

If you are purchasing a domain, you will be choosing who you will be purchasing from. If you are using SBS 2008 to manage the DNS, then you will also be choosing who will be providing the Name Server and DNS functionality for you. If your domain is currently with another provider and you wish to use the SBS 2008 DNS management features, then you will need to transfer your domain to one of the providers listed by the wizard. Domain transfers are often difficult and slow processes that can take a week to complete. If you do take this path, you can configure SBS 2008 now while your transfer happens in the background.

On the **Choose a domain provider** screen, select one of the providers shown and then click on **Next**.

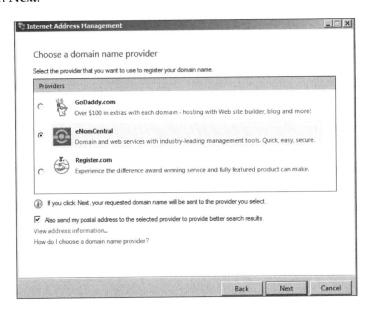

Once you have chosen a provider, a summary of the information is provided along with a button that will open a browser to finish the work of your chosen provider. Click on the **Visit Website** or **Register Now** button to open a browser and follow the process with the provider you selected.

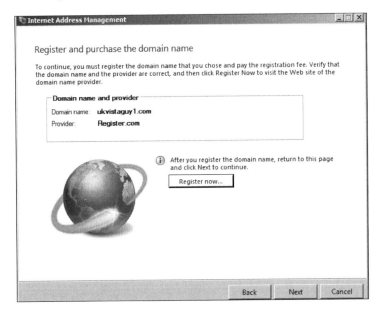

Once you have completed this process, you should have a username and password from your provider that are associated with your Internet domain name. Close the browser window and click on **Next**.

You now need to confirm that the **Domain name and extension** matches the details you agreed with the provider as you may have changed this while on the provider's web site. Once this is confirmed, type in your **User name** and **Password**. This will set the domain that is configured for email and your web site.

To configure the Internet address that will be used for secure web traffic and VPNs, click on the **Advanced settings** link on this page to enable you to change the options. I described this in a little more detail in the earlier section if you chose to not let SBS manage your DNS settings.

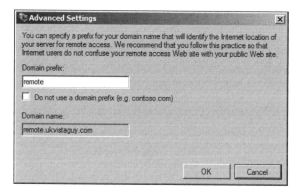

If you entered the **Advanced settings**, then click **OK**.

Click on **Configure** to start the process off. If the username and password entered do not enable SBS 2008 access to your ISP's DNS settings, then you will see an error message like the one below:

Verify your settings and only click on **Yes** if you are either disconnected from the Internet or your account is new and your provider has told you it will take a short amount of time to provision your account. If this is not the case, click on **No** and correct your account information.

Once all the settings are verified, the configuration process will start. It may take a minute or two to configure the system.

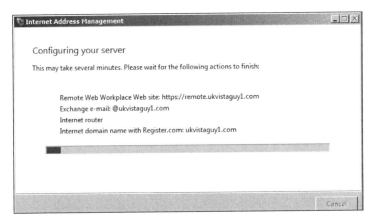

Fixing issues with the Internet Address Management

It is possible that various errors may occur during this process. Some will be benign, such as not being able to configure the router, which will occur if you do not have a UPnP router. The following screenshot shows an example of some errors you might see.

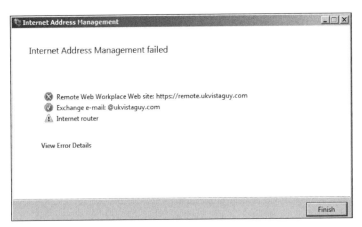

If you look at the error detail by clicking on **View Error Details**, you will get more information about the issue. In the example screen that follows, you can again see that not having a UPnP router is the cause of the second issue, but perhaps not the first.

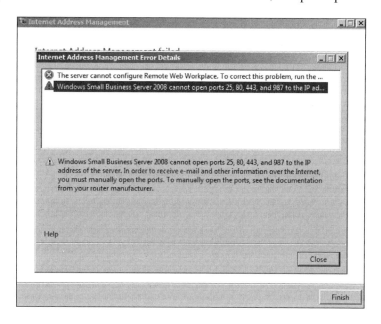

Clicking on **Close** and **Finish** will close the wizard and enable you to investigate more.

SBS 2008 has a great network diagnostics tool that you can access via the **Network** tab in the **Windows SBS Console**. In the tab, click the **Connectivity** section and then click the **Fix my network** button in the task pane on the righthand side. This will start the repair process.

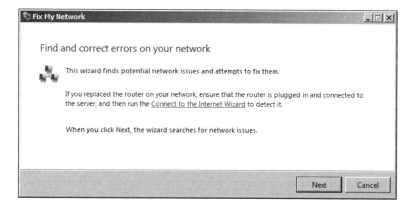

If you click on **Next**, your system will be scanned. This can take a couple of minutes to run; however, the results will enable you to fix most Network issues.

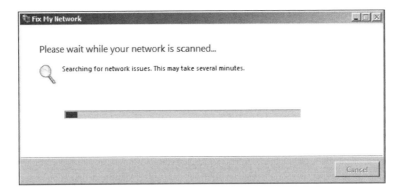

The results will be a number of potential network issues. You can read each one by clicking on it and reading the explanation in the **Details** section in the wizard. To get SBS 2008 to attempt to fix the issues, ensure each issue has a check mark against it and click on **Next**.

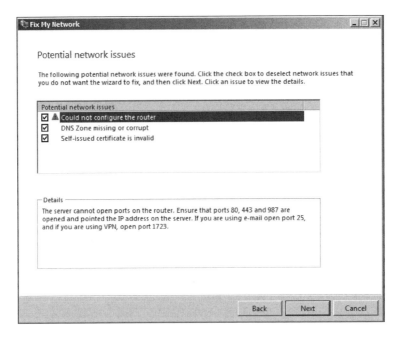

The **Fix My Network** wizard will attempt to fix as many of the issues as it can and will often succeed. With SBS 2003, the most common issues were related to networking and the lessons learned there and from Windows Server 2008 have enabled this tool to regularly deliver.

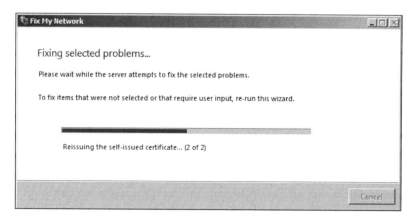

A final summary of the results will be displayed. Again, in the following example, the one remaining issue is that my network router is not UPnP compatible. Click on **Finish** to conclude the process.

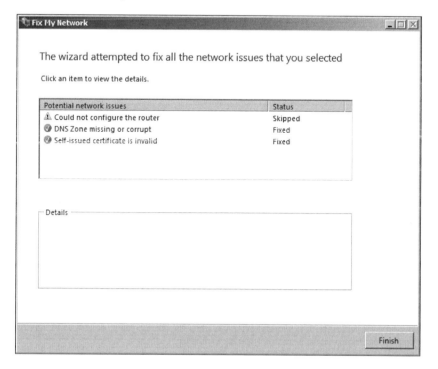

Enabling email routing via your smart hosts

Back at the **Home** tab in the Windows SBS Console, ensure you have checked the tasks you have now completed. Many ISPs require outgoing email to go via their SMTP servers so that they can control spam on their networks. The SMTP server is referred to as a smart host in Exchange 2007 and SBS 2008.

You may be able to skip this section if your ISP allows you to send SMTP email on port 25 without having to route it via their own servers. Many ISPs, including my own, do not allow this, so you have to route mail via their SMTP servers. If you do not use a smart host, then SBS 2008 will route via DNS and make direct connections with the mail servers that you are sending email to.

This should give you a console like this where the next step is to **Configure Smart Hosts for Internet e-mail**.

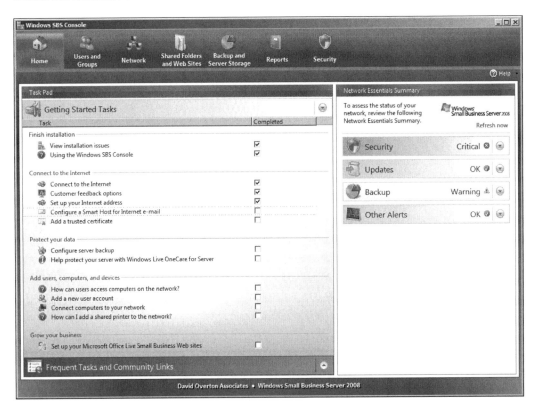

To configure this, click **Configure Smart Hosts for Internet e-mail** and click **Next** at the introductory screen. Select the **I need to configure a Smart Hosts server for Internet e-mail** option and type in the name of the email server your ISP requires you to route through. If your ISP also requires a username and password, then also type these in and then click on **Next**.

 Your ISP will provide you with the details of the SMTP server upon request if you do not know this already.

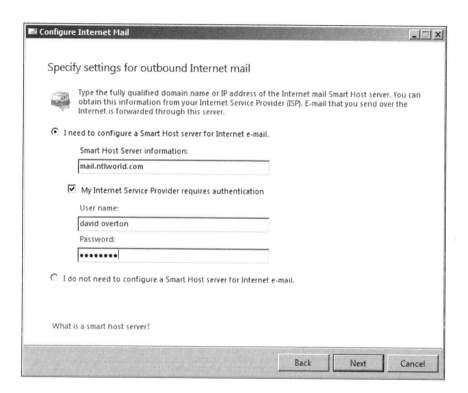

The system will be configured at this point. It is worth sending a test email to check all is configured correctly.

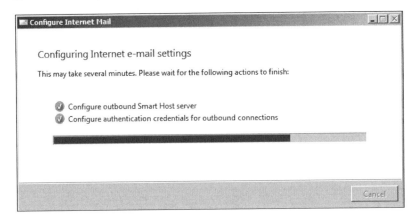

If you use a smart host, you may need to update the SPF record with your DNS provider to include the smart host mail server as a legitimate sender of email. SPF is the Sender Policy Framework and was put in place to reduce spam. Your email will now be sent by a server that is not part of your domain, but one from your ISP's, so can be seen as a spoofed email. SPF enables you to say who will send mail on your behalf and is stored as a DNS record. You can learn more about SPF at the Wiki Page located by `http://davidoverton.com/r.ashx/1E` and create an SPF record at `http://davidoverton.com/r.ashx/1F`.

Configuring Office Live for Small Business for SBS 2008

Office Live for Small Business is a web site that is hosted by Microsoft, often without charge, which your customers can visit as your public web site. It also has a number of applications behind the scenes that you can also use, including Workspaces that you can use to share documents securely with select clients without emailing them back and forth.

Personally, I would recommend you do not try to host your customer web site on your SBS 2008 system. Office Live for Small Business is a convenient way to have your SBS 2008 system collect email and provide remote access to the business while having a public web site on the same domain name that is hosted by someone with greater reliability of communications and more bandwidth.

You can see the current benefits from the web site
`http://smallbusiness.officelive.com`. At the moment they are in summary:

- Free web site—Create a free web site for your business so that customers and prospects can find you online.
- Web hosting and Site Design tool—Start with 500 MB of web site storage and easy-to-use design templates.
- Site Traffic Reports—Track visitor statistics, page views, top referrers, and more.
- Contact Manager—Manage sales opportunities, contact information, and track customer interactions.
- Business Applications—Manage your business with Document Manager, Project Manager, and Workspaces.

To start the Office Live for Small Business process, go to the **Home** tab in the console and select the **Set up your Microsoft Office Live Small Business Web sites**. Click **Next** to move past the getting started screen or click the link on the screen to get more information about Office Live.

 Office Live is not available in all countries, but the web site will inform you when it is scheduled to arrive in your country if it is not listed.

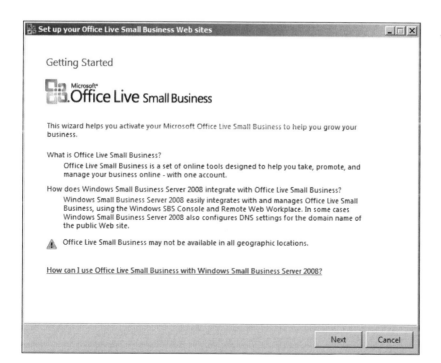

If you already have an Office Live account, select the **Use an existing Office Live Small Business account** option, and click on **Next**. If you don't, or you wish to create a new account for the SBS 2008 system to be connected to, select the **Sign up for a new Office Live Small Business account** option and click on **Next**.

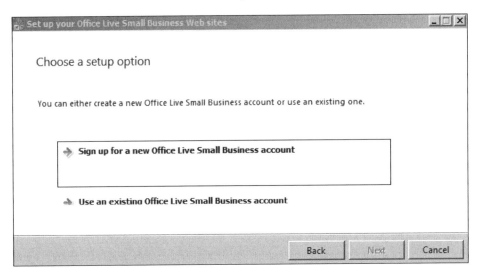

Whether it is a new or existing account, you will be required to decide how your web traffic will be split. This comes back to the same DNS question earlier, in which either you will manage the DNS settings or SBS can manage them for you. The idea is that http://www.yourdomain.co.uk will go to the Office Live site while https://remote.yourdomain.co.uk/remote will give you remote access to your SBS 2008 system.

Select the option that makes most sense. If you have SBS 2008 manage your DNS settings, I would advise you select the option to **Direct Web site traffic for www.yourdomain.co.uk to my Office Live Small Business Web site**. After choosing an option, click on **Next**.

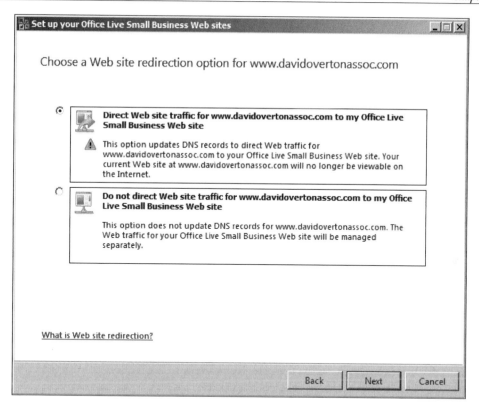

 If you have an Office Live account and have chosen to manage your DNS settings yourself, but want to change it, then the above option will not show itself. To change the settings, re-run the wizard and choose the option to create a new site and then the option will be present. When the Office Live web site appears, close it and then continue as normal.

Signing up for a new Office Live for Small Business account

If you selected the option to create a new account, you will be asked if you would like to open a web browser to complete the sign-up process. You can only continue with the wizard if you select **Yes**.

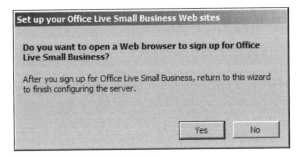

Since you are performing this web browsing task on the server, you will get a security prompt from Internet Explorer on which you can simply click the **Close** button.

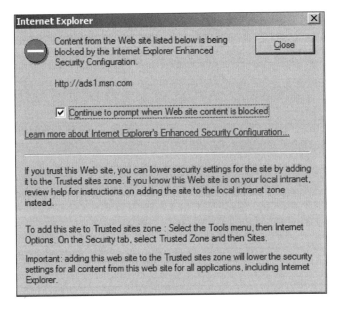

If the web site fails to load as below, you might have to add `http://login.live.com` and `https://login.live.com` to the trusted sites in Internet Explorer. You can remove them later if desired.

Once the web site has loaded, you simply click on the **Sign Up Free** button to complete the process. Once you are finished, close the web browser.

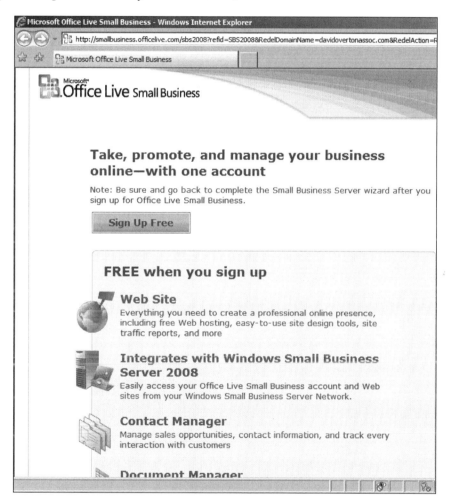

Providing your Live ID for Office Live to SBS 2008

Once the account has been created, or if you selected to use an existing account, you must type in a **Windows Live ID** and **Password** that have administrative rights to your Office Live account. If you have just created the account, it will be the ID you signed in with. Enter these and click on **Sign In**.

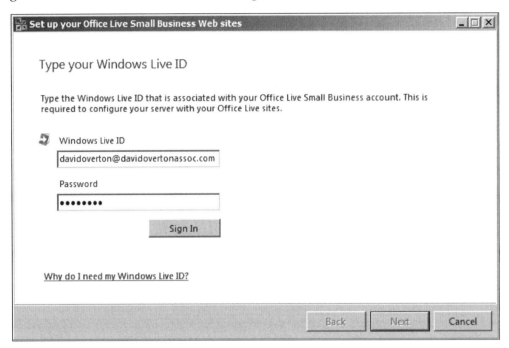

SBS 2008 will configure Office Live Small Business, SBS 2008, and the DNS setting (if requested), and then confirm all was completed successfully.

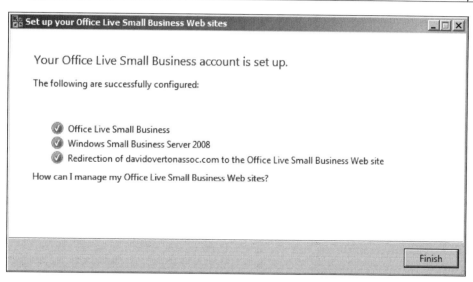

Click on **Finish** to close the Office Live for Small Business wizard.

Configuring a VPN for external access

The Remote Web Workplace enables users to connect to email and the Windows SharePoint Services sites via the browser as well as connect to a Windows computer turned on in the office.

Remote Web Workplace and other user-oriented tools are covered in Chapter 12.

This should enable most people to work remotely without difficulty or the need to connect via a VPN, especially since both Outlook and Windows Mobile can function fully without a VPN.

However, there are scenarios where you need to access the internal SBS 2008 network from another location as if you were sitting in the office. This is configured via a Virtual Private Network that connects over the Internet to `remote.yourdomain.co.uk`.

> One scenario not covered here is when you wish to join two branches together. In this situation, you would normally configure the Internet routers to build a private VPN between the two sites. SBS 2008 is not specifically configured for this to work.

To enable this, go to the **Network** tab in the Windows SBS Console and select **Connectivity**.

You should see that under the **Virtual Private Network** section, the **Status** is **Off** by default to reduce the possibility of someone getting access to the server without your knowledge. Click on this line and select **Configure a virtual private network** from the pane on the righthand side.

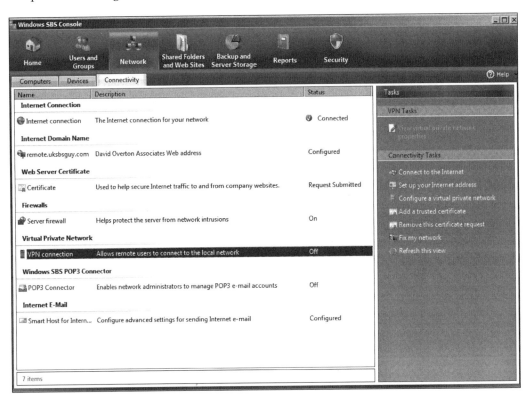

Select the option to **Allow users to connect to the server by using a VPN** and click on **Next**.

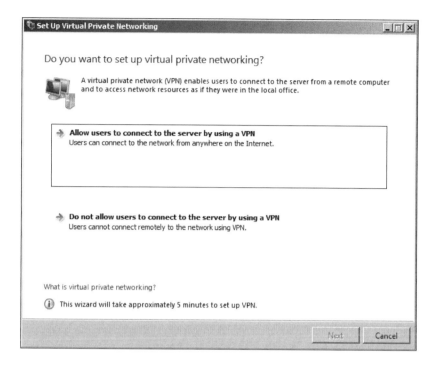

The wizard will configure itself and if possible the firewall to allow port 1723 to be enabled.

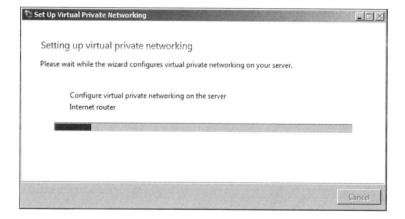

Finally, you will see a status screen that may report an error for the **Internet router** if this is not UPnP configured as it will need the Firewall port manually opening.

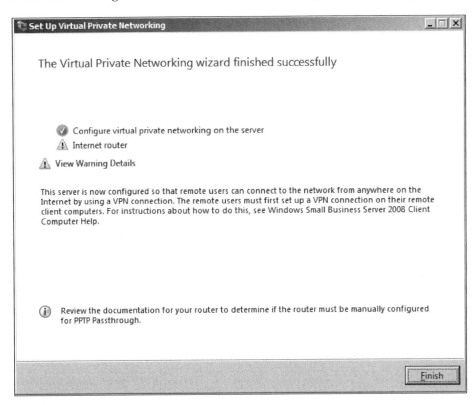

Your users will need to configure their computers to make a VPN connection to the server using the `remote.yourdomain.co.uk address`.

 To provide your users with an automated tool for creating the VPN settings, take a look on my blog at `http://davidoverton.com/r.ashx?19`.

Summary

We have now finished configuring the network services that SBS 2008 will provide to your business both internally and on the Internet. You have also hopefully configured Office Live for Small Business and are exploring a public web site it offers while sharing documents securely with others via the workspaces it offers.

Remote access is configured and will be available once you have finalized the firewall settings in the next chapter. This will give you access to the server from the Internet via the URL: `https://remote.yourserver.com/remote`, which will bring up the Remote Web Workplace. This provides access to email, desktops in the business, and your Windows SharePoint Services site.

The next step is to install the anti-malware software, configure backups, and finally, configure the firewall so traffic from the Internet can reach your server.

10
Securing the Server

This chapter covers the process of finishing the network protection and routing setup and configuring the protection of the data on the server. We will cover:

- Configuring the firewall ports
- Configuring and testing backups
- Configuring anti-malware

To do this, we are essentially completing the tasks in the home screen of the Windows SBS Console, which should look like the following screenshot.

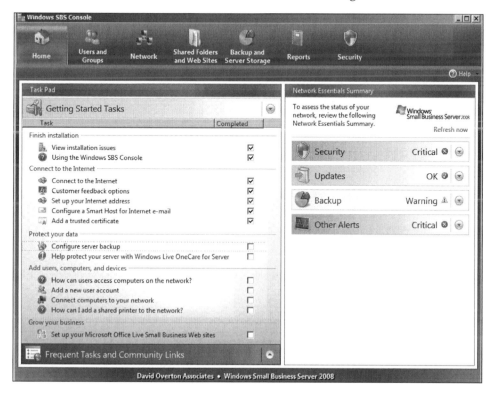

Assumptions

I'm assuming that you understand the concepts of firewalls and ports; otherwise, you will struggle to safely configure your network.

I'm also aware that OneCare, for servers, only provides an introductory offer for anti-malware and another product will be required; however, it is easier to describe the installation of one product rather than trying to answer for all products, so I'm using OneCare as a template. You will, however, need an anti-malware product that is server aware, or need to exclude server product locations such as the exchange data stores and other locations.

Network security configuration

There are a few areas where we can improve the security of the network. They are around the firewall, reducing the traffic that arrives at the SBS 2008 server, and the security certificate that is used to secure and identify the server communications.

Configuring the firewall ports

I did mention the SBS 2003 firewall ports in Chapter 3, but SBS 2008 uses a different collection of network ports to achieve its connectivity. You will need the following ports configured on your firewall to direct traffic to SBS 2008:

Port	Usage
25	Email coming into the server
80	Used to direct traffic to 443 (optional)
443	Secure web traffic, such as Remote Web Workplace and mobile services for phones
587	Secure SMTP (optional), if you have secure SMTP relay enabled, such as for IMAP, then this port is used
987	Secure access to the Windows SharePoint Services site
993	Secure IMAP (optional)
1723	VPN Access (optional)
3389	Remote Desktop (optional), as this can be provided via the Remote Web Workplace that provides a Terminal Server Proxy ability

If you were using SBS 2003, then you can close down ports 444 and 4125, which might have previously been open.

Loading a third-party security certificate

SBS 2008 creates a security certificate to secure its communications. Certificates are only valuable if everybody seeing them trusts the system that issues the certificate. All computers that are part of the SBS 2008 network trust the SBS 2008 server, so trust is achieved in this way. For those that are not part of the SBS 2008 network, a special certificate must be loaded onto those machines so they will trust SBS 2008, else they will provide warnings to users about the integrity of the communication.

There are organizations called Certificate Authorities who have established trust in the marketplace and most IT systems trust the certificates they issue. If you wish to have a more publically trusted certificate, then you will need to purchase one of these.

 One area where third-party certificates are often needed is when using mobile devices, to enable the loading of the SBS 2008 certificate onto the phones. Without the certificate on the phone, synchronization of Outlook information to the phone cannot take place.

Importing a certificate

If you already have a certificate or have purchased one and have been sent a file containing the certificate including the private keys, then you should follow this process.

There are two steps to follow:

- Importing the certificate into the Local Computer Certificate store
- Assigning the certificate using the SBS Console

Importing the certificate

Start **Windows SBS Console (Advanced Mode)** from the **Start** menu and click on the **Network** tab and then the **connectivity** button. As this is the advanced console, you will see extra tasks available on the righthand side.

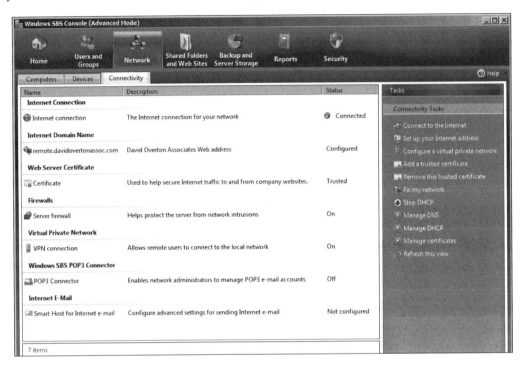

Click on the **Manage certificates** task—if this is not present, check you are running the **Advanced Mode** console: it will say so in the title bar. This will run a management console with the certificates for your computer made visible. Expand the **Personal** tree and right-click on **Certificates** and select **Import** from the **All Tasks** menu item.

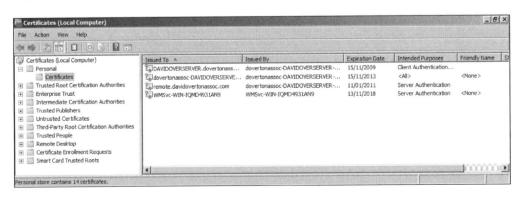

Click **Next** to pass through the welcome screen for the **Certificate Import Wizard** and then click on the **Browse** button to locate the certificate. Then, click on **Next** to continue.

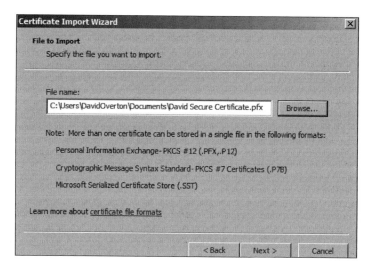

You will now be required to enter your **Password** to enable access to the key. I would put a check mark in the two remaining check boxes to **Mark the key as exportable** to enable you to export the certificate should you need to in the future and include the extended properties. Then, click on **Next**.

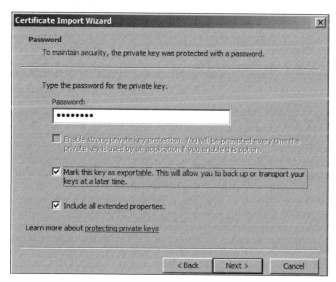

You will be required to confirm the location, which should be **Personal** and again click on **Next**. If it is not set to **Personal**, click on the **Browse** button and change the **Certification store** to **Personal**.

Now click on **Finish** to complete the process and you will see a message stating that **The import was successful**.

Close the Certificates Management console.

Assigning the certificate

In the **Windows SBS Console**, click the task **Add a trusted certificate** to start the process. Click on **Next** to skip past the introduction.

If you have assigned a certificate before, you will be told that **A valid trusted certificate already exists** and you have the choice of renewing your existing certificate or replacing it. Select **I want to replace the existing certificate with a new one** and click on **Next**. If you have not added a trusted certificate before, then you will not see this screen.

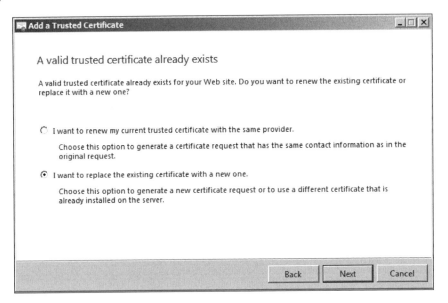

On the **Get the certificate** page, select the option **to use a certificate already installed on the server** and click on **Next**.

The certificate that you installed will show in the list with a **Type** of **Trusted**, while the certificates issued by SBS 2008 will show as **Self-issued**. Select your **Trusted** certificate and click on **Next**.

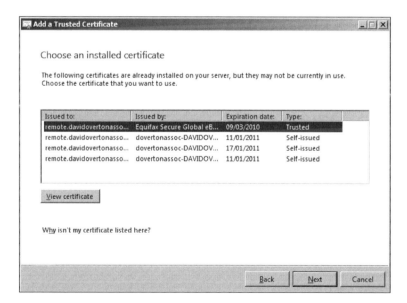

Click on **Next** to start the process and then **Finish** to exit the wizard.

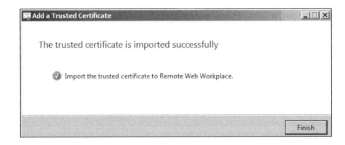

Purchasing a certificate using the wizard

If you wish to purchase a certificate, then the wizard can help provide the information needed to obtain a certificate.

While the wizard facilitates the purchase of a certificate from one of the Microsoft providers, you can use the information provided with most certificate providers.

Start by opening the **Windows SBS Console** and navigating to the **Connectivity** section of the **Network** tab.

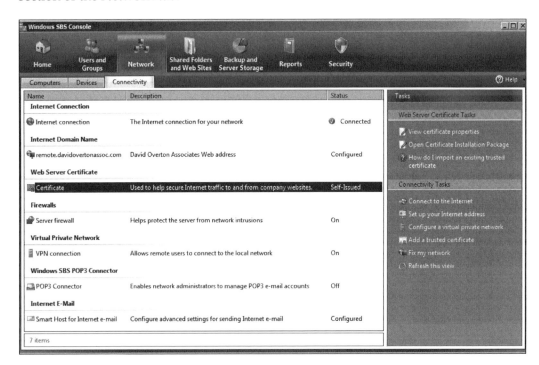

Click on the **Add a trusted certificate** button in the righthand **Tasks** pane to bring up the **Before you begin** screen. If you wish to familiarize yourself with certificates, click on the **What is a trusted certificate** link and read the information.

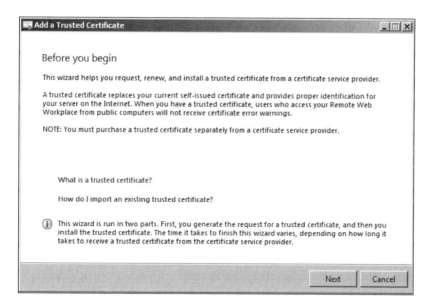

On the **Get the certificate** screen, select the **I want to buy a certificate** option and click **Next**.

You will be asked to confirm several details for your certificate before the request is generated. Confirm the details and click on **Next**.

The SBS 2008 wizard will generate a request that you can either save to file or copy to the clipboard.

If you have chosen a SBS 2008 DNS provider, then you will also be prompted with a link to a site to acquire a certificate. I clicked the link and used the information provided here to request a certificate. The whole process took about 5 minutes with my provider before I had the certificate.

Once you have completed this step, click on **Next** to move on.

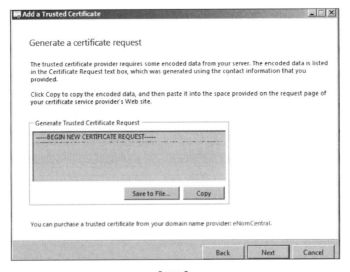

If the request process is taking time, select the top option to give your **provider more time to process the request**, otherwise select **I have a certificate from my certificate provider**. Click on **Next** to continue.

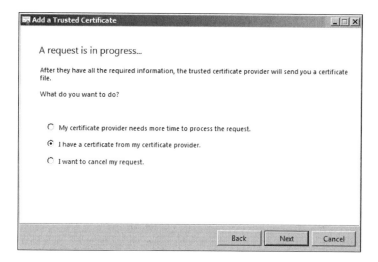

You can either click on the **Browse** button to select your certificate file or click into the text box and paste the encoded text to define your certificate. Click on **Next** to continue.

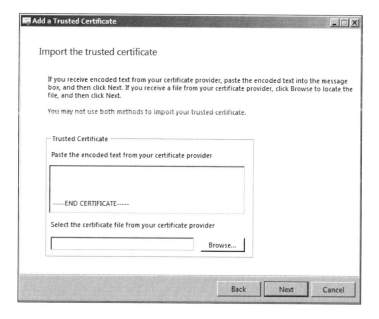

The certificate will be imported into the system and then you will see the screen informing you that **The trusted certificate is imported successfully**.

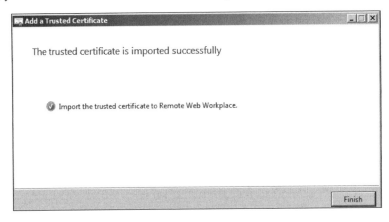

You should now be using a certificate that has its trust authority provided from outside your organization and no longer requires a certificate to be installed.

Configuring backups and running a test backup

Backing up an SBS 2008 system is a vital part of the daily routine. SBS 2008 can reliably automate this for you, without the need for additional software, once the configuration is complete. I would recommend using at least two and ideally, three USB disk drives that can be plugged into the server for the backup, but easily swapped on a regular basis to enable you to take the backup off-site.

These drives would be used only for the SBS backup and are specially configured in SBS. Provided that one of the configured set of drives is attached to SBS 2008, it will continue to take backups.

For security, I would advise that the drives are swapped daily or weekly. Also that the non-active drives are removed from your premises while not connected to the server and stored in a secure, ideally fireproof, location. However, as these systems contain hard disks, they should be handled with care and just like tapes, they are still prone to wear. You should check the health of these drives and plan to replace them once every year or 18 months.

 It is possible to back up to spare internal drives, but these will not give you the "my office caught fire" protection that taking a drive out of the office offers.

If you are running SBS 2008 in a Microsoft Hyper-V version 1 environment, you can still use USB drives, but you cannot disconnect the USB drives without shutting down the server. Hyper-V R2 does enable the removal and attachment of USB drives into SBS 2008.

Most file and email recovery scenarios should be possible without the need to use the backup drives themselves, as SBS 2008 has other facilities that can be used. So, these backups are more commonly used in a disaster recovery scenario when the server is not functioning or has *blown up* and has been replaced. I cover the other recovery mechanisms in Chapter 13.

 SBS 2008 does not support tape-based backup without the need for third-party software. Both tapes and disks wear out, so be prepared to put a drive into storage every 6-12 months and buy a new drive to keep an archival history of your server and data.

Some people are unsure why they will ever need a backup; however, recovering a machine or a vital file from a backup is far quicker and lower in cost than trying to pick up the pieces of a server or disk that has failed. I've known some people who only realize the importance of a backup once all their business data is lost, sometimes dealing a fatal blow to the business.

Configuring backups in SBS 2008

Start at the Windows SBS Console and select **Configure server backup** from the **Home** tab.

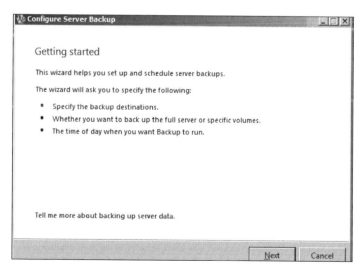

Click on **Next** to skip the **Getting Started** screen and move to the **Specify the backup destination** screen. You should see your connected USB drives in the display. If you are using internal disks, select **Show all valid internal and external backup destinations** and click on the **Refresh** button to show these devices.

If the devices still do not show, check in **Device Manager**, found in the **Start** menu, to see if the drives have been correctly detected and the drivers have loaded. If not, try removing the devices and then re-loading the drivers.

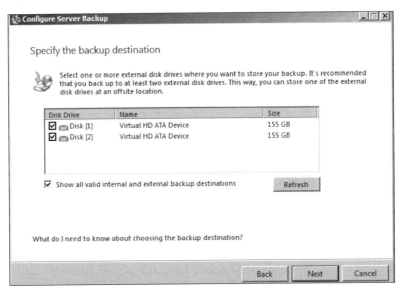

You will then need to label each removable drive so you can recognize which is which. Match the labels that you write on the drives with the entries in the **Disk 1 Label** and **Disk 2 Label** entry boxes on the screen and then click on **Next**.

It is worth the effort of labeling them; otherwise, when you are trying to recover a file and it tells you to insert drive six, finding drive six can be very time consuming.

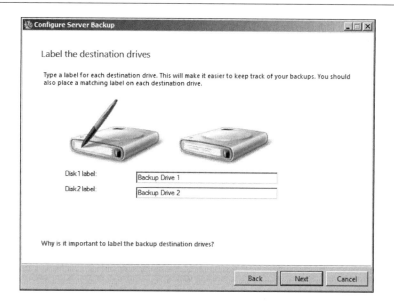

You are now prompted to choose all the devices that should be backed up. You select what gets backed up at the drive level and SBS 2008 handles the rest. If you only have one drive in your system, or a RAID or mirrored set that appear as one drive, then you may not have any options to change on this screen.

Check the drives to back up and then click on **Next**.

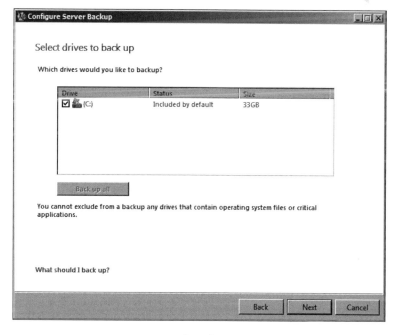

You can choose when SBS 2008 will create backups. While the process may sound confusing, SBS 2008 creates a complete disk backup by combining previous backups with the latest changes. This means that only the parts of a disk that have changed get backed up each day. I've found that I can enable SBS 2008 to create backups several times a day, without impact on the server, and without consuming a huge amount of disk space, but giving me the capability to restore to any of those times rather than the backup from the night before, should I need to. So, in the event of a disaster, I lose less.

For that reason, I configure SBS 2008 to take several backups per day. The less time between backups, the less data that has changed and gets written to the backup drives.

You can chose the pre-defined once and twice a day backup options or choose **Custom** to Check as many time slots as desired. Click on **Next** to continue.

You are now asked to confirm all the details. If you are sure they are correct, click on the **Configure** button. If you are unsure, then click on the **Back** button to change the settings.

When you click on **Configure**, you will be reminded that the backup devices will be formatted. This means that any data on them will be destroyed. If you are happy with this, then click on the **Yes** button.

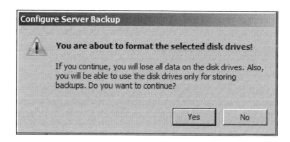

It will take several minutes to format the drives during which time the progress bar will slowly move across the screen.

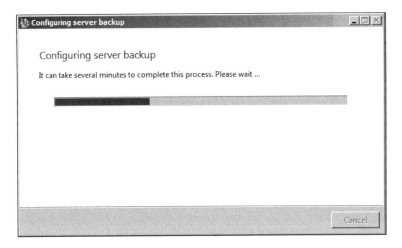

Once all is completed, you will get a confirmation screen where you should click on **Finish**.

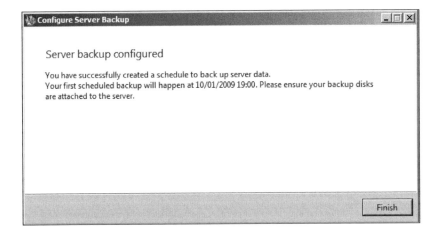

Performing a test backup

There is nothing worse than believing your system has a working backup, but not testing it, so I advise that you now perform a backup to ensure the process works. You should include this in your quarterly maintenance plans to ensure your media is still problem free and working. I've seen too many people think they had a working backup, only to discover they did not, when they needed it.

You should also perform a test recovery of a file. This is covered in Chapter 13.

Within the Windows SBS Console go to the **Backup and Server Storage** tab and you will see the configured backup settings with **Status** of **No previous backups**. Click on the **Backup now** button in the task pane on the righthand side of the screen to start a backup.

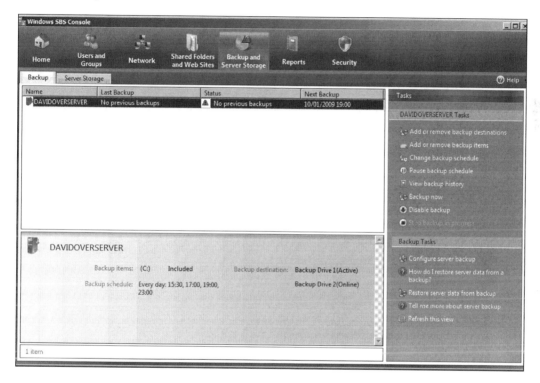

You will be asked if you wish to perform a backup now and you should click on the **OK** button to proceed.

The first backup will take longer than all others to run. The dialog box gives you the option to close the window and continue using the system while the backup runs. Since the purpose is to check the backup works, I would personally not click on the **Close** button, but would take this opportunity to have a short break!

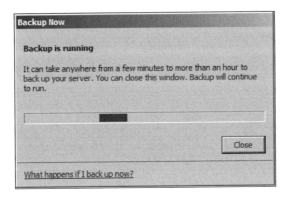

Once the backup has completed, you will see a prompt either telling you that it was successful or that the backup failed. Click on **Close** and if need be, diagnose the reasons why the backup failed, although it is rare that it would.

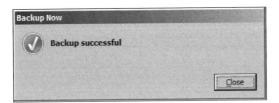

Configuring OneCare for servers or other anti-malware solution

SBS 2008 ships with a trial version of Microsoft OneCare for Servers to provide a three months trial of the Microsoft anti-malware solution. However, the retirement of OneCare has just been announced and no replacement has yet been announced for it, so installing this product is just a stop gap until an alternative arrives.

To this end, I am simply going to say that you configure OneCare from the Windows SBS Console **Home** tab. From here, select **Help protect your server with Windows Live OneCare for Server** and the OneCare configuration screen appears. If you have not subscribed to the update service, it will prompt you to do so.

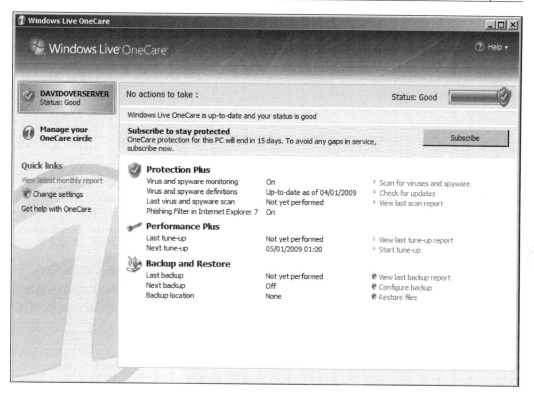

If you are not installing OneCare, then you must install another anti-malware solution. Personally, I do not like those that install alternative firewall solutions as I often turn these off due to the issues they create.

Looking at the OneCare settings, you can see the areas Microsoft recommends your anti-malware software ignores, so it would be advised that you configured the same exceptions:

- `C:\ProgramData\Application Data\Microsoft\Search\Data\Applications\Windows\Windows.edb`

- `C:\ProgramData\Application Data\Microsoft\Search\Data\Applications\Windows\tmp.edb`

- `C:\Program Files (x86)\Microsoft Forefront Security\Exchange Server\Data`

- `C:\Program Files\Microsoft\Exchange Server\Mailbox\First Storage Group`

- `C:\Program Files\Microsoft\Exchange Server\Mailbox\First Storage Group\Mailbox Database.edb`

- C:\Program Files\Microsoft\Exchange Server\Mailbox\Second Storage Group
- C:\Program Files\Microsoft\Exchange Server\Mailbox\Second Storage Group\Public Folder Database.edb
- C:\Windows\ntds\Edb.chk
- C:\Windows\ntds\edb.log
- C:\Windows\ntds\edbtmp.log
- C:\Windows\ntds\ntds.dit
- C:\Windows\ntds\temp.edb.

If you do not configure similar exclusions, then your anti-malware solution may well quarantine the Exchange email database or some other important system.

Summary

We have now finished the configuration of your SBS 2008 server. You can supply IT services to your business such as email, connectivity, and security management. You are also providing Internet services, such as those offered by Remote Web Workplace and Office Live for Small Business. All of this is being delivered in a reliable and secure fashion.

You will able to send and receive emails into SBS 2008 now that the firewall is configured. Remote access should also be working, so accessing the server and services from https://remote.yourserver.com/remote will bring up the Remote Web Workplace, giving access to email and your Windows SharePoint Services site, both externally and internally.

Your anti-virus and anti-malware products should be working and reporting themselves as active and secure on the Security page.

Finally, your backups should be working and tested to ensure they are working.

If you have achieved all of this, then the configuration of your server is complete.

Congratulations!

Next, we need to manage the users and computers connected to the server.

11

Managing Users and their Computers

Yours SBS 2008 system is now fully configured for use by your users. You now need to ensure that your users and the computers that they use are configured in the SBS 2008 system to enable configuration and management. Part of the configuration will enable services, the use of which will be described in the next chapter. You may also wish to, or find that you have to, change settings for existing users as well as add new users or computers.

In this chapter, we will cover the tasks required to add and manage users as well as the tasks to add and manage their desktop and notebook computers.

 You do not use these tools to add additional servers to the network. This is completed using the standard Windows Server domain join and/or promotion tools.

Managing users

You will want to carry out a number of tasks for your users to set them up on the system and ensure they have correct access to data—and that their data is secured appropriately.

Managing roles

When users are created, they are based on one of the templates available for the default settings for a user. These templates are called roles.

Roles define which services a user can interact with from SBS 2008 and the storage limits, also known as quotas, that control how much disk resource each user uses. Roles configure:

- Remote Access via Remote Web Workplace (RWW) and VPN access
- Which sites can be accessed remotely (Outlook and SharePoint besides RWW)
- Whether email quotas are in place and what they are
- Whether storage quotas are in place and what they are
- Whether folder redirection is in place

There are three default roles that you will be able to choose from:

- Standard User
- Network Administrator
- Standard User with administrator links

For most users, the **Standard User** role is the most appropriate as it enables everyone to work on the network, but not access anyone else's content, while also having connectivity via the remote access services.

Before you add users, you might want to add additional roles to give you greater flexibility in the templates used for those users. For example, you might want to grant the management more storage space or users of a certain application access via VPN when others cannot use it.

Adding new roles

Open the **Windows SBS Console** and navigate to the **Users and Groups** tab and then select **User Roles**. Click on **Add a new user role** to create a new role.

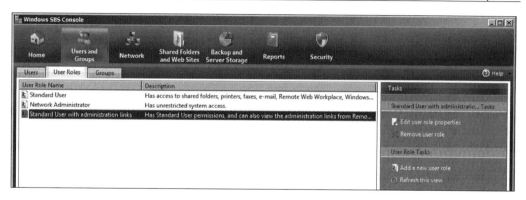

The first step is to name the new role and provide a **User role name** and **Description** to enable easy identification in the future.

Since most roles are basically a few modifications compared to an already existing role, ensure there is a check mark in the **Base defaults on an existing user role** and pick the role to copy settings from in the drop-down list.

Finally, if you want the new role to be the default for new users, ensure there is a check mark in the option **The user role is the default in the Add New User Account Wizard**.

Once all these options are set, click on **Next**.

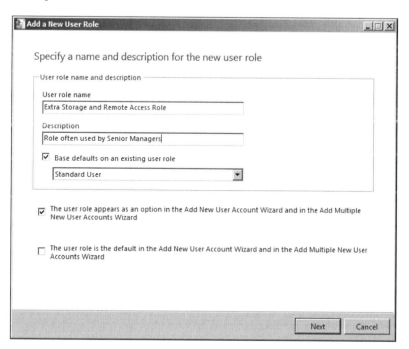

On the next screen, you get to choose **group membership**. Groups enable you to identify users, no matter which role they sit in, and add extra policy or security permissions associated with members of that group. SBS 2008 uses groups to enable access to features; however, as you make choices through the screens after this one, groups will be added or removed from the list, so you do not need to add membership to SBS 2008 groups here.

If you are not familiar with groups and have no requirement to change group settings, then I would strongly recommend that you do not make any changes here. If you do need to add membership to a group, click on **Add**, select from the list, and then return to this screen.

Click on **Next** to continue with the task.

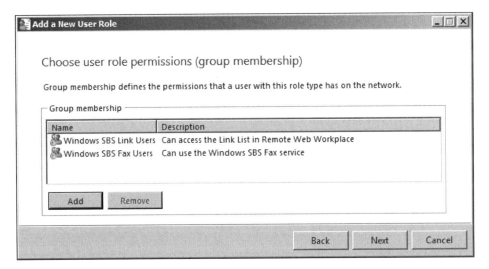

With SBS 2008, users can store significantly larger amounts of email than ever before on the server. Since this can become a burden to the server, you have the ability to enable the **Mailbox quote** by putting a check mark into the **Enforce mailbox quota setting** and choosing the amount of storage that a user may use.

 You cannot set a storage limitation of less than 1 GB.

You can also enable or disable the ability to access email for this user via the Internet and the Remote Web Workplace by checking or clearing the **Outlook Web Access** check box.

Click on **Next** to continue the process.

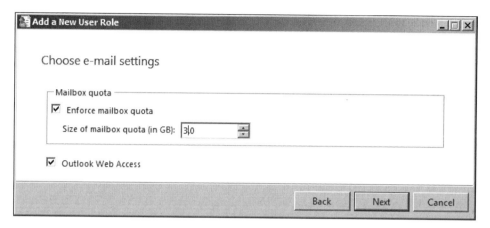

On the **Choose remote access for this user role** screen, you can choose to enable the **Remote Web Workplace** web portal and, if you have configured SBS 2008 VPNs, also access by the user into the network via **Virtual private network**. Once you have enabled or disabled these settings, click on **Next**.

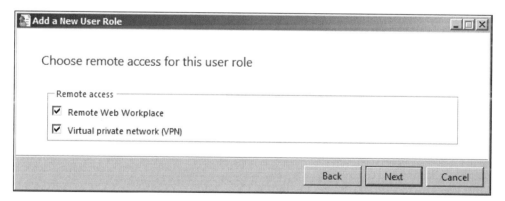

There are two sets of shared folders that you can control on the **Choose shared folder access** screen. Shared folders are those that are stored on the server and are accessed across the network, and SBS 2008 has two sets of shared folders for users. These are:

- **Shared folders** that are used to provide a network area for users to explicitly store files on the server.

- **Redirect user folders to server** that host the user's normal file areas, such as Documents, Favorites, and Pictures. These file locations would normally sit on the user's PC, but this ensures they are centrally managed on the server instead.

The redirected user folders are stored on the server with copies always available on the user's PC, for use when they are working offline. One advantage of this is that the user document store is backed up every time the server is backed up, while the user can continue to work out of the office and the updates only get shared back to the server when the laptop reconnects to the SBS 2008 network.

To enable limitations for these two shared folders, put a check mark in the box for **Quota in GB** and set a limit that is appropriate for the users.

I would strongly recommend the **Enable folder redirection to the server** setting too.

Then, click on the **Add user role** button to create the role as defined by you.

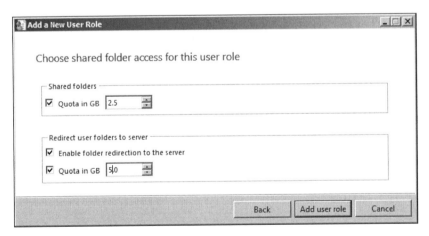

SBS 2008 will take a few moments to create the role before the final **Add a New User Role** screen is presented. Click on **Finish** to exit the wizard.

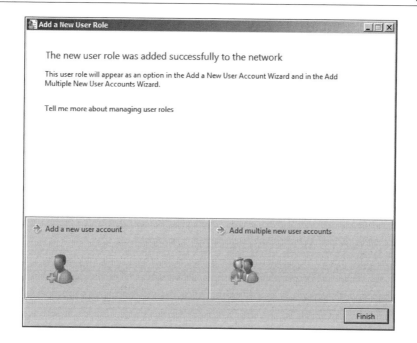

Adding users

The first and most obvious task is to add a new user to the system if they do not already exist. You can either add single users or multiple users, where multiple users all belong to the same role.

To add users, go to the **User and Groups** tab in the Windows SBS Console and select **Users**.

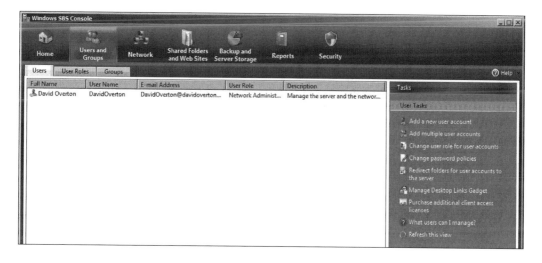

Passwords created by the administrator

The passwords created in these wizards are normally only used to log in. Unless the defaults are changed, each user will be required to change their password, once they log in, to provide the maximum amount of security and ensure that even the administrators do not know the user passwords.

Adding multiple users at once

If you are going to be adding several users, all at once, the best option is to click on the **Add multiple user accounts** button in the righthand task pane, which brings up the bulk load tool. Here, you can choose the **role** your users have on your SBS 2008 network as discussed earlier.

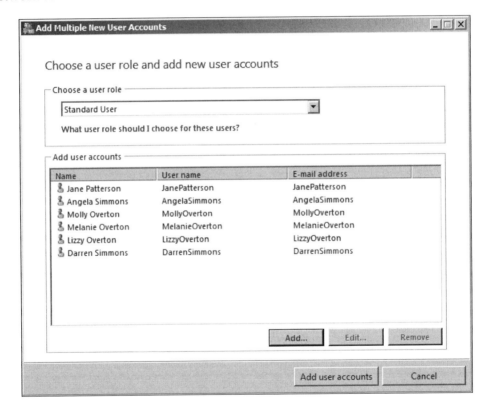

Click the **Add** button to add users. This will bring up the **Add a New User Account** screen as shown in the following screenshot. Enter the **First name** and **Last name** and then pick a username from the drop-down list under **User name**. By doing this, you set the standard by which user's names are generated for each subsequent user. Having a common way to create usernames is a sensible practice, although if you cannot find one that is desirable or if a particular user wants to use a special username, you can simply type a username.

Now, enter the password for your new user in the **Password**, and **Confirm Password** boxes to ensure you typed it correctly and consistently. The password must be complex enough to get both of the check marks green before you can click on the **OK** button.

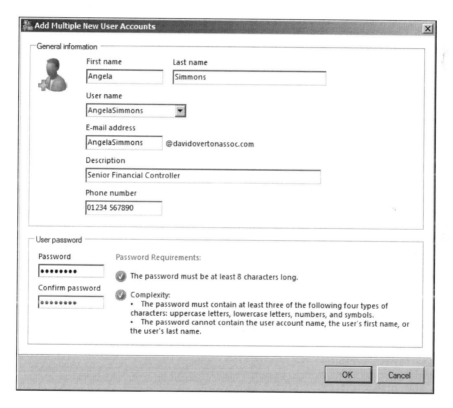

 To make a password complex enough, you must use three different types of characters from the choice of uppercase letters, lowercase letters, numbers, and symbols, and a minimum length of 8 characters. Personally, I like to use a phrase that includes some capitals and numbers for passwords as they are easier to remember and very complex, for example "**I love ice cream!**".

Continue to add users and then click on the **Add user accounts** button to generate all the users.

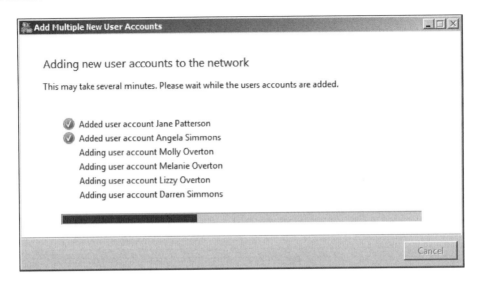

Once all the accounts are generated, you will be offered the option to print a **Getting Started** letter for each user. I think this is quite good and for some, a printed out page that has their username and the web site to convert their PC will be useful. The same information is provided via email for each user too.

While there is a space on the letters for the user's password, it is not printed. You can write it down for the user, but bear in mind that they will change it after the first login.

It is important that they do not write their new password down, otherwise others will find it and security will not be maintained. Since many system attacks are from internal people, passwords should never be written down.

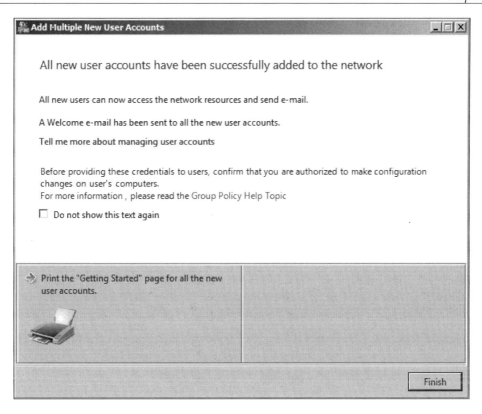

Click on **Finish** to end the process.

Adding individual users

This process is similar to adding multiple users in terms of information required, but slightly different in process, so I shall cover the differences here. From the **Users** tab in the Windows SBS Console, click on the **Add a new user account** button in the task pane.

The **Add a New User Account** screen will appear, which is similar to the multiple user add new user screen except you have to choose the **User role** for the user at the bottom of the screen. Once again, fill in the information as requested and then click on **Next**.

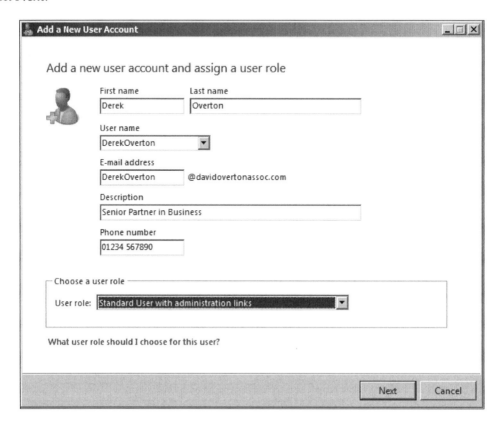

You will then be asked to enter a password for your user, twice, to ensure you type it correctly. The password must be complex enough to get both of the check marks green before you can click on the **Add user account** button. The **Complexity** section describes the requirements for your password to obtain the two green check marks.

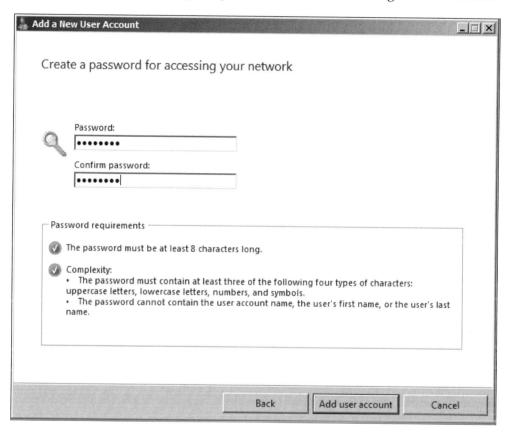

You will see the user account being added, along with other items, before you are offered the opportunity to assign the user to a computer or add a new computer for them. I'll cover adding a new computer later on in this chapter, but if a computer already exists, then you can assign it by clicking on the large **Assign an existing computer to**… button.

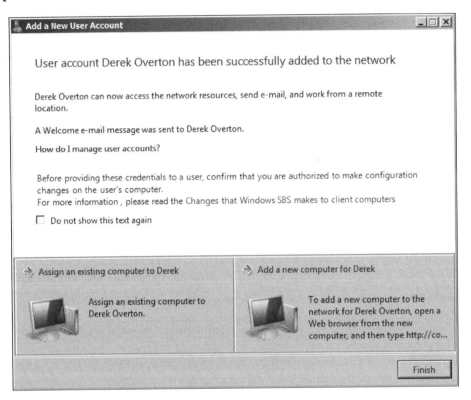

You then pick a computer from the list and select it. If you wish for this user to have local administrative rights on the computer, then change the **Access level** information. If this is a computer that is likely to be left connected to the SBS 2008 network, then SBS 2008 has a feature that might be of use. Users of RWW can take over the screen of some PCs and act as if they were sitting in front of them even though they are not. The list of which users have this right and on which PCs, can be changed here by checking the box for **Can remotely access this computer**.

Clicking on **OK** will finalize the assigning of the user to the existing PC.

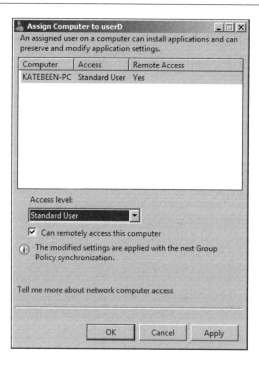

 If you want to print a **Getting Started** page for the user, there is an option to do this by highlighting the user in the Windows SBS Console and clicking the **Print the Getting Started page for this user account** button in the righthand task pane.

Managing users' storage

Each user has three data stores on SBS 2008 that can be limited in the user **Properties**. They are:

- Storage for Exchange 2007, including e-mails, calendar appointments, and contacts
- Shared files
- Redirected user's document files that are stored on the server

You can make broad changes for all users who have the same role by editing the roles from the **User Roles** section as discussed earlier or you can change an individual user as below.

 If you make a change to a Role, it will overwrite any of the customizations that you can make in individual users, such as those described now.

In the Windows SBS Console, go to the **Users and Groups** tab and select the **Users** section. Double-click on the user you wish to change the settings for, or select the task **Edit user account properties** from the righthand task pane.

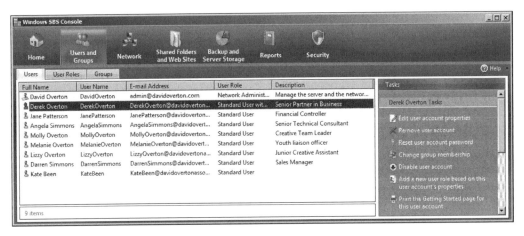

Email storage settings

To change the email quota limits, select **E-Mail** from the navigation pane on the lefthand side and enter a **Maximum mailbox size (in GB)** between 1.0 and 100. You cannot enter a number less than 1 GB. Then, click on **OK** to apply this setting for this user.

 Email storage limits

While repeatedly sending and receiving large emails can be a drain on resources, it is not unreasonable for a user to have between 2 and 4 GB of email storage. However, for better storage management, you should inform your users how to use the file shares and CompanyWeb site to store and share large documents rather than storing them in email. Email does not provide good accessibility to data and file shares, and SharePoint sites provide significantly easier and more efficient collaboration.

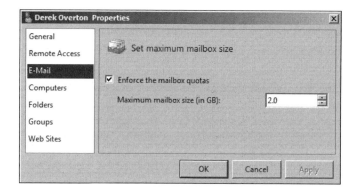

Shared and redirected folder storage settings

In the same dialog box as used for email, move to **Folders** in the left navigation pane. You can now choose to limit how much this user can put in the shared folders on the server by checking the **Enforce shared folder quota** option and enter a limit in GBs. To remove the limit for this user, uncheck the check box.

 I always enable redirecting user's folders to ensure the business has a backup of their key data and that they can access it from anywhere.

You then have the option to redirect the user's folders to the server. This means that when the user saves a file to his/her document folder, it actually saves to the server and a copy is also stored on their hard disk. This has several benefits:

- User documents are backed up with the server, so even if a user's computer fails, their files are safe.

- If a user logs in at another computer, they can immediately access their files in the documents folder without having to do anything.

- They can access the files remotely, even if they cannot access their computer.

- They can work offline and when they reconnect to the server, all changes are replicated to the server.

- The files are secured against access from other standard users, although a user with administrative access can gain access to the files should it be required.

To enable redirection, check the **Enable folder redirection to the server** check box. This will then allow you to say if the user has a limit on the amount of storage on the server they can use, again in GBs.

 When you turn on folder redirection, ensure that you don't have items you do not want appearing on the server in your documents and desktop folders. As these will need to be synchronized with the server, it can take a considerable amount of time if the user has a large video file on their desktop. As the user, move these to somewhere else on the computer's hard disk to avoid this issue.

Once you have set the email and file storage options, click on **OK** to apply the settings and close the window.

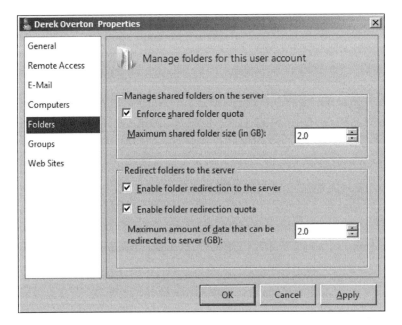

 Folder redirection time delay

Once you have configured folder redirection, the policy will need to be applied to the computer and then the files copied across. This will happen at the next log on event. To force this, run the command GPUPDATE/target:User/Sync from an administrative Command Prompt and follow instructions to log off. Then, log back on to start the update.

Managing computers

Once the users have been added to SBS 2008, you will need SBS 2008 to manage the computers in your business. To achieve this, you must make SBS 2008 aware of them and enable those computers to enforce the policies and security requirements from the SBS 2008 server. This is achieved by joining them to the SBS 2008 domain. While you can do this manually, SBS 2008 simplifies this process and provides additional migration features.

> If you manually join a computer to the SBS 2008 domain, it will not show in the console until you move it to the MyBusiness\Computers\SBSComputers organizational unit in Active Directory.

I will cover how to:

- Add computers to the network
- Ensure they are up to date with security patches

Adding computers to the network

Adding a computer to the network is required for both existing computers that a user has been using with files and applications installed, and new computers fresh from the manufacturers. SBS 2008 provides a utility to achieve this that can be accessed by your web browser or copied to a USB device. Since the computer must be connected to the SBS server to perform this task, I will only describe the browser-based process.

> To copy the tool to removable media, go to the **Network** tab in the Windows SBS Console and select **Connect computers to your network**. When prompted, select the option to copy the program to portable media and then run this on your computers. The process will be the same as that described below once you have connected to the web site.

Besides copying the utility, all the steps in this task will be carried out sitting down at the computer that you wish to join to the domain.

Before you can use this utility, you need to ensure your computer complies with the software requirements. While these are not formally presented anywhere, I have found them to be:

- Windows Vista
    - Service Pack 1 or above
    - .Net Framework 2.0 (normally pre-loaded on Windows Vista)
    - KB 930995 — `http://support.microsoft.com/kb/930995`, which is not loaded on all machines

- Windows XP
    - Service Pack 2 or above
    - .Net Framework 2.0 (visit the Microsoft Update web site if it is not installed. You will need to visit again after it has installed to load the required service packs).

Once the pre-requisites are installed, log in as an administrator on the machine and connect to `http://connect` in the browser.

If you cannot connect to `http://connect`, but your network is working, then it is probably your DNS suffix. To correct this, look at Microsoft support article KB 957708 at `http://support.microsoft.com/kb/957708`.

You will possibly see the yellow bar security warning at the top of **Internet Explorer** regarding **Intranet settings are now turned off by default**, which can be ignored. Click on the **Start Connect Computer Program** button in the browser and run the downloaded tool. Information on running the tool is provided in the browser window too.

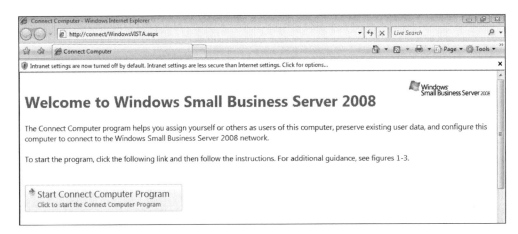

You can now choose to install the computer for a different user to the one logged on, or for the person who is logged on. If you choose **Set up this computer for myself** then the current desktop and files will be preserved for the user you chose to use on the SBS 2008 network. If you are setting the computer up for others, then the files and settings of the logged in user will not be added to the named user.

To copy the files and settings across, select **Set up this computer for myself**; otherwise select **Set up this computer for others**.

 The user who will be using this computer should have already been created on the SBS 2008 system as previously described.

Click on **Next** to continue.

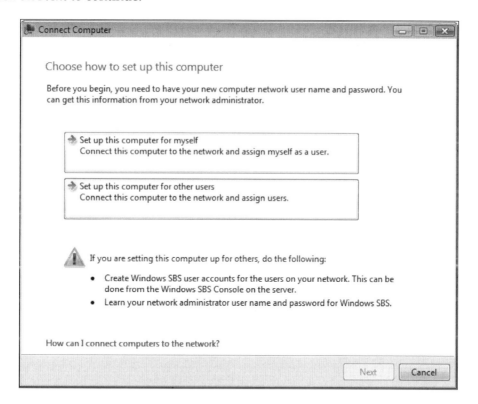

The computer is now checked to ensure it meets all the pre-requisites and if so, you can click on **Next** to continue. If one of the pre-requisites is missing, you will get an alert informing you of the missing software. You will have to resolve the issue and restart the **Connect Computer** wizard.

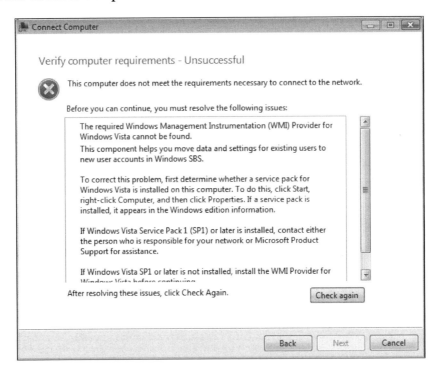

You must now enter the SBS 2008 **User name** and **Password** for the user you are enabling on that PC and moving the files for, and click on **Next**.

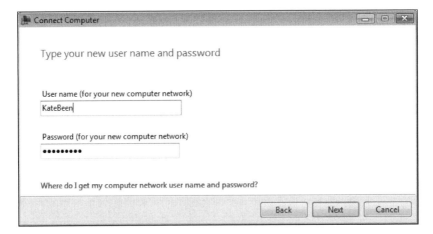

You are now given the chance to change the computer name and description to make them more useful. Once you have made any changes, click on **Next**.

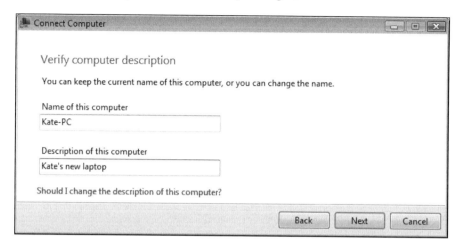

To move your existing files and settings, select the user you wish to move and then click on **Next**. This will select the files and settings that are copied to the network if folder redirection has been enabled, and will also preserve your application settings, such as your desktop background and Office settings.

 If the user you are looking for is not in the list, it could be because your profile is marked as private. Follow the information in Microsoft support article KB 886210 — http://support.microsoft.com/kb/886210, which explains how to set the options on your folders. This article was written for SBS 2003, but the process is the same for SBS 2008.

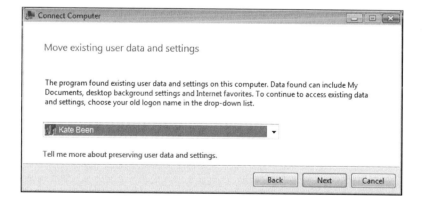

Finally, confirm all the settings are correct and click on **Next**.

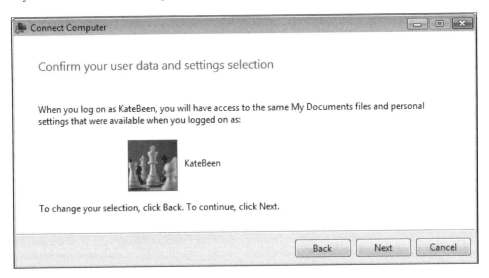

Your computer will be restarted at least once during the process. Confirm that you are ready to restart your computer and then click on **Restart**.

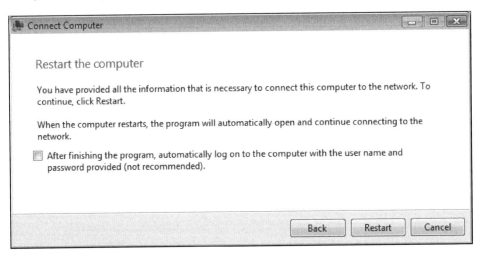

The **Connect Computer** wizard will now start processing your files settings. This may take a while.

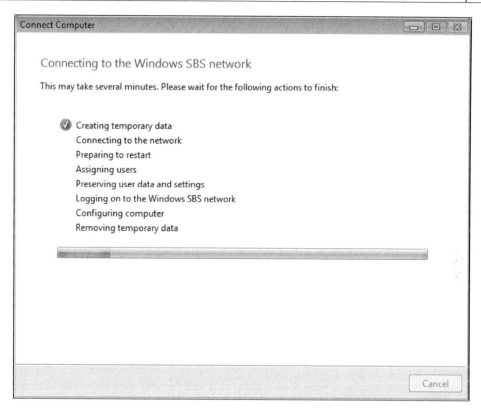

Once the process is finished, you will be required to log back into the computer and if everything is successful, you will see the success screen. Click on **Finish** for the normal Windows configuration and log in to complete.

Having gone through this process, you should now find that the following settings have been configured:

- A new group called **Windows SBS** will be on the **Start** menu and it will contain a link to your SBS internal web site.
- The home page will point to your SBS internal web site.
- Favorites will have been added for the SBS 2008 web sites (internal and external).
- Your PC firewall will have been configured if you are using the Windows Firewall.

- Your system updates will be configured to use your SBS 2008 automatic update services.
- SBS 2008 components will have been installed.
- The SBS 2008 Desktop gadget for Windows Vista will be installed into the gallery, but not enabled.

Ensuring computers are up to date with updates

It is vital that a computer applies updates to provide protection from Malware. With SBS 2008, the list of updates to be deployed is managed in the Windows SBS console and the process of accepting these updates is documented in Chapter 13.

However, sometimes you want to check that the updates are being correctly applied on a client PC. Again, in Chapter 13, I highlight the reports that will show if a computer is not being updated, but I'll describe the process here.

On the client computer, go to the **Start** menu and find **Windows Update**. It will normally show that all updates are applied, just like the following sample screenshot.

 Ensure that it states **You receive updates: Managed by your system administrator**. If it does not, check the *Security* section of Chapter 13 to ensure that the computer has its updates managed by the server.

To force a check to see if any updates are available, click on the **Check for updates** action in the lefthand pane.

 If you believe that SBS 2008 is not offering the right updates, click the link **Check online for updates from Microsoft Update** to see if the Microsoft servers are offering updates that you think should be applied, but are not visible via SBS 2008.

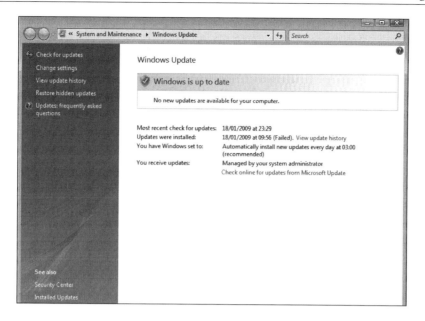

Once the check for updates has completed, you will sometimes see a list of updates that need to be installed. High priority security updates should install automatically, but optional items will not. To view and potentially select the optional items, click on the **View available updates** link to select items from the list and then return to this screen. To perform the installation of the pre-selected or selected items, click on the **Install updates** button.

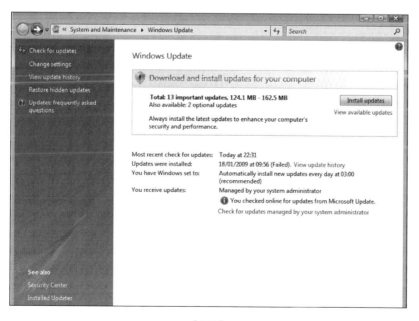

Summary

You should now have your client PCs configured to use SBS 2008. Since the users now belong to the SBS 2008 domain, policies about security, access times, and well-being can now be centrally controlled. This includes ensuring that all their security updates are applied to keep company data protected.

As their files, if desired, are now backed up and managed by SBS 2008, even if a computer completely fails or is lost, users can work and see their files, email, calendar information, and contacts when using another user's computer signed in as themselves, and when they get a new computer it will all appear there too.

Users can also be productive in and out of the office with a range of remote access tools that SBS 2008 provides.

The next step in this journey is to understand how a user interacts with the services that SBS 2008 offers to ensure both the business and the users get the most out of the investment in SBS 2008.

12
Working with SBS Services as a User

Your SBS 2008 server, network, computers, and users will now be configured for use. However, to get the business benefit, you will need to embed the use of the services and facilities into the user's psyche to enable them to benefit from it and use it.

In this chapter, we will cover the following areas:

- E-mail, Calendar, and Contacts
- File Management
- Remote access to the server, network, and services

E-mail, Calendar, and Contacts

SBS 2008 includes Exchange 2007, which provides E-mail, Calendar, and Contact functionality. This is available through Outlook, over the Web via Outlook Web Access and on mobile devices. If the user makes a change to one, it will be replicated to Exchange and then to the other locations. How to access from the other locations will be covered later in this chapter.

I'm going to presume that you understand how to send and read email and create and use contacts, but I will share some useful scenarios that many small businesses benefit from, but don't always understand are present in SBS 2008. Some of these will rely on Office 2007 with Outlook, while others can be seen via the web-based interface too. The scenarios are:

- Viewing your calendar and other people's calendars
- Scheduling a meeting for multiple people and ensuring their diaries are all free for the time period
- Telling people when you are going to be away or unavailable
- Finding emails that have been filed
- Recovering emails that have been deleted and removed from the deleted items folder

 All of the actions in this section are carried out on a user's computer, logged in as that user. Only where SBS 2008 is explicitly mentioned, is there an action that is carried out on the server.

Outlook 2003 and 2007 connection configuration

To configure Microsoft Outlook 2007, you should simply have to open Outlook as it should auto-configure itself. Outlook 2003 will require configuring, but I'm only going cover the important sections here. For full instructions, click on the link **How do I use Outlook Anywhere**, on the Remote Web Workplace main screen.

The links on Remote Web Workplace point to addresses that begin with `https://sites/...`, which is not accessible from outside the SBS 2008 network. This should be changed to `https://remote.yourdomain.co.uk/...` as described later in this chapter. If this has not been done and a user needs access to the information, then they can edit the address in their browser replacing the first part of the URL as described above.

If you need to manually configure Outlook, you will need to select the server as an Exchange server. The name of the **Microsoft Exchange Server** is the name of your SBS 2008 server. In the following screenshot, the name of my SBS 2008 server is **davidoverserver** and this is entered into the **Microsoft Exchange Server** section, along with the **User Name** of the user I am logged in as on their computer.

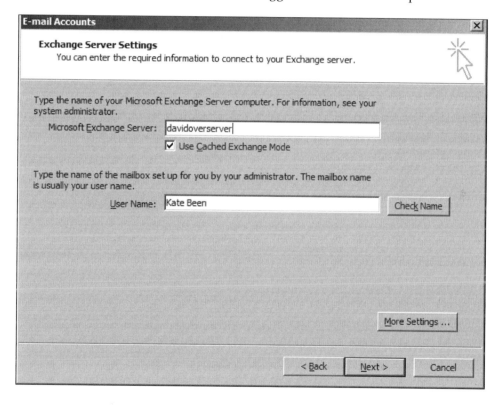

You can either click on **Next** to finish the settings, or if this is a laptop or a machine that may access SBS 2008 from a remote location, click on **More Settings**. Click on the **Connection** tab and then put a check mark in the **Connect to my Exchange mailbox using HTTP** check box. Finally, click the button **Exchange Proxy Settings**. Once the proxy settings are open, you will need to type in the remote access URL for your server and also check the **Mutually authenticate the session when connecting with SSL**, and then enter the name of your remote access server, preceded by **msstd:**.

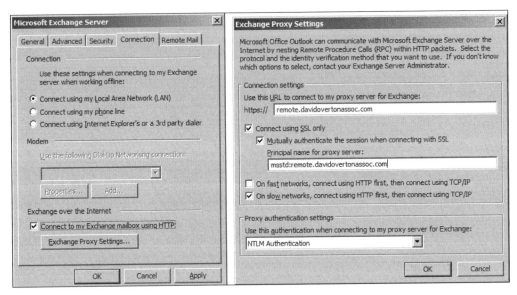

Clicking on **OK** will enable you to finish the configuration.

Once these changes have been enabled, Outlook will connect to the network without any further action—provided you have an Internet connection, and should work offline until it gets an Internet connection.

Calendar management

SBS 2008 provides each user a calendar that they can use to manage their diary and which they can choose to share with colleagues if they desire. The level of details shared can be from very basic free and busy time slots through to enabling someone else to have the ability to see and change the diary.

 This availability of information does concern some users, which is why they can also mark any appointment as private and no details will be shared with others, even if the calendar has been fully shared.

Outlook on the desktop enables access to both your and other's calendars, while Outlook and Windows Mobile devices offer much less, if any, access to other people's calendars. I will only describe each task from Outlook in this section, and will provide more information on using Outlook Web Access later in this chapter.

Viewing Calendars

Start **Outlook** from the **Start** menu. Once Outlook has loaded, click on the **Calendar** button or go to the **Go** menu and select **Calendar** from the menu.

You will see your calendar displayed, normally in the **Day** format with today showing. In the example below, you can see the padlock for the private appointment that others can't see, two normal appointments, and the tentative appointment that is not confirmed at 17:00.

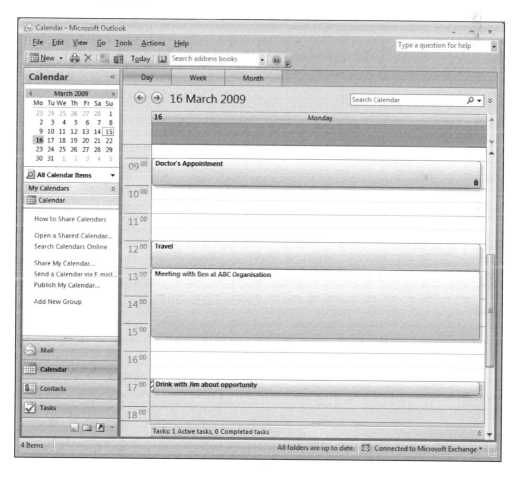

To open another person's calendar, click the **Open a Shared Calendar** link on the lefthand side and then type in the name of the person whose calendar you want to see. If you have permission to view their calendar, you will see both calendars side by side as follows:

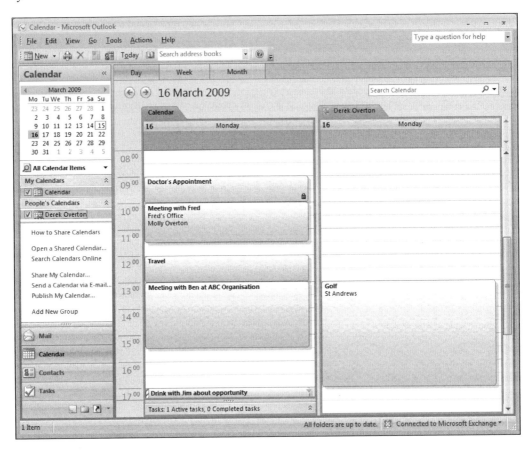

If you do not have permission and you are running Outlook 2007, you will be prompted to send an email requesting permission. The email will look like this:

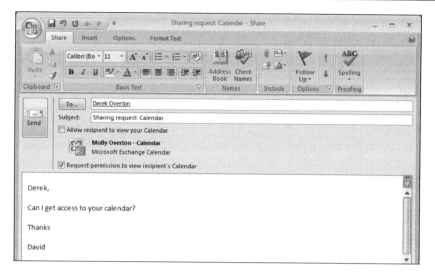

If the person receiving this email has Outlook 2007, they simply click on **Accept** to enable you to view the calendar.

If you or they have an earlier version of Outlook, then the person whose calendar you want to view will need to carry this task out by hand. To do this, get that individual to open **Outlook** and then their **Calendar** and right-click on **Calendar** under **My Calendars** and then select **Properties** from the menu. When the properties appear, go to the **Permissions** tab and either add the user and assign specific permission, or to make life easier, simply set the default access to reviewer.

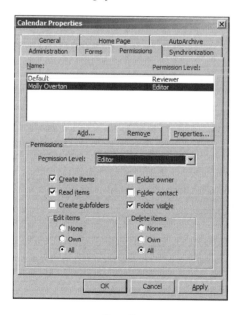

You can now view both your and other's calendars to identify opportunities to meet. You can open more than one other person's calendar, but things can get confusing with so many open.

 With Office 2007, you can overlay the calendars by clicking the arrow next to someone's name. For all versions of Outlook, you close a calendar by removing the check mark next to their name in the lefthand navigation pane.

Using Calendars to schedule a meeting

Add appointments to your calendar by clicking on the time (when you want the appointment to start) shown on the lefthand side, and then dragging your mouse to select the time period. Right-click the selection and choose **New Appointment** to block the time in your diary.

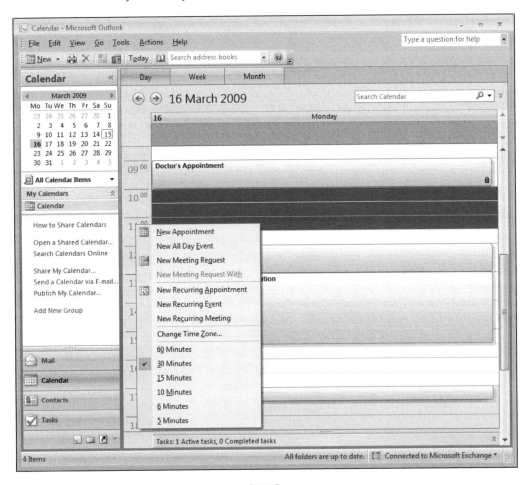

You then fill out the details of the appointment, ensuring that the **Subject**, **Location**, and **Start time** and **End time** are all correct. I normally also put in some details in the pane below so I know why I am meeting and what the agenda is.

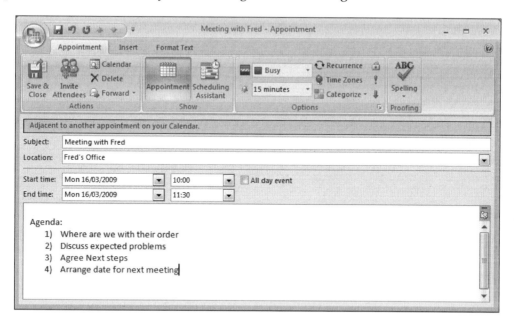

To send this to other people without viewing their calendars, click on the **Invite Attendees** button and add their email addresses.

If you need to schedule people from your own business whose calendars you do have access to, click on the **Scheduling Assistant** button on the ribbon bar. This will enable you to see if others are free or busy during the planned timing. You can see in this example that Kate has given us the ability to see more details from her calendar than David.

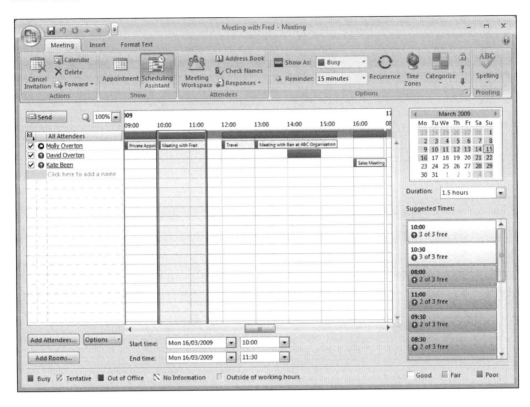

To get back to the appointment, click on the **Appointment** button and you will now see that the **To** button and list have been provided. If you had clicked on the **Invite Others** button, then you would not have been shown other calendars, but you would have the option to invite others by adding their email addresses to the **To** list.

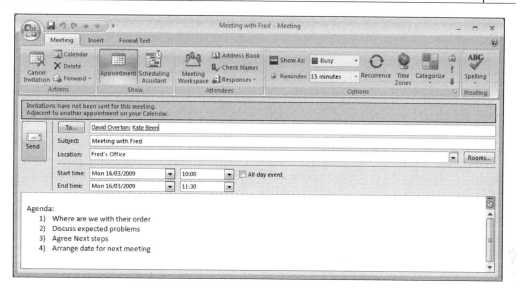

To send this to the list of people who you want to attend, click the **Send** button. They will then either accept, decline, or tentatively accept your request.

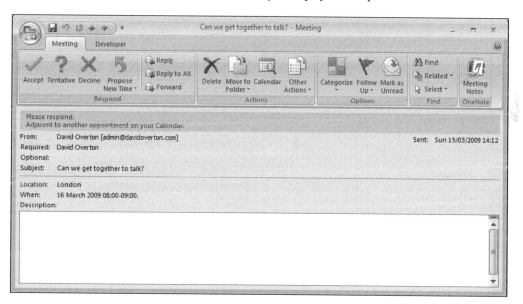

Telling others when you are unavailable

The **Out of Office Assistant** is not a calendar feature; however, setting expectations as to when you might be able to respond is a good business practise. Whether you are going to be in a deep planning meeting, on holiday, or just very busy telling people what to expect sets the correct level of expectation and often leads to more satisfied customers and colleagues. You can also tell them who to contact in the interim.

To access the assistant, go to the **Tools** menu in the person's Outlook and select **Out of Office Assistant**. You can then set up the message, when it should start and stop, and if desired, any rules. Once you have completed this, click **OK**.

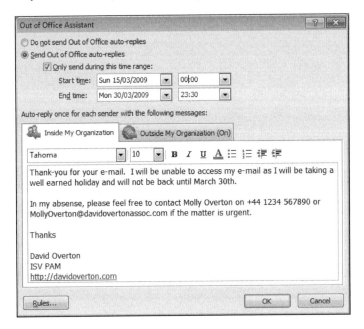

 This can also be configured using Outlook Web Access.

Finding information using search

I used to find myself filing everything in Outlook, but then trying to find it was a difficult task, especially if I was searching for the information in a different location to where I filed it. Now, Outlook has Instant Search, which can search across all folders in Outlook in a second or two. To use it, type a few key words into the search box and it will search the current folder.

To search with greater granularity, click on the double arrow to the right of the search window and the drop-down query builder will appear. Typing in any of those text boxes will refine the search.

Finally, if you do want to search all folders rather than just the current one, click the link **Try searching again in All Mail Items**.

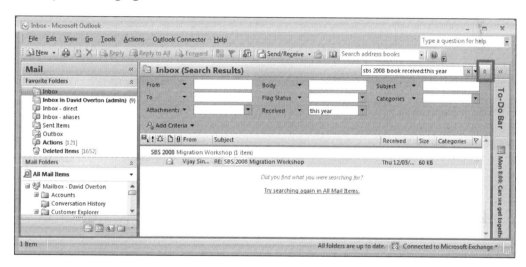

User email recovery

Being asked to recover something from a backup is a slow process for the administrator and user. However, as a user, you can recover deleted items without having to ask anyone to get involved.

When you delete an item, it is placed into the **Deleted Items** folder. If you then empty your **Deleted Items** folder, it appears to have gone; however, you can recover these items for another 30 days by going to the **Tools** menu and selecting **Recover Deleted Items**. This will show you all the mail items that were permanently deleted from that folder. For most situations, this means you must be in the **Deleted Items** folder before you go to the **Tools** menu. You will then be presented with a list of items that you can mark for recovery by selecting them and clicking on the button with the picture of the envelope and an arrow on it. The emails will be restored back to the folder they were deleted from, so normally the deleted items folder again.

Managing files

One service that SBS 2008 provides for users is a secure place to store files. Both web sites and file shares are provided by default to assist with this.

Enabling collaboration on documents, where multiple people will want to read or update a file is best delivered using the CompanyWeb site. The CompanyWeb site is the internal web site and it is built on Windows SharePoint Services technologies.

In this section, I will explore:

- File management aspects of CompanyWeb
- Searching across the network for information
- User file recovery

Internal Web Site Access

SBS 2008 provides an intranet for sharing information. This site is called the CompanyWeb and can be accessed internally by visiting `http://companyweb`. To access it remotely, click on the **Internal Web Site** button that will open up the URL `https://remote.yourdomain.co.uk:987`. It is important that you note the full URL with **:987** on the end, otherwise you will not see your CompanyWeb.

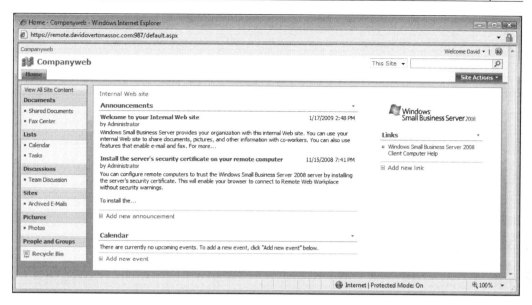

CompanyWeb, in its simplest form, is a little like a file share, but has considerably more functionality such as the ability to store more than just files, be accessible over the Internet and your local network, host applications, and much more.

For file management, it enables flow control such as document check-in and check-out for locking of updates and an approval process for those updates. It can also inform users when changes have taken place, so that they do not need to check on the web site as it will tell them. Finally, it can enable multiple people to work on a document and it will arbitrate the updates so the owner can see all the comments and changes.

While we are looking at CompanyWeb from a file management perspective, it is worth pointing out that any Windows SharePoint Services site also has the capability to run surveys, provide groups, web-based calendars, run web-based applications that are built on top of the SharePoint services, host blog and wiki pages, and perform as your fax center.

In looking at file management, I will briefly explain how to:

- Upload a document via the web interface
- Add a document via email attachment
- Edit a document stored in CompanyWeb
- Check Out/In a document
- Recover a deleted document

Uploading documents

Navigate to `http://CompanyWeb` in your browser and then to the **Shared Documents** section.

 You can create other document libraries by clicking on **Site Actions** in the righthand corner of the screen and then selecting **Create**.

From here, you can upload documents in three different ways. You can upload single or multiple documents from the **Upload** menu.

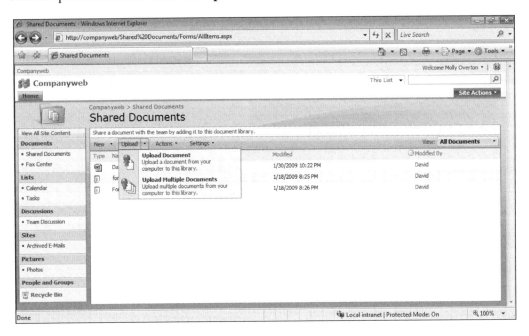

If you chose this option, you will be prompted to **Browse** for a single file and then click on **OK** to upload the file.

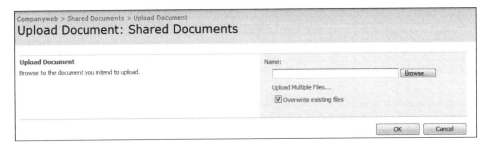

If you chose **Upload Multiple Documents** from the menu or the **Upload Document** screen, you will be presented with the multiple upload tool. Navigate to the folder with the files you wish to upload, check the items, and click **OK** to start the upload.

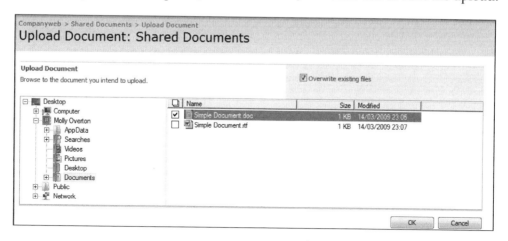

The final mechanism to load documents is to choose to **Open with Windows Explorer** from the **Actions** menu. This will open an Explorer window that you can then copy and paste into as if you had two local folders open on your computer.

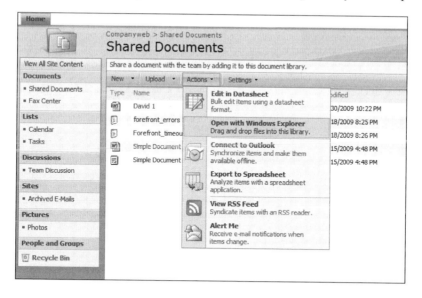

Uploading using email

I know this might sound a little strange, but the process of emailing documents backwards and forwards between people, for ideas and changes, can make "keeping up to date" very confusing for everyone. Using CompanyWeb in this way enables each user to update their copy of the document and then merge them all together so the differences can be accepted or rejected by the owner.

To upload a document via email, create a new email in Outlook and attach a document as per normal. Then, go to the **Insert** tab and click on the small arrow on the bottom right of the **Include** section.

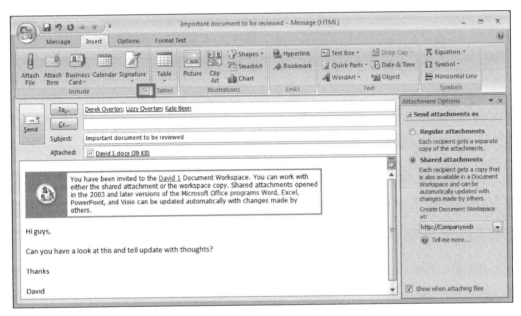

In the task pane that opens on the righthand side, change the **Attachment Options** to **Shared attachments** and type **http://CompanyWeb** into the box labeled **Create Document Workspace at:**.

This will create the additional text in the mail and include a link to the site that was created under CompanyWeb. This site is secured so that only the people on the **To** line and the person who sent it have access.

Send the email, and the attachment will be loaded to the special site. Each user can open the attachment as per normal, save it to their hard disk, and edit the document. The user can make as many changes as they like and finally, save the updates to the CompanyWeb site. If their changes are to an earlier version, they will be asked to either overwrite or merge the changes.

The following sample shows the writing from Molly and Lizzy in two different colors so that the document owner can read and consider all the changes and then accept all or some of them.

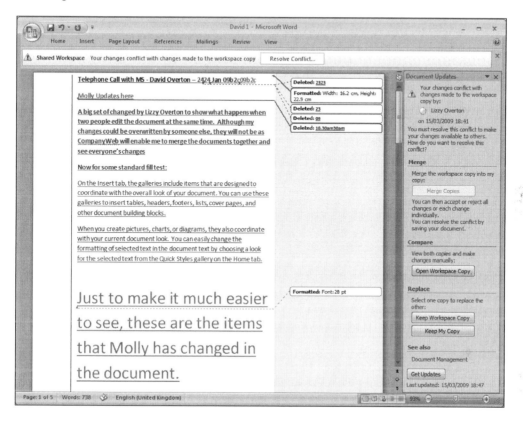

Opening documents and Checking Out and In

Once you have documents stored on the CompanyWeb site, you can open them by simply clicking on the links. You will be prompted if you want to open a **Read Only** copy or **Edit** the document. Click **OK** once you have selected the right option.

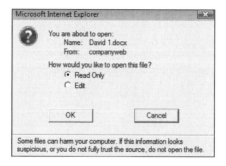

This simple mechanism is fine where there is no control, but you might want to ensure that no one else can modify the document while you are doing so. In the previous section, I showed the conflict resolution process, but this can be avoided by individuals checking documents in and out. When a document is checked out, you can only view the document unless you are the person who checked it out, in which case you can edit it.

To check a document out, hover over the document and click on the downward arrow that appears on the right of the filename. A menu will appear and you can select **Check Out** from that menu.

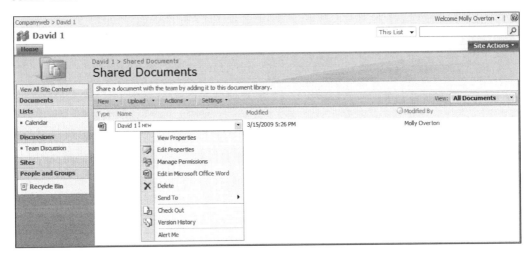

You can then edit the document while others cannot. Once you are finished, you need to check the document back in. This can be done from Word or back on the web site on the same drop-down menu where you checked it out.

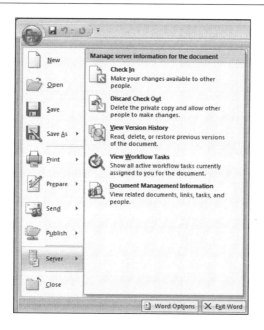

Recovering a deleted document in CompanyWeb

If you delete a document in CompanyWeb, there is a recycle bin to recover documents from. On almost all lefthand navigation panes is the **Recycle Bin** link. Click this and you will be asked to select the documents to recover and then click on **Restore Selection**.

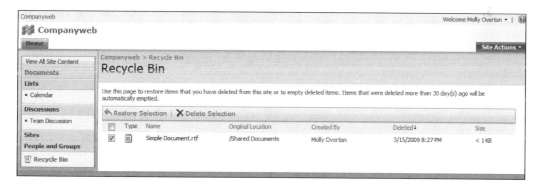

Searching for information

You can search for any file, email, calendar appointment, or document stored on your hard disk with SBS 2008 and Windows Vista or Windows XP and Windows Search. Just as with the email search facility, you can also search for any file, or the contents of any file on both the CompanyWeb site and on your computer.

To search on CompanyWeb, type the key words that you are interested in into the search box in the top right corner and then click on the magnifying glass.

This will then display you a varied set of results as you can see in the following example.

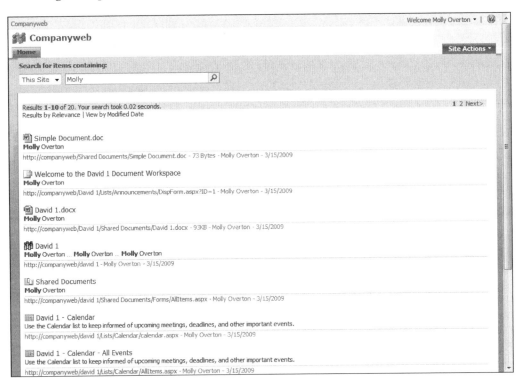

If you are using Vista, you can type a search into the **Start** menu or select **Search** from the **Start** menu and again type the key words you are looking for in the top right corner. The Windows search will search your files, emails, calendar and contacts, and browser history to find a list of matches for you.

You can get the latest version of Desktop Search for Windows Vista and Windows XP by following `http://davidoverton.com/r.ashx?1K`.

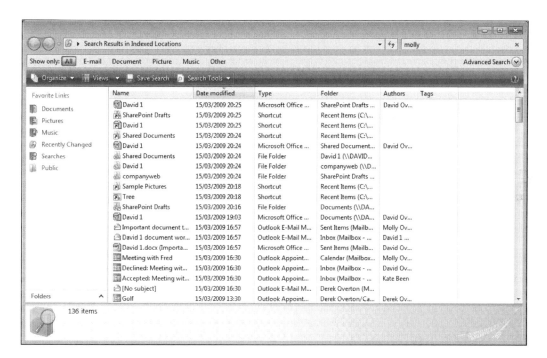

User file recovery

We have already covered how you recover deleted emails and documents in CompanyWeb, but users need something a little more sophisticated with file recovery on their desktop.

Generally, when an administrator is asked to recover a file for a user, it is either because they have just deleted it and it is not in the recycle bin or they still have the file, but it has become corrupt or they wish to undo changes made over the last day or two. When you turn on folder redirection or when you are using Windows Vista, users get the ability to roll back time to a version of the file or folder that was copied over the previous few days. This means that not only can we undelete files from the recycle bin, but we can revert back to an earlier copy of a file that has not been deleted from 3-7 days previous without needing to access the backups.

If the file has been deleted, we can look into the folder from an earlier time snap-shot as opposed to just the still existing files.

To access this facility, right-click on the folder for which you want to get an earlier version and select **Properties**. Now, move to the **Previous Versions** tab. You can now **Open** the folder to view, as is shown on the right below, **Copy** the folder to a new location, or **Revert** the folder to the selected version, overwriting the current files.

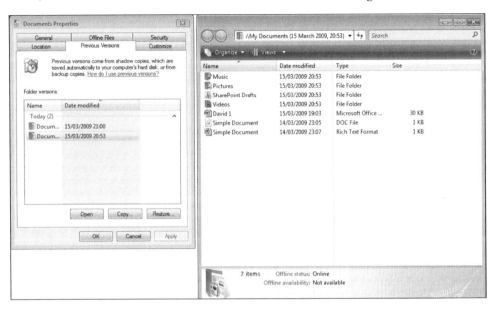

Remote access

Now that the client computers are configured to work with SBS 2008, you need to check that the remote access tools are working. These are:

- Remote Web Workplace
- Outlook Web Access
- Internal Web Site Access
- Connecting to a PC on the SBS 2008 LAN
- Connecting via a Virtual Private Network (VPN)

Remote Web Workplace, remote email, and intranet access

The Remote Web Workplace is the primary location to use to access computers and services inside your SBS 2008 network when you are not yourself connected to it. To access the site, open your browser and go to `https://remote.yourdomain.co.uk/remote`.

If you forget the `/remote` from the URL, you will get a **403 – Forbidden: Access is denied** error.

You will be presented with a sign-in screen where you enter your **user name** and **password**.

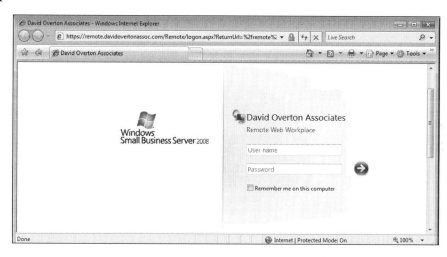

Once you are through the login screen, you will see options for the provided three sections and a number of links.

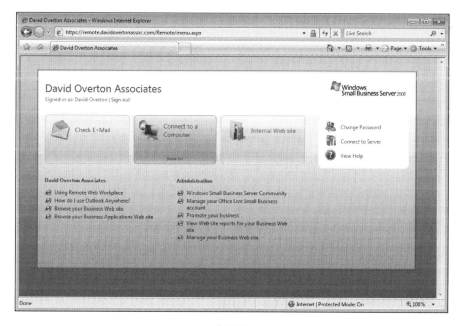

Customizing Remote Web Workplace

You can customize the information that is present on the Welcome screen of the Remote Web Workplace, including the links shown, the background bitmaps, and company icons.

Two of the links shown on the Welcome Page have a URL that starts with `https://sites`, which will not work from the Internet, so these will need to be changed. To do this, go to the **Shares Folders and Web Sites** tab and select **Web Sites**.

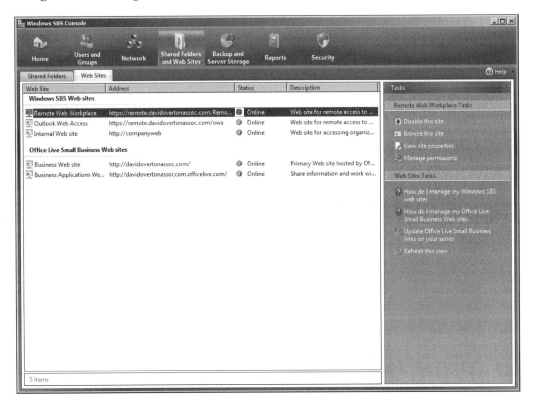

Click on the **View site properties** button in the righthand task pane and navigate to the **Home page links** section. From here, you can choose what is displayed on the front page, removing options if desired. To alter the URLs of the links, click on the **Manage links...** button.

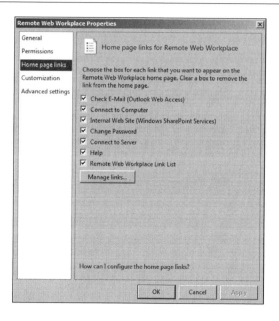

The **Remote Web Workplace Link List Properties** window will open. On the
General page, you can enable or disable links. On the **Permissions** page, you can
control who can access what from the site. The page that we need to change is the
Organization links where the top two links need changing.

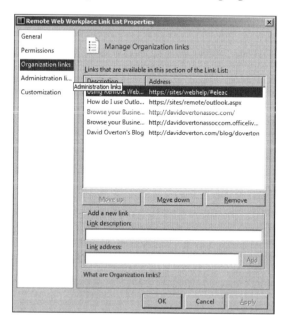

Select **Using Remote Web** and click on **Remove** and then **How do I use Outlook Anywhere** and then click on **Remove** again. Add the following information by completing the **Link description** and **Link address** where you replace yourdomain.co.uk with your correct domain name.

Link Description	Link address
Using Remote Web Workplace	https://remote.yourdomain.co.uk/webhelp/#eleac
How do I use Outlook Anywhere	https://remote.yourdomain.co.uk/remote/outlook.aspx

You can change the other settings in this page, such as the name of the **Administration links** section, or even add in a link to my blog at http://davidoverton.com/blogs/doverton. Click on OK once you have completed these changes.

To change the Organization's name on the home page or to add a logo, go to the **Customization** section and change the details here. Note that the logos and backgrounds are stored in C:\Program Files\Windows Small Business Server\Bin\Webapps\Remote\Images, so any file will need to be copied here before you can choose it by clicking on the **Choose** button.

Close the dialog box by clicking **OK**.

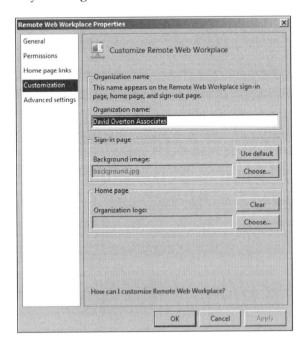

Outlook Web Access

SBS 2008 offers both web-based access to your email account and access from Outlook 2003 and 2007 even when you are not connected to your SBS 2008 network, such as when you are using a wireless LAN at home or while travelling.

To access the web-based email, click on the **Check E-Mail** button from Remote Web Workplace, which will open up a window to `https://remote.yourdomain.co.uk/owa`. From here, you can access your email, calendar, and contacts as well as send new emails and search for information.

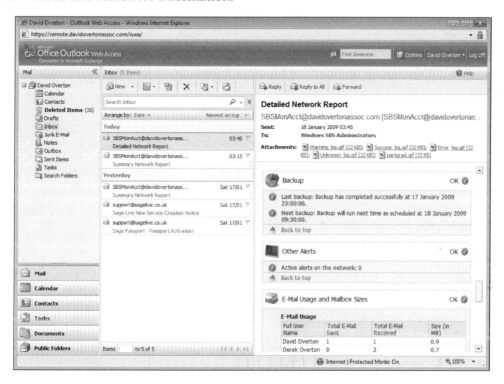

Outlook Mobile Access via ActiveSync or Windows Mobile phones

Users can now also use one of the many phones with Windows Mobile or that supports the ActiveSync protocol to read and respond to emails, check their calendar, and have a single copy of their contacts. Setting up a user on a mobile phone is as simple as knowing their email address, username, and password. On older Windows Mobile phones, they will also need to know the remote access address, which would be `remote.yourdomain.co.uk`. That is it!

Connecting to a PC on the SBS 2008 LAN

Sometimes, you need to sit at your PC in the Office, even though you are not there. This can be especially useful if there is an application or data on that machine that you cannot access any other way. SBS 2008 can enable access to the PCs running within the SBS 2008 network remotely. This can also be used by administrators to access the server console remotely. By default, you have access to your own PC although you can configure which PCs you have access to in the **Network** tab inside Windows SBS Console.

To connect to a PC, click on the **Connect to a computer** button in the Remote Web Workplace. This will produce a list of computers that you can connect to. Select one and click on **Connect**.

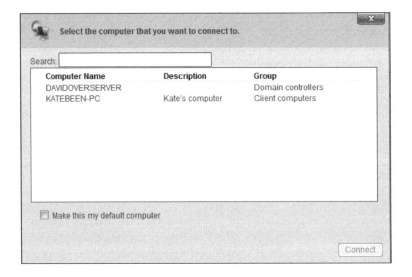

You will then be asked if you want to confirm the connection and if so, if you want your clipboard (cut, copy, and paste functionality between the remote machine and your local machine) to be enabled as well as the remote machine being able to print to any locally attached printers. I normally keep both these checked and then click on **Connect**.

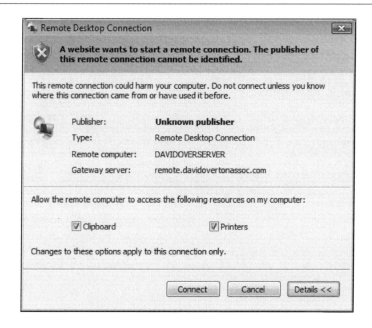

Finally, you will be asked for your username and password again. If you check the **Remember my credentials** box, then you will not need to enter them again. Click **OK** to start the session.

It is likely that the connected session will take over your whole screen. If you look at the screen, you should have a small tab area with the name of the computer that you have connected to and window minimize and close buttons on the righthand side. Use the machine and when finished, either log out from the **Start** menu or hit the cross button to close the window.

Connecting via a Virtual Private Network (VPN)

Sometimes, even with all the options listed above, you need to connect your PC to the network as if it were physically there. This is delivered using a Virtual Private Network, which creates a secure connection to your work network.

 The performance of this link is limited by the speed of both your local Internet connection and that of your SBS 2008. Don't expect the same performance as if you were literally in the office; removing background pictures and unnecessary user interface tools, such as the Sidebar will improve the situation.

The Settings for a VPN can either be configured on each Windows client PC or you can create a downloadable tool that many users can run, which will provide the settings for them. In either case, you must have enabled the VPN in the network settings and configured the user to be able to access them. Once you have done so, the user will connect to remote.yourdomain.co.uk with just their username, domain name, and password.

I have documented how to create a VPN by hand at http://davidoverton.com/r.ashx?1I and to create a tool that will create them for your users at http://davidoverton.com/r.ashx?1J.

Summary

You users will gain benefits from professional email, calendars, and contacts using Exchange 2007 with Outlook, over the Web or on a mobile phone. This level of connection anywhere often enables significant business benefit by itself.

CompanyWeb will provide a fantastic centralized store for documents and team working and should reduce the "back and forth" email trails.

Finally, your users should be able to work just as productively whether they are in or out of the office.

The final step is to ensure that users remember to use these tools. The welcome email that is sent to each user is a good start. However, if you are not a technologist yourself, remember to use a Small Business Specialist Community Microsoft partner to learn much more and get the most out of your SBS 2008 system.

13
Introduction to SBS 2008 Management

SBS 2008 is now configured for use, technically, and enabled for users. Besides using the solution, you will also need to manage it. All computers, like cars, need regular maintenance, but unlike cars where this can be a once a year exercise and perhaps even once every two years, this needs to be done more frequently with SBS 2008. Because hardware, software, or security issues can arise at any time, it is advised that you have a daily routine of checks and some knowledge of how to carry out the basic administration tasks. The good news is that SBS 2008 makes many of the tasks simple to complete and daily checks can be completed in just a few minutes—providing all is running as it should.

In this chapter, we will cover:

- Daily maintenance checks via the built-in reports.
- Maintenance areas.
- Troubleshooting common problems.

Administration tools

There are a number of tools that you will need to be aware of, to simply administer your SBS 2008 server. Rather than describing how to find each one of them, as we go along, I will quickly recap those we have seen already and introduce the new tools. They are:

- Windows SBS Console
- Windows SBS Console (Advanced Mode)
- Windows SBS Native Tools Management
- Exchange Management Shell
- Command Prompt run as Administrator

Windows SBS Console standard and advanced mode

The Windows SBS Console provides access to all reports and settings for managing SBS 2008. It hides the complexity of the underlying sub-systems and gives you a number of wizards to manage those systems.

The console comes in two flavors—standard and advanced mode.

In the advanced mode, you are given links to tools that can assist, but break out of the console. Both are found on the **Start** menu. An example would be the **Network** tab that provides links to **DNS**, **DHCP**, and **certificate management** outside the console. Below is a screenshot of the console in advanced mode.

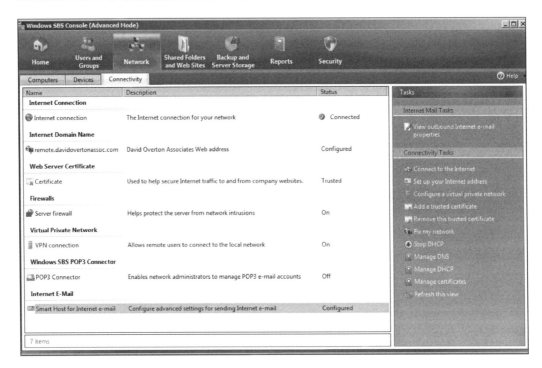

Windows SBS Native Tools Management

Once your needs grow beyond the Windows SBS Console, you will need to access the underlying native management tools for the technologies that SBS 2008 relies on. This single tool gives you access to the Server, network, security, Exchange, and Internet Information Services consoles that you would normally load individually.

You can customize this tool to meet your own needs, so I normally add in the Windows Server Backup console and remove the Fax console, for example. The console can be found in the **Windows Small Business Server** folder on the **Start** menu.

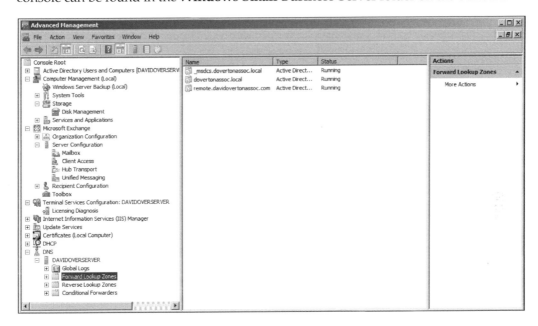

Exchange Management Shell

While you can manage Exchange via the graphical tool that is embedded into the Windows SBS Native Tools Management, I also like to use the command-line tools. To access these, you will need to locate the **Exchange Management Shell** on the **Start** menu under **Microsoft Exchange Server 2007**.

To learn more about the commands available, type get-excommand into the shell for a full list.

Command Prompt run as Administrator

The final command-line tool is the simply the **Command Prompt** as found on the
Start menu. However, if you simply click on the command prompt, you cannot run
any administrative commands. To do so, you must find **Command Prompt** on the
Start menu and then right-click on it and choose **Run as Administrator**.

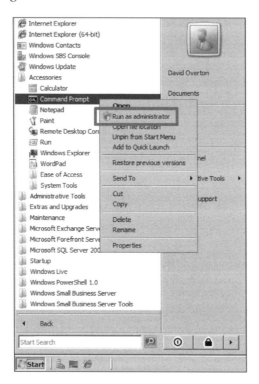

You will know if you have it right as the title bar will state **Administrator:
Command Prompt**.

Daily maintenance check via reports

You should get a summary daily report emailed every day and a detailed network report emailed every week. These give simple high-level points as to where you should focus any maintenance work on your SBS 2008 system. While there will often be nothing to worry about, keeping an eye on the gauges of the engine is worthwhile.

The data in the emailed reports is available and can be updated at any time from the Windows SBS Console in the **Reports** tab. Click on **Generate report** to create a new report and **Generate and e-mail report** to also send it via email. In the following example, there are some security alerts that will require attention. Looking at the detailed report will provide more information.

The daily reports are just that—which means that they are generated each day. The detailed report is only generated once a week, which means that you will need to generate it as it can be up to 6 days old when you are reading it in the console.

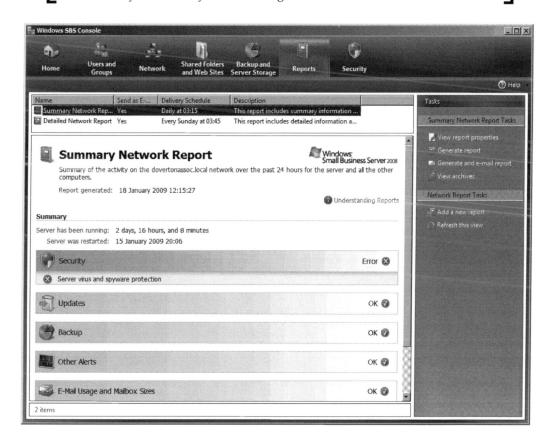

Maintenance areas

From the report, you will see a number of areas to focus attention on. I'll offer advice on diagnosing issues with each section below.

Security

One of the most important items to be monitored on your SBS 2008 system and the network in general is security. An insecure system will become compromised. The impact of a compromised system could be anything from loss of data to theft or the use of your computer resources for criminal activities.

The **Security** tab in the Windows SBS Console provides further areas for investigation. You will need to examine each area where there is not a green check mark. In the following sample screenshot, we have two Windows PCs without up-to-date Anti-virus software and out-of-date software on the server too. This would require immediate attention.

 Remember that all anti-malware software requires a subscription to keep it up to date. While there are a few free services out there, it is better, in my opinion, to invest here rather than regret later.

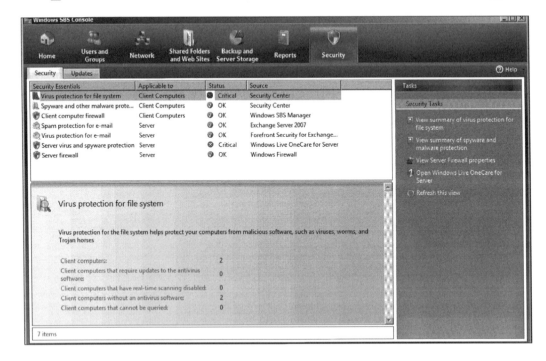

The second area to check around security it that all the updates are made available to end users as soon as possible. When Microsoft makes an update available on the Internet, the SBS administrator is required to approve it before the computers in your network are required to install it. If you look at the **Updates** tab in the following screenshot, you will see that there are two optional updates that need to be approved or declined.

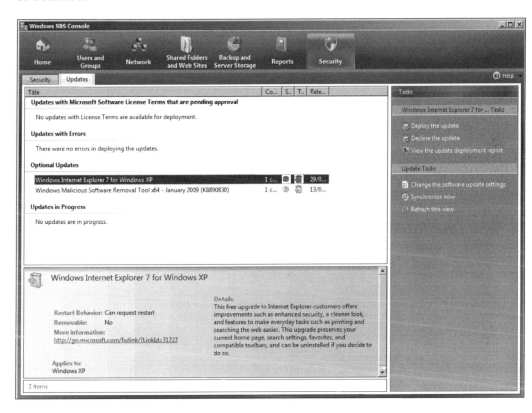

You can choose how many approvals you need to do by hand, and many are automatically approved for you by changing the settings. If you click on the **Change the software update settings** button on the righthand task pane, you control which level of updates are automatically deployed on both servers and Windows client computers. The only time when a critical update will not automatically approve itself for distribution, is if the license terms have been updated. In this case, you must click **Updates with Microsoft Software License Terms that are pending approval** to enable those updates.

I set all updates to High for both clients and servers as this ensures the best level of protection for my systems. It is unlikely, but not impossible that an update may cause a problem on a computer. However, I would rather be calling the free Microsoft support services for dealing with an issue should an update break an application, rather than having to deal with a virus or malware outbreak.

If you do choose to change the update settings, you can change what gets automatically installed, when it happens, and which computers are managed by the system.

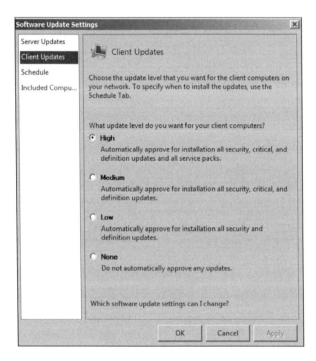

To approve an update, such as the **Malicious Software Removal Tool** in the console image earlier, select the item and click on the **Deploy the Update** button in the task pane. You will then be asked to confirm your request and you must click on the **OK** button for it to continue.

You will then have to approve the license terms for the update. To continue, you need to click on the **I accept** button; otherwise, it will not be approved.

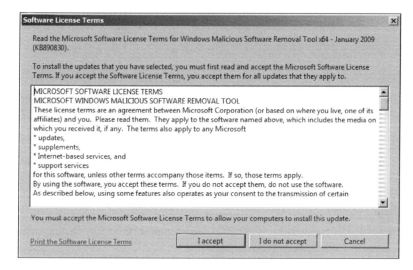

You will then see confirmation when the process is complete.

 It can take up to 24 hours for an approval to be deployed to the target machines, and they must be connected to the network for the update to be processed.

 Updates when not connected to the SBS network

If a user is disconnected from the SBS server, but needs to apply updates, they can go to the **Windows Update** item in the **Start** menu and then click **Check online for updates from Microsoft Update**.

Backup and Recovery

Security is not just about keeping bad software off the system, but also includes keeping good backup copies. If you go to the **Backup and Server Storage** tab in the Windows SBS Console, you can see the status of the backup and the backup devices.

 Remember to regularly remove one of the backup devices off-site and to replace it with another one to ensure that you always have a recent copy of the system off-site in the event of a disaster on site. Ideally, this should be carried out on a daily basis.

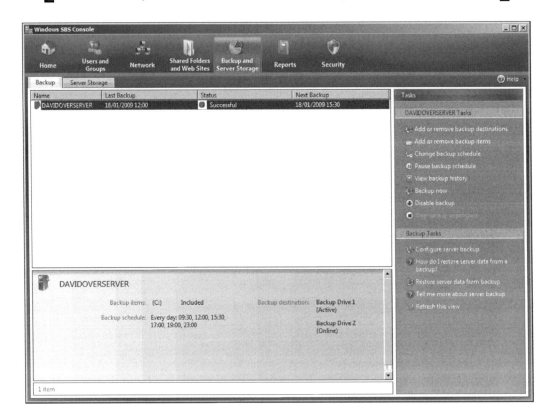

To check the history of the backup, click on the **View backup history** button in the task pane. From here, you should be able to see what has been backed up and by navigating to the **Backup History** item, see all the successful backups.

To learn more about the backup, which was configured in Chapter 10, including how much storage is used on each device, as well as to restore data from a backup, click on the **Restore server data from backup** button from the task pane.

In this window, you can select a backup to restore data from as well as check how much storage is used on each device. In the sample shown here, I have 28 backup slots on my first device using a total of just under 50 GB. When the device runs out of storage, the backup routine will start overwriting the oldest backups. For this reason, you should have a regular archival process of the USB devices to enable long term historic data recovery, perhaps in the event of a legal question years after the system was installed.

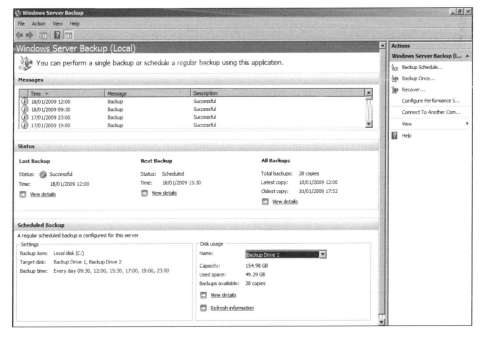

If you need to perform a full system restore, then you will need your SBS 2008 boot disks to boot into the recovery environment, otherwise you can use the wizard above to recover files. I'll discuss both below.

File and data recovery

If you are simply hoping to recover files or data, click on the **Recover** option from the task pane on the right. Choose which server you will be recovering the data from. In most circumstances, this would be **This Server** and click **Next**.

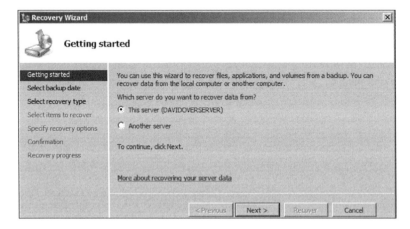

You can then select the date from the backup that you would like to roll back too. The darker dates on the calendar have backups on them, and since SBS 2008 defaults to at least two backups per day, you can then pick the **Time**. Then, click **Next**.

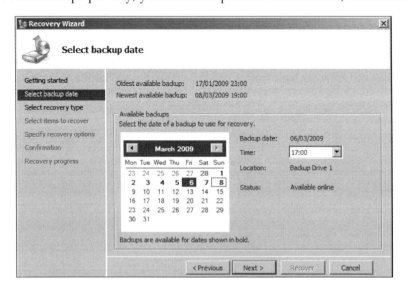

You then have a choice of the recovery type. In each case, you can restore the data over the top of the current data or to a new location so that you can move it yourself. The **Files and folders** option enables you to pick files from directories and restore them. The **Applications** option enables you to restore the data files associated with Exchange 2007 or Windows SharePoint Services (CompanyWeb) and finally, the **Volumes** option restores whole disks, although it cannot restore the main system disk as discussed in the next section. Pick the option for you and click on **Next**.

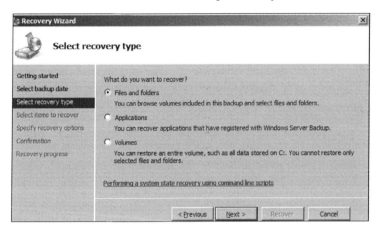

Recovering files

If you are recovering files, you must first find the files you want to restore and highlight them. Once you have selected the files, click on **Next**.

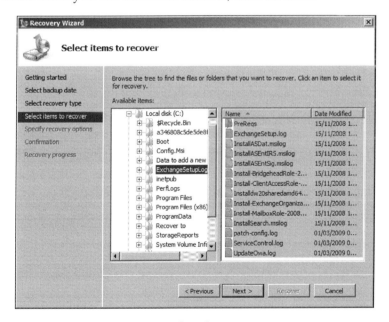

You must then choose whether you will be restoring to the **Original location** or **Another location**. If you are restoring to the original location, then you must decide what to do if existing files are found. If you are restoring to an alternative location, click on the **Browse** button to choose the folder to restore the files to. Once you have completed these choices, click on **Next** to continue.

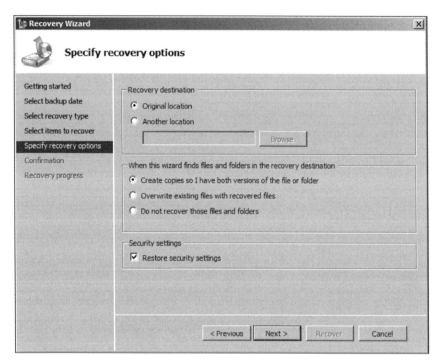

The Recovery Wizard will show a list of all the files that are to be restored, where they will be restored to, and other settings. If you are comfortable with the settings, click on **Recover**.

 You must be cautious when recovering to the **Original location** and overwriting existing files as you could damage your system in the process if you overwrite good files with out-of-date files.

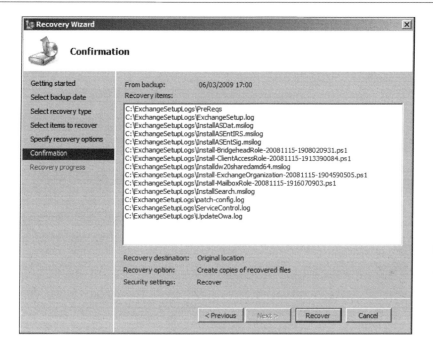

Recovering Exchange or CompanyWeb

If you choose to recover applications, then you must choose from the **Applications** list. Pick the choice that is right for you and then click on **Next**.

 Note that this is just the recovery of the files for that application and not any other associated settings, such as registry or Active Directory settings.

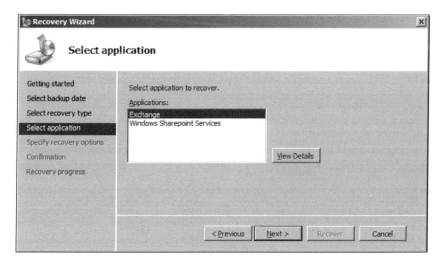

Chose if the Wizard is to **Recover to original location** or **another location** and then click on **Next**.

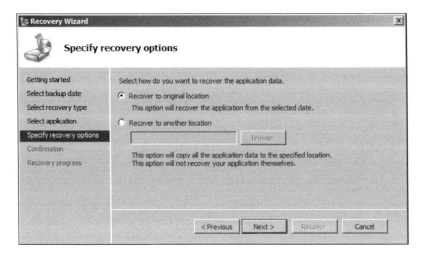

You will be asked to confirm the selection and click on the **Recover** button to start the process.

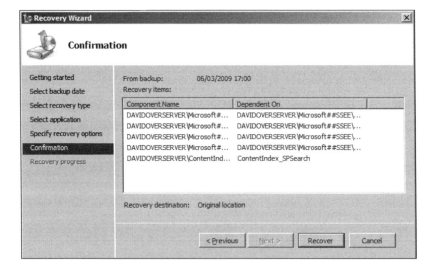

Full volume recovery

If you wish to restore a whole disk, you'll be asked to choose the destination disk to hold the recovered disk. Note that you cannot restore the system disk to the current system drive using this method.

Check the **Source Volumes** you wish to restore and the appropriate **Destination Volumes** that will hold the data, noting the fact that all the existing data on the **Destination Volume** will be removed. Click on **Next** to continue the recovery.

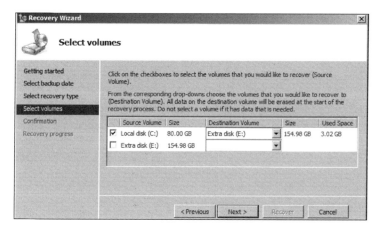

Full system recovery

If your server is in need of full recovery where you roll back the system disk and everything else on it, you will need to boot from the SBS 2008 DVD and select **Repair your computer** from the initial menu after you have chosen the keyboard country.

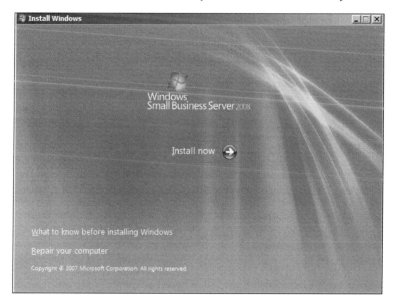

In most SBS 2008 systems, you only have one **Operating System**, so you should be able to click on **Next** to continue. If your system drive is not showing, it could be because you need to load non-standard RAID drivers. Insert your drivers disk or CD and click on **Load Drivers**, let it find the disk and then click on **Next**.

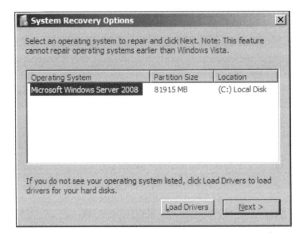

Click on the **Windows Complete PC Restore** link to start the system disk restore process.

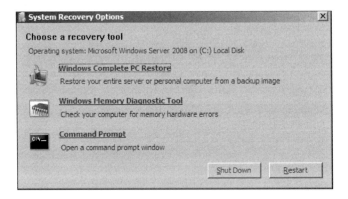

In many cases, you will want to restore the latest backup as you are recovering from a system failure. If you wish to roll back a system to an earlier time, select the **Restore a different backup** option and click on **Next**.

When picking an older backup to restore from, select the backup device that you will be restoring from and then click **Next**. If you have to swap backup devices or add the right device to the server, click on **Refresh** once the device is installed and pick the correct device.

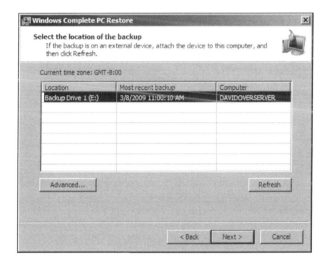

You can then pick any backup that is available from the device you chose. Pick the backup and click on **Next**.

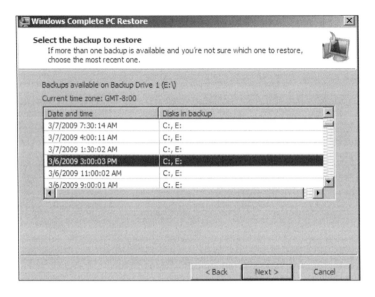

Since we are restoring the system disk at the minimum, I would recommend you **Format and repartition disks** as a minimum. If you have your data and system partition separate, then it will be possible to recover the system disk without losing any user data.

Click on **Next**, once you have checked the boxes you need.

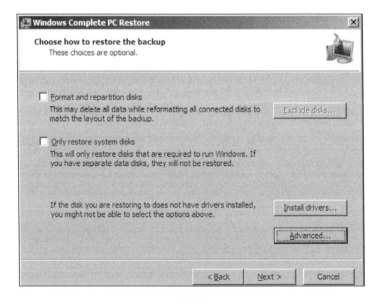

You will see a confirmation screen to double-check the settings for the backup on which you will need to click **Finish** to continue the process. You will also need to confirm that you are happy that data will be erased from the disks if you continue. Click on **OK** and the restore will start.

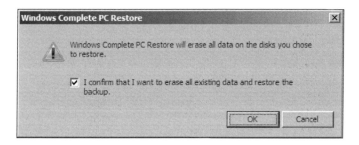

The system restoration process will show a progress bar. It took a little over an hour for me to roll back my server to a backup that was created 3 days earlier. Once the restore is finished, you will be prompted to restart the server. Once restarted, everything should function as normal.

Forefront Updates

The final place where security is determined is in the optional component of Microsoft Forefront Server Security. Sometimes you can find errors in the event log with an ID of 6012. These generally point to a timeout when trying to download the Forefront updates. Following is an example of the error message you might see in the event viewer.

You can find the **Event Viewer** in the **Administrators Tools** on the **Start** menu or by running **eventvwr** from a Run prompt.

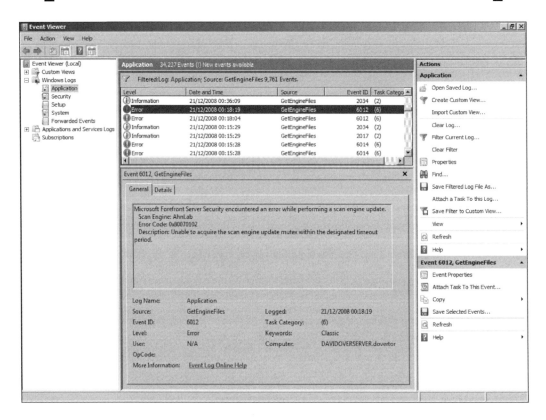

There are two stages to fixing this error. The first is to make a change in the Windows Registry to enable the downloads to take longer, and the second is to kick off the downloads again. To update the registry, run this command from a command prompt run as administrator.

```
REG ADD "HKLM\SOFTWARE\Wow6432Node\Microsoft\Forefront Server
Security\Exchange Server" /V EngineDownloadTimeout /T REG_DWORD /v
0X708 /f
```

This will add the registry key required, overwriting the existing value. It is very important that you do not make other changes to the registry without ensuring they are supported. The 0x708 value in the command line is the number of seconds ForeFront will allow a download to take in Hexadecimal—0x708 is 1800 seconds or 30 minutes.

You can then either wait for the next download or you can manually start one by starting the **ForeFront Server Security Administrator** from the **Start** menu. Navigate to the **Scanner Update** and click on **Update Now** on the items that have not recently updated.

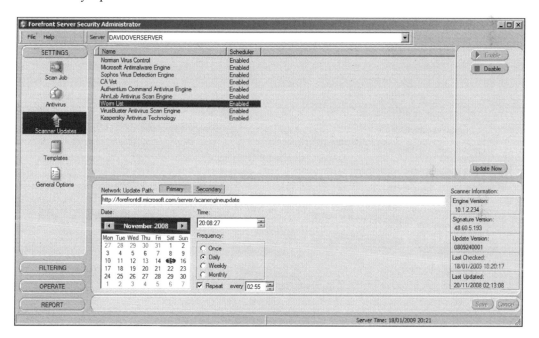

Storage

Over time, your users will fill the storage capacity of the disks inside your SBS 2008 server if they are not regulated by disk quotas or if the business needs require the quotas to be made larger. This can be alarming if usage grows at a rapid rate, but this should not be the case, which means that you need to regularly monitor using the **Backup and Server Storage** tab in the Windows SBS Console to ensure it is not creeping up towards a full disk. Ideally, you want your disks to be no more than 80%-85% full to give you the time to add additional storage without impacting the users.

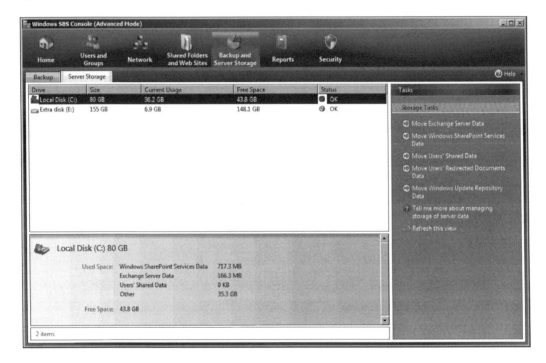

The summary will tell you how your storage is looking. If you do need to add more storage, you can either add additional drives to your server or you can replace an existing drive with a larger disk set. If you do replace a small drive, you must replicate all data from the small disks to the new larger disks. All disk configurations should be configured to be resilient to a single disk failure so that you do not lose your data. Disk mirroring is the normal configuration used to achieve this.

Once more drives are added to the system, you will be able to relocate the data stored on the SBS 2008 server with the **Storage Tasks** in the task pane.

These tasks used to be very complex; however, SBS 2008 simplifies the movement of the following to the simple task of picking which drive to store the data on. This might involve anything from moving SQL databases to changing shared folder. The data stores that can be moved are:

- Exchange Server Data
- SharePoint Services Database
- User Shared Data
- Redirected Documents Data
- Windows Update Repository

To start the process, pick one of the **Storage Tasks** to move data from the **Tasks** pane. You will have to click on **Next** to move past the introduction screen. You will be asked if you wish to perform a backup before you move the data. Depending on the time since the last backup, click on either **Yes** or **No** depending on the risk of data loss should the system fail during the data move.

You will then be presented with a list of disks on your system where you could move the data too. In the example below, I am moving from the **Local Disk (C:)** to the **Extra disk (E:)**. Select the drive and click on **Move**.

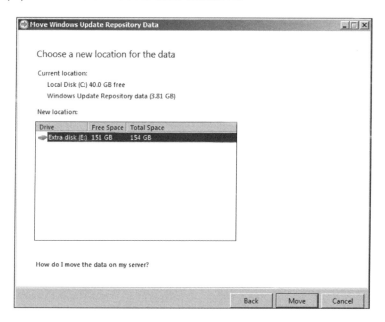

The system will move the data for you and reconfigure the applications. Once it is completed, you can click on **Finish** to return to the Windows SBS Console where you will see the moved storage reflected in the information on the **Server Storage** tab.

Event Log messages

You can get more detail about the event log errors by looking in the **Event Viewer**, either in the **Administrator Tools** menu or in the **Windows SBS Native Tools Management**. You can then find any errors and warnings in the tool to further diagnose them.

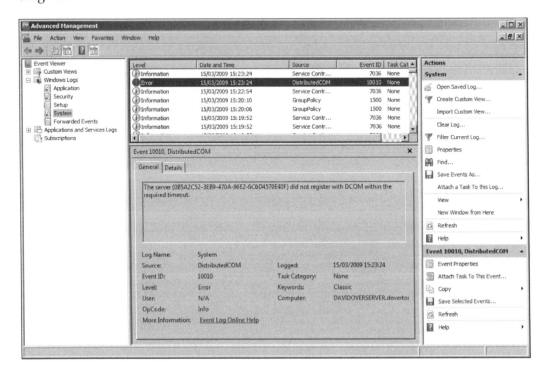

There are three steps I recommend to deal with these items. The first is to click the **Event Log Online Help** link in the event log event itself. If this does not yield the result you are after, then enter the **Event ID** and **Source** into the Microsoft support site search engine at `http://support.microsoft.com/search`. If that does not work, then I perform a general search via a web search engine for the **Event ID**, **Source**, and key words from the **General** description.

Troubleshooting common problems

In this section, I will try to provide some very basic diagnostic areas I would look at to fix issues in specific parts of the system.

External network

If the internal network is working fine and people can connect to the Internet, but others cannot connect into your system, I would first check the firewall and router. Assuming that the basic connectivity checks are all OK, I would start with the **Fix my network** option in the Windows SBS Console under **Network**. Click on **Next** to start the wizard off and wait a few minutes as it can take some time to run.

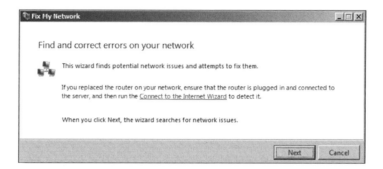

Once the wizard has run, it will show you the issues it finds. If your router is not a UPnP router, you will always get a top issue of **Could not configure the router**. This can be ignored in this case, but other issues need further investigation. Some issues do not have a full description and the only way to understand the problem further is to type the link into a browser to find out more. Clicking on **Next** will start the automated attempts to fix the issues with the check boxes filled in,

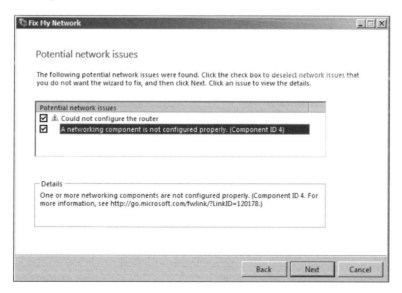

You will be asked to confirm that you wish to continue with the automatic resolution process and you will need to click on the **Yes** button to continue.

Once all the fixes are in place, you will get a final summary screen to inform you whether you have any further issues to worry about.

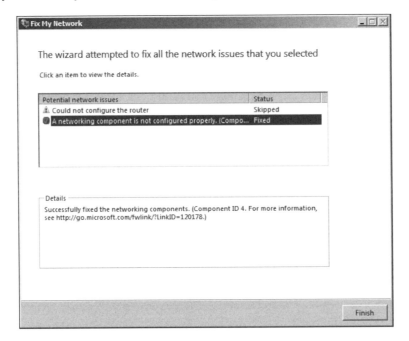

Internal network

Not only can the connection between your server and the Internet stop working, but also the connection between your server and other machines on your network.

Before delving too deeply into the software side of the network, it is always worth double-checking the cables, switches, and hubs and ensuring they all have their green lights on. I've seen many network issues being resolved by pushing a cable home properly.

In an attempt to diagnose this, I would recommend first checking the **Networking and Sharing Center** in **Control Panel** and ensuring that it has a good connection through to the **Internet**. This check can be carried out on a problem PC, but more importantly, on the server too.

If there is a problem listed there, then you need to fix this before proceeding. The **Diagnose and repair** option in the **Tasks** list will attempt to resolve this problem for you.

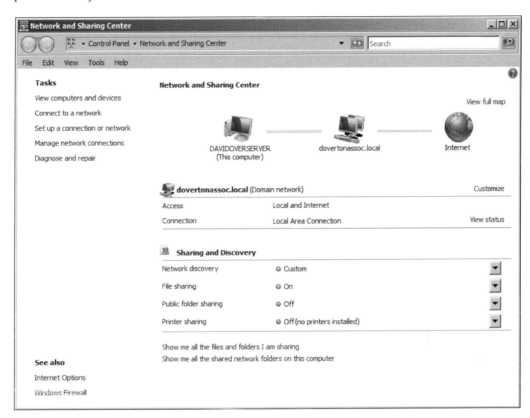

There are two services on your server that are important for the smooth running of your internal network, so I would next check these. They are the DHCP and DNS services. Both tools can be found as part of the **Windows SBS Native Tools Management** or under the **Administrators Tools** item on the **Start** menu.

DHCP is responsible for allocating IP addresses to computers and if this is not running, it can cause issues. Go to the **DHCP** console and check that it is running and has a green arrow in the IPv4 server symbol. If not, try starting the service. If it will not start, this normally points to the fact that another device with a DHCP server has been plugged into the network. You will need to find this new addition and disable DHCP on that device.

If that was not the issue, then check that the IP address **Scope**, **Router**, **DNS Server**, and **DNS Domain** **N**ame are correct. The **Scope** is the address range that your computer clients will be allocated IP addresses from. The **Router** setting should point to your Internet router, the **DNS Server** should have the IP address of your server, and the **DNS Domain Name** should be the name of your domain.

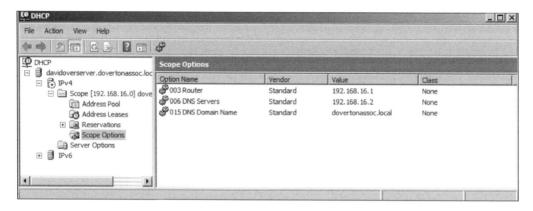

The final check is that the DNS service is up and running. You should see a screen similar to the one below with plenty of entries under the domain name. If not, try restarting the DNS service, otherwise you have a significantly painful DNS corruption that will require knowledge beyond this book to repair.

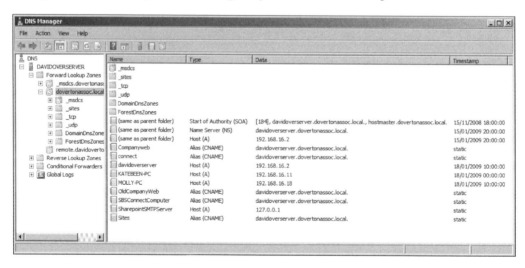

There are two checks you can carry out on the DNS settings. The first is to run the built-in monitoring tool and the second is to check if the DNS is set to send queries to forwarders.

Right-click on the server name in the navigation pane and select **Properties**. Select the **Monitoring** tab and put a check mark in the **simple** and **recursive query** boxes and then click on **Test Now**. If the DNS servers are all responding correctly, you will see two **Pass** responses in the **Test results** section.

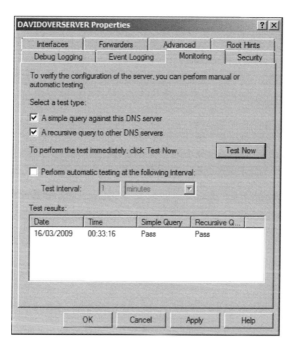

If the **Simple Query** has a **Fail**, you should restart your DNS service. If the **Recursive Query** shows a fail, you need to check your **Forwarders**.

Select the **Forwarders** tab and note if there are any items listed. If none are listed, you can ask your ISP for the DNS forwarders you should use as it is possible that your queries are timing out. If you have **IP Addresses** listed, then you should confirm with your ISP that they are still valid and that they are working correctly.

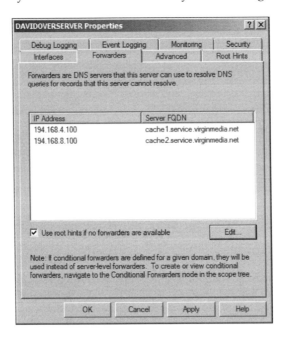

 Some people do not trust the security of using forwarders, so they either leave this section blank or they use another provider, such as OpenDNS.

Spam

Spam, that is mail that is not wanted or requested, is a waste of system resources, users' time , and is potentially harmful. It is not possible to simple say "no spam" in an email system, so various rules exist to manage spam within Exchange 2007 and Outlook. Should too much spam get through to users, they will find it annoying and potentially offensive. However, on the flip side, if the rules are set too stringently, then valuable email will be stopped as spam and could cost you your business if important communications were lost.

On SBS 2008, spam filtering is delivered as part of Exchange 2007. To understand how much spam is being stopped, look at the **Security** tab in the Windows SBS Console and select the **Spam protection for e-mail** line. In the pane at the bottom of the screen, you will see how much spam has been stopped.

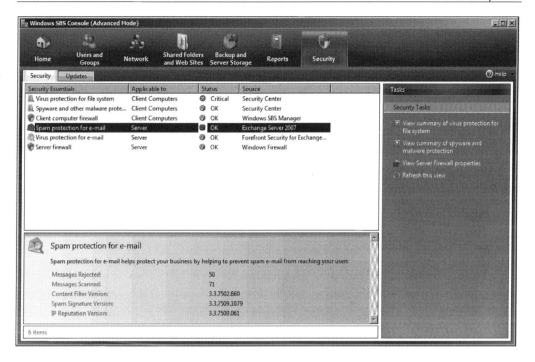

To change the settings, perhaps to enable more spam to be quarantined rather than just deleted, you need to start the **Exchange Management Console** from the **Start** menu.

Navigate to the **Hub Transport** under **Organization Configuration** and then select **Anti-Spam** in the main information pane.

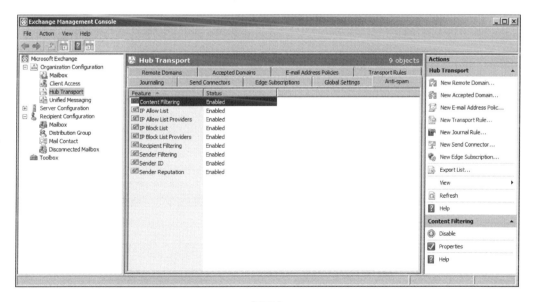

It is worth looking at all the options; however, the **Content Filtering** option has the most useful settings to be changed. Select **Content Filtering** and then click on **Properties** to bring up the settings for the content filtering. In the **Action** tab, you will see options for spam. By default, spam is deleted, which makes me nervous that I might miss an important email, so I would recommend making a spam quarantine email account and directing all spam above 6 or 7 (the spam rating) into the quarantine and rejecting mail that is very spam like in content, such as 8.

With these settings, if someone thinks an email might have been rejected as spam, you can log into that account and check it out.

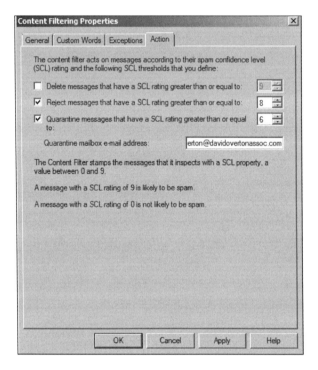

Poor performance

Poor performance is a nightmare scenario for most people managing a server as tracking down the culprit can be very complicated and time consuming. I am not about to be able to simplify it, so I wanted to give you a first pass glance at a system. Start **Performance Monitor** from **Administrative Tools** on the **Start** menu to get an overview of what your server is doing.

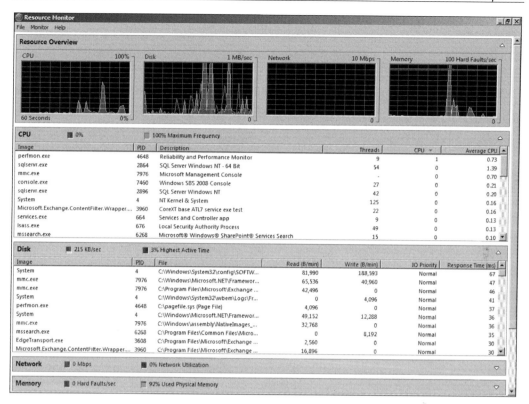

Check each section to find out if it is particularly active. **CPU**, **Disk Active Time**, and **Networks Utilization** that are close to 100% are signs of stress on your SBS 2008 system. **High Maximum Frequency** and **Used Physical Memory** are not normally signs of problems. A high **Hard Fault/sec** for memory is something to worry about, especially if it is tied with high **Disk Active Time** as this would suggest not enough memory.

However, even when you know what area of the system is under stress the action is very dependent on the cause. If you are unsure how to take this further, talk to a Small Business Specialist Community Microsoft Partner to gain some assistance.

Summary

In this chapter, you should have started to get an idea about how to do simple maintenance for your SBS 2008 server. You will need to check the reports on a daily basis and then drill further into issues to resolve them before they become a showstopper for your business.

All areas of maintenance have been touched upon so that you should be able to perform basic maintenance for security issues, backups, storage, networking, email, and performance.

This means that you now not only have a working server and network, but you are able to maintain this solution.

This is not the end of the journey though; this is the beginning of running your business differently with the aid of new technology. If it is not used and maintained, it may not deliver the benefits you hoped for.

I hope you have enjoyed this process as much as I have. If you have questions, I can always be contacted through my web site—http://davidoverton.com, but be aware that I cannot answer all questions, although I do try.

Index

V

versions, software updates
  .NET framework 2.0 installation,
      checking 40
  checking 38
  exchange 2003 Service Pack 2 installation,
      checking 39, 40
  Microsoft Core XML Service version,
      checking 41
  SBS 2003 - at Service Pack 1 or greater,
      checking 38
  Windows Server - at Service Pack 2 or
      greater, checking 38
  Windows SharePoint Service 2.0. Service
      Pack 3 installation, checking 41, 42
  Windows SharePoint Service 2.0. Service
      Pack 3 usage, checking 41, 42
Virtual Private Network. *See* **VPN**
VPN 342
VPN Server
  changing 33

W

Windows SBS Console 13
Windows Server 2008 12
Windows SharePoint Services 12
Windows Software Update Services 13

Thank you for buying
Small Business Server 2008
Installation, Migration, and Configuration

About Packt Publishing

Packt, pronounced 'packed', published its first book *"Mastering phpMyAdmin for Effective MySQL Management"* in April 2004 and subsequently continued to specialize in publishing highly focused books on specific technologies and solutions.

Our books and publications share the experiences of your fellow IT professionals in adapting and customizing today's systems, applications, and frameworks. Our solution based books give you the knowledge and power to customize the software and technologies you're using to get the job done. Packt books are more specific and less general than the IT books you have seen in the past. Our unique business model allows us to bring you more focused information, giving you more of what you need to know, and less of what you don't.

Packt is a modern, yet unique publishing company, which focuses on producing quality, cutting-edge books for communities of developers, administrators, and newbies alike. For more information, please visit our website: www.packtpub.com.

Writing for Packt

We welcome all inquiries from people who are interested in authoring. Book proposals should be sent to author@packtpub.com. If your book idea is still at an early stage and you would like to discuss it first before writing a formal book proposal, contact us; one of our commissioning editors will get in touch with you.

We're not just looking for published authors; if you have strong technical skills but no writing experience, our experienced editors can help you develop a writing career, or simply get some additional reward for your expertise.

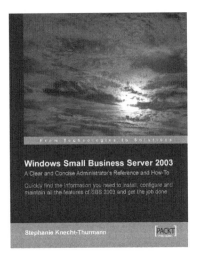

Windows Small Business Server SBS 2003

ISBN: 978-1-904811-49-7   Paperback: 494 pages

Quickly find the information you need to install, configure and maintain all the features of SBS 2003 to get the job done

1. Comprehensive coverage

2. Structured for speed. Find it, do it, finish

3. Perfect companion to the MS Docs and KB

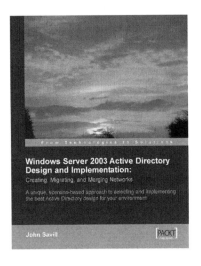

Windows Server 2003 Active Directory Design and Implementation

ISBN: 978-1-904811-08-4   Paperback: 356 pages

A unique, scenario-based approach to selecting and implementing the best Active Directory design for your environment

Understand the principles of Active Directory design

1. Create new networks or evolve existing Active Directory installations

2. Create the best Active Directory design for a broad range of business environments

3. Implement your Active Directory designs

4. Migrate and merge Active Directory structures

Please check **www.PacktPub.com** for information on our titles